CONTRACT ADMINISTRATION

TOOLS, TECHNIQUES AND BEST PRACTICES

GREGORY A. GARRETT

SUSTAINABLE FORESTRY INITIATIVE

Certified Fiber Sourcing

www.sfiprogram.org

Wolters Kluwer

Law & Business

Editorial Director: Aaron M. Broaddus
Cover Design: Don Torres
Interior Layout: Don Torres

Copyright Notice

Notice of Trademarks

Product No.: 0-4722-400

ISBN: 978-0-8080-2215-2

TABLE OF CONTENTS

Preface v

Dedication vii

Acknowledgments ix

About the Principal Author xi

Introduction xiii

Chapter 1   Contract Administration: Personnel, Workload,
and Processes (Gregory A. Garrett) 1

Chapter 2   Integrated Project Management (IPM)
Discipline (Gregory A. Garrett) 21

Chapter 3   Opportunity and Risk Management
(Gregory A. Garrett) 45

Chapter 4   Contract Changes Management
(Dr. Rene G. Rendon) 69

Chapter 5   Contract Financing, Payment, and Profitability
(Gregory A. Garrett and Dr. Juanita Rendon)..... 89

Chapter 6   Contract Claims and Dispute Resolution
(Peter A. McDonald, Esq., C.P.A.) 119

Chapter 7   Managing Subcontracts: Challenges and Best
Practices (Gregory A. Garrett) 145

Chapter 8   Government Property Management: Challenges
and Best Practices (Dr. John I. Paciorek) 161

Chapter 9   Earned Value Management Systems (EVMS)
(Gregory A. Garrett) 193

Chapter 10 How It All Ends: Contract Terminations and
Closeout (Tom Reid, Esq., CPCM) 221

Chapter 11 Mitigating the Risk of Litigation (Robert Burton,
Esq., Paul Debolt, Esq., and Terry Ellig, Esq.)... 249

Chapter 12 Contract Interpretation, U.S. Government
Contracts Policies, Reviews and Audits
(Gregory A. Garrett) 271

Chapter 13 The Future of Contract Administration: Purpose
Driven Governance (Eric Esperne, Esq.)........... 289

Glossary of Key Terms...315

References...347

Index 353

PREFACE

The art and science of managing U.S. federal government contracts after they have been awarded can be highly complex indeed. For more than 30 years, I have observed how much time and attention both U.S. government agencies and government contractors spend in determining requirements, developing acquisition strategies, preparing proposals, selecting the right contractor(s), negotiating the deal, and forming the contract. Unfortunately, I have also noticed how little time and resources government agencies and contractors devote to successfully managing the contracts after award. Stated simply, post-award contract management, commonly called contract administration, is vital to the successful delivery of quality products, services, and solutions in support of the mission of nearly every government agency. Thus, the topic and focus of this book is critical for helping improve the government and industry contract administration process and communicating the importance of the functions performed.

While many books have been written about developing winning proposals to obtain U.S. government contracts, very few books have focused on how to apply proven tools, techniques, and best practices to contract administration. Once again my friend Gregory A. Garrett has done an outstanding job of writing and assembling a team of 10 top experts in contract management, accounting, project management, supply chain management, government contract law, and government property management to author this unique text.

I consider this book a practical, informative and compelling reference guide for everyone involved in U.S. federal government contract administration! I have been asking Gregg for many years to write a book focusing on contract administration tools, techniques, and best practices and he has done it!

Deidre Lee
Executive Vice President of Federal Affairs and Operations
Professional Services Council &
Former Administrator, Office of Federal Procurement Policy

DEDICATION

I dedicate this book to all the men and women within the U.S. federal government and industry who devote countless hours to ensure that the promises made in contracts are actually delivered!

To Carolyn

I cannot imagine my life without you and our children. Thank you for your friendship, love, and support.

To Dr. William C. Pursch

I appreciate and value your friendship, coaching, and support for the past 20+ years. You are an Officer and a Gentleman.

ACKNOWLEDGMENTS

I would like to thank the following people for their support and contributions to this book!

Robert Burton, Esq.

Paul Debolt, Esq.

Terry Elling, Esq.

Pete McDonald, Esq., CPA

Dr. John Paciorek, CPPM

Tom Reid, Esq., CPCM

Dr. Juanita Rendon, CPA

Dr. Rene G. Rendon, CPCM, C.P.M., PMP

I would like to extend a special thank you to the following people for their outstanding and professional administrative support services.

Barbara Hanson

Julie McKillip

ABOUT THE PRINCIPAL AUTHOR

Gregory A. Garrett is a Managing Director of the Navigant Consulting, Inc., Government Contractor Services, practice in the Vienna, Virginia, office. An internationally recognized expert in government contracting, cost estimating, contract pricing, risk management, and project management, he is also a best-selling author and highly acclaimed speaker. During the past 25+ years, he has managed more than $30 billion of large complex contracts and projects for both the U.S. government and industry. He has taught and consulted with more than 25,000 professionals in more than 40 countries and is the recipient of numerous national and international business awards for his writing, teaching, consulting, and leadership.

Mr. Garrett provides client support in assessing business risk and makes recommendations for performance improvement of contractor purchasing systems, cost estimating systems, bid/proposal management practices, contract pricing systems, contract administration practices, earned value management systems (EVMS), supply-chain management processes, and program management methodologies. He also serves as an expert witness in support of client claims and/or litigation.

A highly successful industry executive, prior to joining Navigant Consulting, Mr. Garrett served as Chief Operating Officer (COO) for Acquisition Solutions, Inc., where he led some 200 consultants providing professional services to more than 30 U.S. federal government agencies. He served nine years with Lucent Technologies, Inc., as Chief Compliance Officer and VP of Program Management for all U.S. federal government programs. Previously, he was Partner and Executive Director of Global Business at ESI International. A highly decorated military officer of the U.S. Air Force, Mr. Garrett's service included program manager, Space Systems Division; warranted contracting officer, Aeronautical Systems Division; professor of contracting management, Air Force Institute of Technology; and acquisition action officer, HQ USAF at the Pentagon. A prolific writer, Mr. Garrett has authored 15 books and published more than 80 articles on bid/proposal management, government contracting, project management, cost estimating, contract pricing, contract negotiations, risk management, supply-chain management, and leadership.

INTRODUCTION

This book is intended as a practical and informative reference guide for U.S. federal government agency business professionals and government contractors involved in managing contracts. It is a comprehensive guide to the contract administration process that is required for U.S. federal government contracts. A team of 10 leading experts in contract management, project management, supply chain management, accounting, law, and property management have worked together to develop this one-of-a-kind publication.

Our hope is that you will find this text to be a valuable resource that explains and informs about what it takes to effectively manage government contracts. This book provides a wide range of discussion regarding the functional skills, tools, techniques, and best practices that are available and adaptable to help improve performance results.

CHAPTER

CONTRACT ADMINISTRATION: PERSONNEL, WORKLOAD, AND PROCESSES

INTRODUCTION

For more than three decades, U.S. government audits conducted by numerous agencies and watchdog groups have indicated the real and compelling need for improved post-award contract administration by government and industry. In both the public and private business sectors, contract administration is often an afterthought, usually insufficiently staffed as to both the quality and quantity of resources (contract manager, project manager, technical managers, property managers, supply-chain/subcontract managers, etc.). Typically, government and industry focus their time, attention, and key resources on soliciting, proposing, negotiating, and forming the contract—simply stated, getting the deal. As a result, there are often very limited resources to manage, administer, and close out the deal.

While project management and earned value management have received significant focus and attention in recent years for the value-added capabilities they can provide, few organizations have paid much attention to post-award contract administration and closeout activities, which are equally vital to business success.

In this chapter, we focus on the importance of having the appropriate people and processes in place to manage the growing number, value, and complexity of contracts to ensure that U.S. government agencies are able to obtain quality products, services, and/or solutions from government contractors and subcontractors.

CONTRACT ADMINISTRATION: PEOPLE AND WORKLOAD

U.S. government agencies and contractors both are highly focused on awarding/receiving contracts and spending money. Yet, both currently suffer from a shortage of human talent to effectively and efficiently manage the massive growth of U.S. government spending. Since fiscal year (FY) 2000 the U.S. government's spending has increased from $219 billion to more than $538 billion in FY 2008 (see Figure 1-1). In addition, the number of transactions or contracts awarded by U.S. government agencies during the same period of time has grown from 500,000 in FY 2000 to over 7.7 million in FY 2008 (see Figure 1-2).

Figure 1-1

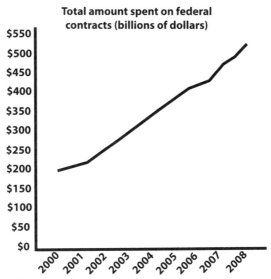

Total amount spent on federal contracts (billions of dollars)

Source: Federal Procurement Data Systems, 2008

Figure 1-2

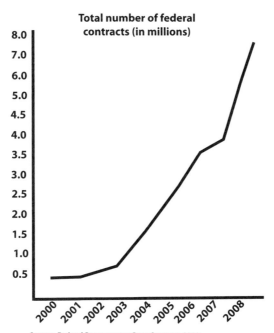

Total number of federal contracts (in millions)

Source: Federal Procurement Data Systems, 2008

This tremendous spending growth during the Bush administration was largely the result of numerous converging factors, including

- the global war on terrorism;
- creation of the Department of Homeland Security;
- significant natural disasters;
- demographics – aging of the baby-boomers;
- rising health care costs; and
- economic recovery expenses due to recession.

Since the start of the Obama Administration, U.S. government spending has risen to even higher levels, especially in the U.S. Department of Health and Human Services, Housing and Urban Development, Treasury, Labor, Education, Energy, Transportation, and the Environmental Protection Agency, to provide for the growing demand for services, economic stimulus, and bailouts of financial institutions; Freddie Mac; Fannie Mae; automobile manufacturers; and others.

Thus, during the past decade U.S. government contracts have grown dramatically in

- number/quantity – up 14 times since FY 2000;
- dollar amount/value – triple since FY 2000; and
- complexity/integration of hardware, software and professional services.

Those who plan, negotiate, award, manage, administer, deliver/fulfill, and close out the contracts and related projects, both in U.S. government and industry, have either remained the same or decreased in number. In addition, both government and industry lack sufficient education and training to keep abreast of the dramatic increase in the complexity of the government's requirements and its increased spending.

From the U.S. government's perspective, the following job titles/roles are critical to its ability to acquire and manage products, services, and solutions from industry to meet the needs of the respective agencies (see Table 1-1).

Table 1-1	
Key Government People/Roles	
• Program Manager	• Contract Specialist/Administrator
• Systems Engineer	• Government Property Manager
• Contracting Officer	• Budget/Financial Analyst
• Contracting Officer's Technical Representative	• Quality Assurance Specialist
• Lawyer	• Logistics Manager
• Cost/Price Analyst	• Others

During the past decade many of the people who have performed these vital government acquisition functions have retired, transferred to other positions within government, moved to a position within industry, or changed career fields.

From the industry or government contractor's perspective, the following similar job titles/roles are critical to the ability to win and successfully deliver on U.S. government contracts, subcontracts, and related projects (see Table 1-2).

Table 1-2	
Key Industry People/Roles	
• Program Manager	• Logistics/Supply Chain Manager
• Systems Engineer	• Lawyer
• Contract Manager	• Project Control Manager
• Subcontract Manager	• Business Development Manager
• Bid/Proposal/Capture Manager	• Account Manager
• Cost/Price Analyst	• Accountants/Financial Manager
• Contract Administrator	• Property Manager
• Buyer/Purchasing Specialist	• Others

U.S. government agencies and industry both have heavily invested in numerous technology-based tools to improve their buying and selling, including software applications, hardware platforms, enterprise resource planning (ERP) systems, and other information technology- (IT) related systems. However, many of these IT- and ERP-related investments have never achieved the promised results. Clearly, the U.S. government's buying and industry's selling of commercially available off-the-shelf products and services was tremendously expedited by the expansion of the following:

■   Internet-based business
■   Electronic Data Interchange (EDI)
■   Electronic Funds Transfer (EFT)
■   Electronic signatures
■   Electronic sales catalogs

- Federal Supply Schedules (FSS)
- Government-Wide Acquisition Contracts (GWACs)
- Blanket Purchase Agreements (BPAs)
- Indefinite Delivery Indefinite Quantity (IDIQ) contracts

While a majority of the U.S. government's contracts are firm-fixed-price (FFP) and are utilized to acquire relatively simple commercially available off-the-shelf products and services, these typically comprise less than 50 percent of the dollars spent by some government agencies. Conversely, a minority of the U.S. government contracts are cost-reimbursement or time and materials (T&M) contracts, typically used to acquire highly complex systems, integrated solutions, and a vast array of professional services. Yet these cost-reimbursement type contracts and time and materials (T&M) type contracts together often account for over 50 percent of the dollars spent by some government agencies.

What is driving the growing amount of money being spent by the U.S. government's acquiring complex systems, integrated solutions, and professional services? The answer lies in the following converging factors:

- Increased and evolving threat of global terrorism,
- Communication technologies,
- High integration cost for hardware and software,
- Increased customer demands,
- Less government personnel with needed professional services expertise,
- Less government technical expertise to develop more detailed/defined requirements,
- Increased gap between government and industry compensation for key professional services,
- Increased reliance on information technology platforms, related hardware, and software applications, and
- Other factors.

Why Does the Type of Contract Matter When It Comes to Contract Administration?

The answer is simple. When a firm-fixed-price (FFP) contract is awarded, the U.S. government has very low financial risk, because the contractor has agreed to perform the contract for a fixed amount

ONE

of money. If the contractor can adequately perform the work for less, then it makes a higher profit. If, however, it takes the contractor more than the fixed amount to accomplish the work, then the contractor loses money. Thus, government agencies typically perform little contract administration on FFP contracts, because the contractor has the greatest financial risk.

Conversely, when a cost-reimbursement (CR) type contract or a time and materials (T&M) contract is awarded, the U.S. government has higher potential financial risk. In the case of the cost-reimbursement type of contract the government has agreed that the nature of the work is too difficult to adequately define at the outset. Thus, on a cost-reimbursement type of contract the government is essentially purchasing the contractor's best efforts and promising to reimburse the contractor for all of its allowable, allocable, and reasonable expenses. Depending on the type of cost-reimbursement contract there may be an incentive fee, award fee, and/or fixed fee, which is subject to specific Federal Acquisition Regulation (FAR) limitations.

In the case of a T&M contract the government has agreed that the nature of the professional services is too difficult to adequately define and scope out at the start. Thus, on a T&M contract the government is purchasing the contractor's best efforts for specific services in specific labor categories, plus related materials. In a T&M contract the time consists of a fully-loaded wrap-rate (direct cost, indirect cost, and profit) for each specific labor category on an hourly-rate basis. In a T&M contract the material consists of the total material costs, plus any related handling costs, but it does not typically include any profit, which is prohibited by the FAR.

Since cost-reimbursement and T&M contracts place greater financial risk on U.S. government agencies, they are less preferred. Despite the fact that cost-reimbursement and T&M contracts are not preferred, they are and have been for many years the types of contracts on which the U.S. government agencies spend most of their money to buy systems, services, and integrated solutions. As a result, the U.S. government agencies have struggled to provide the necessary contract administration support services and appropriate surveillance to help guide contractors, mitigate risks, and ensure successful programs.

CONTRACT ADMINISTRATION PROCESS

Contract administration can be straightforward or complex, depending on the nature and size of the project. Administering a contract entails creating a contract administration plan and then monitoring performance throughout the many, varied activities that can occur during project execution. Key contract administration activities include ensuring compliance with contract terms and conditions; practicing effective communication and control; managing contract changes, invoicing and payment; and resolving claims and disputes. A contractor's getting paid more money for doing more work than was originally agreed upon in the contract is both fair and reasonable. Similarly, if a contractor fails to properly perform the work or fails to comply with the terms and conditions of the deal, there should be an appropriate remedy. Tailored project management and contract administration procedures are essential to ensure that both parties know what is expected of them at all times; to avoid unpleasant surprises and reduce risks regarding requirements, costs, or schedule-related issues; and to solve problems quickly when they occur.

However, government customers do sometimes consider contractors who effectively manage their contracts and actively pursue payment for contract changes to be "nickel-and-diming" them. Some contractors will intentionally "low bid or underprice" the initial bid in order to get the contract on the bet that they can make enough follow-on sales to offset the initial loss and create a profitable long-term business relationship. Often, government buyers are so motivated to reduce initial capital expenditures to fit their reduced budgets that they will essentially entice sellers into an initial low bid/buy-in business model.

Effectively managing the contract scope of work, through proven project and contract management best practices, is wise and financially prudent for both the government and industry. The government needs to ensure that it gets what it paid for and when it needs it! Contractors need to ensure that they provide the products and/ or services as and when they agreed to deliver.

Post-award contract administration is the process of ensuring that each party's performance meets contractual requirements. On larger project with multiple product and service providers, a key aspect of contract administration is managing the interfaces among the various providers. Because of the legal nature of the contractual relationship, the project team must be acutely aware of the legal implications of actions taken when administering the contract.

Effective contract administration is critical to effective project management because an organization's failure to fulfill its contractual obligations can have legal consequences. Thus, someone must monitor performance of contractual obligations. That person is the contract manager, who must always be aware of the legal and financial consequences of an action or failure to act, and who must take steps to ensure required actions are taken and prohibited actions are avoided. In a real sense, a contract manager is a project manager, and the principles of project management apply to his or her work.

Each party to a contract appoints a contract manager who monitors not only its own organization, but also the other party to ensure that both parties are keeping their promises. The contract manager must maintain these two perspectives throughout the contract performance.

The post-award phase of the contract management process (shown in Figure 1-3) includes applying the appropriate contract administration and project management actions to the contractual relationships and integrating the output from these best practices into the general management of the project.

Figure 1-3		
Post-Award Contract Administration Process		
Key Inputs	Tools & Techniques	Desired Outputs
Contract Project plans + schedules Work results Contract change requests Invoices	Project management discipline Opportunity and risk management Contract changes management Contract analysis + planning Kick-off meeting or pre-performance conference Contract claims and dispute resolution Supply chain management Government property management Performance measuring + reporting (earned value management system) Contract closeout checklists	Documentation Contract Changes Payment Completion of work

Input

Input to the post-award phase of the contract management process consists of the contract, project plans and schedules, work results, contract changes requests, and invoices.

Contract

The contract document is the primary guide for project execution and administration of the contract.

Project Plans and Schedules

The project manager prepares appropriate plans to ensure that work is properly completed on time, on budget, and meets contractual requirements. Such planning could include a work breakdown structure (WBS), organizational breakdown structure (OBS), responsibility assignment matrix (RAM), schedules (Gantt charts, milestone charts, project network schedules, etc.), and an earned value management system (EVMS). In addition, the contract manager should develop a contract requirements matrix (see Form 1-1).

Form 1-1				
Contract Requirements Matrix				
Deliverables				
Description	Contract Reference	Delivery Date or Services Date	Work Breakdown Structure Element	Other Reference

Work Results

The results of performing the requirements will affect contract administration. Chapter 2 discusses integrating a project management discipline into the planning and execution of all work.

Contract Administration: Personnel, Workload, and Processes

11

ONE

Contract Change Requests

Contract change requests are a common element of most contracts. An effective process for managing contract changes must be in place to ensure that all requests are handled smoothly. Contract changes may be called amendments, modifications, change orders, supplemental agreements, add-ons, up-scopes or down-scopes. Contract changes are opportunities either to increase or decrease profitability for the seller. Changes are a necessary aspect of business for buyers because of changed needs. Chapter 4 provides practical guidance on managing contract changes.

Invoices

An efficient process must be developed for handling invoices throughout contract administration. Few areas cause more concern to sellers than late payment. Buyers can realize savings by developing an efficient and timely payment process, especially as sellers are often willing to give discounts for early payment. Chapter 5 discusses the importance of timely and proper invoices and methods of payment by government agencies to contractors.

Tools and Techniques

A variety of tools and techniques are used for successful contract administration. A brief introduction of each follows.

Project Management Discipline

All work to be performed should be appropriately led, planned, scheduled, coordinated, communicated, tracked, evaluated, reported, and corrected, as necessary, using the basic guidelines of the Project Management Institute's (PMI) *Project Management Body of Knowledge (PMBOK)*. Chapter 2 discusses the importance of creating an integrated project management discipline.

Contract Analysis and Planning

Before contract award, each party should develop a contract administration plan and assign the responsibility of administering the contract to a contract manager. To whom should the job be assigned? A project manager could do double duty as the contract manager. However, in most large companies contract administration is a specialized function usually performed by someone in the contracting department, because the job requires special knowledge and training. Contract administration is an element of both contract management and project management.

Kick-Off Meeting or Pre-performance Conference

Before performance begins, the government and industry should meet (via teleconference, videoconference, Web meeting, or face-to-face) to discuss their joint administration of the contract (see Form 1-2). The meeting should be formal, agenda should be distributed in advance, and minutes should be recorded and distributed. Each party should appoint a person who will be its organization's official voice during contract performance. At the meeting, the parties should review the contract terms and conditions and discuss each other's roles. The parties also should establish protocols for written and oral communication and progress measurement and reporting, and discuss procedures for managing changes and resolving differences. Government and contractor managers with performance responsibilities should attend the pre-performance conference or at least send a representative. Important subcontractors should also be represented. The meeting should be held shortly after contract award at the performance site, if possible.

Form 1-2
Pre-performance Conference Checklist

Project Name	
Prepared by (Print)	Date Prepared:
Customer	Contract
Contact Telephone/E-mail	

☐ Complete requirements analysis – verify and validate the requirements stated in the contract to ensure that the project, when completed according to the requirement statement, will meet the needs of both parties.

☐ Summarize contract requirements – complete a contract requirements matrix (see Form 1).

☐ Establish the project baseline – ensure that the baseline and specifications are established.

☐ Develop in-scope and out-of-scope listings – develop lists of items that the government and contractor consider within and outside the scope of the contract.

☐ List the contractor's assumptions about the government's requirements and understanding of the end-user's expectations.

☐ Establish preliminary schedule of meetings between the parties.

☐ Inform your team and other affected parties – brief the team members who will attend the meeting, ensuring that they understand the basic requirements of the contract and the project.

☐ Review meeting findings with all people affected in your organization.

☐ Document who attended, what was discussed, what was agreed to, and what follow-up actions are required – by whom, where, and when.

☐ Prepare and send pre-performance conference meeting minutes to the other parties.

Performance Measuring and Reporting

During contract performance, the project manager, contract manager, and responsible business managers all must observe performance, collect information, and measure actual contract progress. These activities are essential to effective control. The resources devoted to these tasks and the techniques used to perform them will depend on the nature of the contract work, the size and complexity of the contract, and the resources available. On large, complex contracts, the government often requires the contractor to apply an earned value management system (EVMS), which is discussed in detail in Chapter 9, to ensure that all aspects of cost, schedule, and technical performance are effectively integrated and successfully implemented.

Payment Process

Every contract must establish a clear invoicing and payment process. The government and the contractor must agree to whom invoices should be sent and what information is required. Contractors must submit proper invoices in a timely manner, and the government is then required to pay all invoices promptly. Chapter 5 provides a comprehensive discussion of contract financing, payment, and profitability.

Contract Change Management Process

As a rule, any party that can make a contract can agree to change it. Changes are usually inevitable in contracts for complex undertakings, such as system design and integration. No one has perfect foresight—requirements and circumstances change in unexpected ways, and contract terms and conditions must often be changed as a result. Chapter 4 provides a wealth of additional information on contract changes management.

Dispute Resolution Process

No one should be surprised when, from time to time, contracting parties find themselves in disagreement about the correct interpretation of contract terms and conditions. Such disagreements typically are minor and are resolved without too much difficulty. Occasionally, however, the parties find themselves entangled in a seemingly intractable controversy. Try as they might, they cannot resolve their differences. If the dispute goes unresolved for too long, one or both of the parties may threaten, or even initiate, litigation.

Litigation is time-consuming, costly, and risky. You can never be entirely sure of its result. Rarely is the outcome a truly satisfactory resolution of a dispute, and it sours the business relationship. For these reasons, litigation should be avoided. One goal of business managers and contract managers should be to resolve disputes without litigation whenever possible.

For effective dispute resolution, one must

- Recognize that contract documents are not perfect,
- Keep larger objectives in mind,
- Focus on the facts,

- Depersonalize the issues, and
- Be willing to make reasonable compromises.

When disputes become intractable, seeking the opinion of an impartial third party can sometimes help. When this approach is formal, and the decision is binding on the parties, it is called arbitration. Many government agencies now include a clause in their contracts that make arbitration the mandatory means of resolving disputes. Chapter 6 discusses the topic of contract claims and various dispute resolution methods.

Supply Chain Management

Chapter 7 provides an interesting discussion of the challenges of supply chain management typically encountered by government prime contractors and some of the many proven effective best practices to improve performance results.

Government Property Management

Chapter 8 offers an enlightening review of the key aspects of government property management, pursuant to FAR Part 45, and the numerous challenges often encountered by U.S. government agencies and government contractors. In addition, the chapter provides a review of numerous demonstrated best practices from both government agencies and industry.

Contract Closeout Process

Contract closeout refers to verification that all administrative matters are concluded on a contract that is otherwise physically complete. In other words, the contractor has delivered the required supplies or performed the required services, and the government has inspected and accepted the supplies or services (see Form 1-3). Chapter 10 provides a comprehensive discussion of contract terminations and contract closeout.

Form 1-3				
Contract Closeout Checklist				
Project Name				
Prepared by (print)			Date Prepared	
Customer			Contract	
Contract Telephone/E-mail				
1.	☐ yes ☐ no ☐ n/a	All products or services required were provided to the buyer.		
2.	☐ yes ☐ no ☐ n/a	Documentation adequately shows receipt and formal acceptance of all contract items.		
3.	☐ yes ☐ no ☐ n/a	No claims or investigations are pending on this contract.		
4.	☐ yes ☐ no ☐ n/a	Any buyer-furnished property or information was returned to the buyer.		
5.	☐ yes ☐ no ☐ n/a	All actions related to contract price revisions and changes are concluded.		
6.	☐ yes ☐ no ☐ n/a	All outstanding subcontracting issues are settled.		
7.	☐ yes ☐ no ☐ n/a	If a partial or complete termination was involved, action is complete.		
8.	☐ yes ☐ no ☐ n/a	Any required contract audit is now complete		

Output

The output functions resulting from contract administration include appropriate documentation, payment, and completion of the work, each of which is highlighted below.

Documentation

It is essential to provide proof of performance, management of changes, justification for claims, and evidence in the unlikely event of litigation. The most important documentation is the official copy of the contract, contract modifications, and conformed working copies of the contract. Other important forms of documentation include:

- **External and internal correspondence**. All appropriate contract correspondence should be saved electronically by the contract manager and project managers, with separate files for external and internal correspondence. Each piece of correspondence should be dated and properly electronically stored.

- **Meeting minutes**. Minutes should be recorded electronically for all meetings between the seller and buyer. The minutes should state the date, time, and location of the meeting and identify all attendees by name, company or organization, and title and describe all issues discussed, decisions made, questions unresolved, and action items assigned. Copies of the minutes should be provided to each attendee and to others who were interested in the meeting but unable to attend.

- **Progress reports**. Progress reports should be saved electronically and filed chronologically by subject.

- **Project diaries**. On large projects, the project manager and contract manager should keep a daily diary to record significant events of the day. They should update their diaries at the end of each workday. The entries should describe events in terms of who, what, when, where, and how. Preferably, the diary should have daily entries and be kept in electronic form or in a perfect-bound book with pre-numbered pages. A diary supplements memory and aids in recalling events and is also useful as an informal project history when a new project manager or contract manager must take over. It can also be of great assistance in preparing, negotiating, and settling claims or in the event of litigation. However, a diary may become evidence in court proceedings, so a diarist should be careful to record only facts, leaving out conclusions, speculations about motives, and personal opinions about people or organizations.

- **Telephone logs**. Another useful aid to memory is a telephone log, which is record of all incoming and outgoing phone calls. It identifies the date and time of each call, whether it was incoming or outgoing, and if outgoing, the number called. It lists all parties to the call and includes a brief notation about the discussion.

- **Photographs and videotapes**. When physical evidence of conditions at the site of performance is important, a photographic or videotape record can be helpful. This record will greatly facilitate communication and provide an excellent description of the exact nature of the site conditions. Whenever a contract involves physical labor, the project manager, contract manager, or other on-site representative should have a camera and film or digital camera available for use. The purpose of documentation is to record facts and reduce reliance on human memory. Efforts to maintain documentation must be thorough and consistent.

- **Contract changes**. As a result of changes in a buyer's needs, changes in technologies, and other changes in the marketplace, buyers need flexibility in their contracts. Thus, changes are inevitable. Sellers must realize that changes are not bad, that they are in fact good, because changes are often an opportunity to sell more products or services.

Payment

Payment is important as sellers want their money as quickly as possible. The government should seek product and service discounts for early payments. Likewise, contractors should improve their accounts receivable management and enforce late payment penalties.

Completion of Work

The last step is the contractor's actual accomplishment of the government's requirement for products, services, systems, or solutions. Ensuring that the parties to a contract communicate with each other is important. A contract is a relationship. Because virtually every contract entails some degree of interaction between the parties, each party must keep the other informed of its progress, problems, and proposed solutions, so that the other can respond appropriately.

Like all human relationships, contracts are dynamic. As performance proceeds and events unfold, the parties will find that they must modify their original expectations and plans to adjust to real events. As they do so, they must modify the contract terms and conditions to reflect the current status of their agreement. Changes are an inevitable part of contracting, because no one can predict the future with perfect accuracy. However, the parties should make changes consciously and openly, so that they remain in agreement about what should be done. Lack of communication can result in dispute over what each party's obligations really are.

An important part of communication and control is the effective management of changes. Effectively managing contract changes includes establishing formal procedures for modifying the contract and limiting the number of people entitled to make changes. It also entails establishing recognition and notification procedures in response to authorized changes. Finally, it requires establishing procedures for identifying, estimating, and measuring the potential and actual effect of changes on all aspects of contract performance. Form 1-4 provides a checklist of tips for successful contract administration.

Form 1-4
Checklist of Tips for Successful Contract Administration
☐ Develop and implement a project management discipline to ensure on-time delivery and flawless execution.
☐ Comply with contract terms and conditions.
☐ Maintain effective communications.
☐ Manage contract changes with a proactive change management process.
☐ Resolve disputes promptly and dispassionately.
☐ Use negotiation or arbitration, not litigation, to resolve disputes.
☐ Develop a work breakdown structure to assist in planning and assigning work.
☐ Conduct pre-performance conferences or a project kick-off meeting.
☐ Measure, monitor, and track performance.
☐ Manage the invoice and payment process.
☐ Report progress internally and externally.
☐ Identify variances between planned versus actual performance – use earned value management.
☐ Be sure to follow up on all corrective actions.
☐ Appoint people to negotiate contract changes and document the authorized representatives in the contract.
☐ Enforce contract terms and conditions.
☐ Provide copies of the contract to all affected organizations.
☐ Maintain conformed copies of the contract.
☐ Understand the effects of change on cost, schedule, and quality.
☐ Document all communication – use telephone logs, faxes, correspondence logs, and e-mails.
☐ Prepare internal and external meeting minutes.
☐ Prepare contract closeout checklists.
☐ Ensure completion of work.
☐ Document lessons learned and share them throughout your organization.
☐ Communicate, communicate, communicate.

SUMMARY

Contract administration is an important aspect of successful business. Simply stated, contract administration is the joint government and contractor actions taken to successfully perform and administer a contractual agreement, including effective changes management and timely contract closeout. The ongoing challenge is to maintain open and effective communication, timely delivery of quality products and services, responsive resolution of problems, compliance with all agreed-upon terms and conditions, and effective changes management. After a project is successfully completed, proper procedures are instituted to close out the contract officially. Of course, the goal of nearly every contractor is to capture the government's follow-on business, which is far easier to do if the contract and related project were properly managed by both parties. Achieving a true partnership between a government agency and industry requires dedication and discipline by both parties—not just one!

Recognize, too, the power of precedent. Your organization is always evaluated based on your past performance and the precedents it sets. Your contract administration actions taken years ago affect your organization's reputation today. Likewise, in both government and industry the contract management actions you take today form your organization's reputation for tomorrow.

This first chapter has merely set the stage for the rest of this book, which discusses all of the concepts, functional areas, tools, and best practices outlined in this chapter in far greater detail.

QUESTIONS TO CONSIDER

1. How well does your organization select and staff post-award contract administration?

2. How effective is your organization in managing post-award contract changes?

3. On a scale of 1 (low/poor) to 10 (high) how do you rate your organization's ability to efficiently and cost-effectively conduct contract administration and ensure successful contract results?

CHAPTER **2**

INTEGRATED PROJECT MANAGEMENT (IPM) DISCIPLINE

INTRODUCTION

Every U.S. federal government contract and related project has a customer or multiple customers, sometimes called end-users. By definition every U.S. government outsourced or contracted project is a goal-oriented undertaking of multiple tasks, often interdependent in nature, increasingly involving multiple parties, including a U.S. government agency, prime contractor, subcontractors, and other third parties, to develop or provide products, services, or solutions within a given period of time. One of the key reasons U.S. federal government outsourced or contracted projects fail is because the project leaders, in both government and industry, lose focus on what is important. Too often projects suffer from vague and constantly changing U.S. government agency requirements and funding combined with inadequate or incomplete customer acceptance criteria, which leads to project failure. Everyone involved in the planning and execution of a U.S. government contract must maintain focus on the end-user's goals. Projects only succeed if the end-user's needs are met or exceeded.

Creating an integrated project management (PM) discipline across multiple parties involved in a U.S. government contract, after the contract has been awarded, does not happen overnight. In fact, based on our research, most government contractors that have effectively implemented integrated PM discipline have spent years evolving from functional or product/service-oriented organizations to integrated project management organizations. Further, based upon research and experience it has been determined that many organizations that have effectively developed an integrated PM discipline to support contract management and contract administration have evolved through five distinct phases of the integrated project management (IPM) life cycle: (1) awakening, (2) implementing, (3) professionalizing, (4) enterprising, and (5) integrating (see Figure 2-1).

Figure 2-1				
Integrated Project Management (IPM) Life Cycle (5 Phases)				
Awakening Phase	**Implementing Phase**	**Professionalizing Phase**	**Enterprising Phase**	**Integrating Phase**
• Awareness of Need for PM • Leadership Involvement (Champion) • Core Team or Project Management Office (PMO) Formatio	• Process Development • PM Staffing • PM Training • Focus on Key Projects	• PM Rigid-Flexibility • Widespread PM Application • Focus on PM Certification • Sharing PM Best Practices	• Standardization of ERP Database • Link to other Processes • PM Health Checks	• Multi-party • Customer • Principal Supplier(s) • Supply- Chain Partners • Integrated • Project Practices • Project Tools and Techniques • Project Training • Project Leadership

Awakening Phase

The first phase that a government contractor creating an institution-alized integrated project management discipline experiences is the *Awakening* phase. During this phase of development, leadership's involvement and support is crucial because it is during this phase that project management's effect on the business is evaluated. The application of the integrated project management discipline across multiple related projects has proven successful for improving business performance in numerous organizations and companies. Improved business performance is typically viewed or translated to include reduced costs of operation, reduced cycle-time, increased revenues, increased profitability, and greater customer satisfaction. Many organizations and companies, including ABB, AT&T, Bechtel, Boeing, Cisco, EDS, Ford, IBM, NCR, Northrop-Grumman, NTT, and USAA, have moved rapidly to take advantage of project management's (PM) promise during the past 10 years, initiating its implementation as a discipline within their organization. Most of the companies formed a headquarters core PM team or project management office (PMO) charged with establishing a constant but flexile PM discipline that could be quickly applied to all of the organization's projects.

In the awakening phase, leadership is crucial. In non–project-based organizations, functional processes such as engineering, manufacturing, installation, and sales have traditionally operated independently from their peer units. For PM to be successfully implemented, organizations must change from a functional or product-oriented operating structure to one that is project oriented.

To ensure that the entire organization benefits from the implementation of PM, the executives of several companies, including AT&T, NCR, and Hewlett-Packard, among others, established a corporate-wide Project Management Leadership Council comprising directors from every business unit. This council was chartered to provide a forum to foster the growth and development of a world-class corporate project management resource for the project management community. Companies with a Project Management Leadership Council have helped foster project management's attributes by sharing lessons learned and best practices throughout their respective companies.

Implementing Phase

The second phase that a government contractor will experience is *Implementing* project management, the most expensive and labor-intensive phase in creating an integrated PM discipline. In most organizations, the core PM team, sometimes called a PM Center of Excellence or Project Management Office (PMO), is critical to the success of the implementing phase. Staffed with a small team of experienced project managers from both internal and external sources, this core PM team or PMO focuses on developing processes and training as well as supporting large programs. To help jump-start the effort, many organizations have supplemented the team's or PMO's knowledge by bringing in experienced external PM consultants. Initially, most organizations outsource program/project management training to one or more of the many university or training firms. The training, essential in the implementing phase, must focus on project management principles and practices and customer requirements management. The intent of the PM curriculum, which should be based on the Project Management Institute's (PMI) Project Management Body of Knowledge (PM-BOK), is to provide managers with sufficient knowledge to begin applying the PM discipline in their work environment.

During the implementing phase, the main function of the core PM team or PMO is typically to provide experienced project managers to augment newly formed PM teams, sometimes temporarily. In this phase, PM implementation is usually concentrated on selected large projects. The driver behind placing experienced project managers on selected projects is the belief that concentrating talent on the largest projects leads to the highest return. Choosing highly visible projects to internally showcase and document PM successes and lessons learned is vital in this phase. Internal support can only be obtained by successfully performing these showcase programs.

Professionalizing Phase

The third phase a government contractor will undergo is the *Professionalizing* phase, in which the project management discipline is strengthened and project management tools are improved. During the professionalizing phase many organizations establish the concept of rigid-flexibility to ensure that key PM practices, based upon the PMI PMBOK, are successfully executed. In addition, during the professionalizing phase PM application becomes widespread throughout the organization, and specific PM objectives are created to proactively manage scope, schedule, cost, and customer relations. Setting clear PM objectives is essential in the first steps towards widespread application of the discipline.

During the professionalizing phase, most companies like Cisco, IBM, and USAA have undertaken several actions to improve their level of PM professionalism, including encouraging project managers to obtain the Project Management Institute's Project Management Professional (PMP ®) certification. To further support communication and professionalism several companies, including Hewlett-Packard, and USAA, conduct a yearly project management conference, which serves as an important medium for communicating and applying PM lessons learned throughout the organization. Many companies, such as CH2M Hill, have also improved professionalism by creating an intranet Intranet PM website to facilitate dialogue within their PM community. In addition, companies like Bechtel and Northrop-Grumman have introduced project control specialists to help them improve the efficiency of their respective project managers by allowing them to focus on customer and management issues instead of on data collection. In the professionalizing phase, most organizations continue to develop their internal PM process documentation to facilitate rapid and consistent implementation and sharing of best practices.

Enterprising Phase

Enterprising is the fourth phase of creating an integrated project management discipline. Connecting the various projects and programs is pivotal for taking company-wide advantage of every business opportunity. Effective use of company resources across multiple projects can be obtained if processes and tools are compatible among these projects. Standardization of progress reports and tools to generate them is the first step in this phase. Another important step in enterprising is standardization of resource codes and names used in planning tools. In organizations that manage large, complex, outsourced projects that consume hundreds of resources, the tracking of these resources is often accomplished using resource categories (for example, engineers) instead of specific individual resources. It is essential that there be cross-project agreement on how to use and code these resources before enterprise project management can become a success.

Linking PM processes with other processes within an organization, such as engineering, manufacturing, installation, customer service, logistics, asset management, financial management, and contract management, is essential within the enterprising phase. Many organizations have worked in partnership with companies like Microsoft, Oracle, and SAP, among others, to develop an integrated PM implementation database and process description. In this process all interfaces, such as those between PM and contract management, are agreed to and documented. This integrated process description also includes an analysis of current information systems and outlines the target system architecture for the business. The successful implementation of a viable and certified earned value management system (EVMS) is also a key element of the enterprising phase of the IPM discipline.

A few companies, including EDS, IBM, and others, have used the integrated process description in "health checks," or project team assessments. During a PM health check, members of the headquarters organizations or PMO visit project teams and evaluate or audit their performance against the organization's integrated process and systems architecture description. Typically, the desired outcome of these health checks is a road map to migrate the project to standard processes and systems and to document PM best practices. An important difference between a financial audit and this health check is that the health checks are conducted on request in a team-building environment. This collaboration between the project teams and the core headquarters organization or PMO uses the strengths of both and signifies a high-level PM discipline.[1]

Integrating Phase

Integrating is the fifth and final phase for a government contractor in creating an integrated project management (PM) discipline. The integrated PM discipline is based on the premise that for projects to be successful in an outsourcing environment involving multiple-parties—U.S. government agency, prime contractor, and subcontractors (lower tiers)—everyone needs to be unified and focused on achieving customer goals. Integration means that all of the parties involved in a large, complex, outsourced project work together to achieve customer goals. There are four essentials to achieve an integrated PM discipline: (1) project practices, (2) project tools and techniques, (3) project training, and (4) project leadership.

Case Study: NCR

During the period 1993-1996 NCR, at that time an AT&T company, formerly known as AT&T Global Information Solutions (AT&T/GIS), experienced a transformation as it successfully instituted an integrated project management discipline throughout its worldwide services organizations. AT&T/GIS aimed to provide customer-focused solutions to help businesses better understand and serve their customers by more effectively obtaining, transferring, and using customer information. Achieving this goal placed great pressure on the company's project management community.

The company had hundreds of project managers worldwide who collectively managed thousands of information technology projects. These projects ranged from relatively common installations of off-the-shelf computer hardware to highly complex multinational systems integration and professional services undertakings. The company also had thousands of other employees who served as members of project teams. The company developed and implemented various means of fostering effective interaction among its project teams. The following information about these best practices may prove helpful to other companies that seek to enhance such interaction in their own work environments.

First Best Practice: GlobalPM®

AT&T/GIS empowered its project managers through the creation and implementation of a state-of-the-art project management methodology called GlobalPM®. GlobalPM® practices and techniques gave the company's project managers a clear, concise, and consistent set of organizational processes and conceptual and documentation tools. Throughout the world, they provided project managers and the team members who worked with them a consistent approach to managing highly challenging projects involving total business solutions.

Second Best Practice: Customer-Focused Teams

The company formed several hundred customer-focused business teams to implement a new customer-focused business model. A customer-focused team is a multi-functional unit dedicated to understanding a specific customer's needs and interests and working to deliver solutions fitting the customer's unique organizational profile. Each team was headed by a team leader and made up of representatives from a variety of functional areas. All team members were focused on helping the customer reach its business goals. The team had the decision-making authority, responsibility, and accountability needed to be fully responsive to the customer's business needs. Its goal was to work together with shared values and a common bond to delight the customer.

Third Best Practice: Early Involvement of the Project Manager in the Business Process

The company has learned that early involvement of their project managers in pre-contract award activities is a proactive means of mitigating risk. Often project managers can give sales and marketing managers critical insights into the value of certain requirements and the realistic opportunities of achieving the results that the customer desires. Project managers can, for example, assess whether cost and schedule estimates are realistic, analyze the risks and the opportunities a project provides, and recommend special terms and conditions for tailoring the contract to the project goals.

Fourth Best Practice: Shared Lessons Learned

"If you always do what you always did, you will always get what you have always got!" The project management team and customer must work together to document the successes and failures of their endeavors so as to learn from the past. The company recognized that it needed to improve its efforts to ensure that lessons learned were shared on a consistent basis.

Fifth Best Practice: Professional Development Programs and Certification

The company promoted and provided professional development programs for its project management teams globally. It sent hundreds of its managers to a comprehensive professional development program in project management offered by George Washington University. Also, the company actively promoted professional certification in project management via the Project Management Institute's (PMI), Project Management Professional (PMP) certification. Clearly, the leadership of NCR, formerly AT&T/GIS Worldwide Professional Services, saw the value of integrating the project management discipline within the company, which evolved over several years through the phases of the integrated project management process.[12]

Case Study: Hewlett-Packard

Hewlett-Packard (HP) learned many years ago the value of implementing project management (PM) and integrating the PM discipline throughout its business. Between the late 1980's and 1990's HP's revenues doubled. During that time period the company's worldwide customer support system recognized that customer requirements were becoming increasingly customized and complex. HP's customers needed flawless execution of complex outsourced projects to provide total business solutions. Various HP support services were becoming more important and were at times being viewed as key market differentiators. HP's executives decided to expand the company's customer support sales organization and develop project management as a core competency.

HP formed a Project Management Office (PMO) within their support organization. By charter, the PMO was to develop PM expertise throughout the company to meet the challenging needs of

HP's customers. To facilitate the implementation of PM, an aggressive PM training and mentor program was established. The mentor program partnered experienced project managers with newly assigned project managers to help support the latter's professional development. As professionalism in project management grew at HP so did the company's efforts to achieve industry recognition through PMI's Project Management Professional (PMP) certification. Today, HP is widely recognized for its demonstrated expertise in managing complex outsourced projects and meeting or exceeding customer expectations. Like NCR and many other companies, HP understands and values the importance of execution. HP has shown their customers that the joint use of proven project practices, project tools and techniques, project training, and project leadership improve performance and help to leverage customer loyalty.[3]

INTEGRATED PROJECT MANAGEMENT (IPM) LIFE CYCLE: LESSONS LEARNED

An integrated project management organization should view every internal and external business activity as a project and the grouping of related projects as programs. A true world-class organization uses the power of the integrated project management discipline to set proper customer expectations and leverages its suppliers to reduce cycle-times, reduce costs, improve on-time delivery, and ensure customer satisfaction. Almost any organization and its related customers and suppliers can evolve through the awakening, implementing, professionalizing, enterprising, and integrating phases of the IPM life cycle, given executive support and resources. The real key to creating an integrated project management discipline is the ability to do it well, do it fast, and exceed customer expectations.

Based on years of extensive experience and research, there are five project elements that must be accomplished to successfully manage complex outsourced projects and achieve the fifth and final level or phase of the IPM life cycle. The five projects elements required to achieve IPM are

- Customer Needs & Goals
- Supplier Value-Chain
- Project Communications
- Project Teamwork
- Integrated Project Management Discipline

The combination of the above five project elements form the Integrated Project Management (IPM) Model (see Figure 2-2). The IPM Model is a visual tool designed and intended to help every member of a project team, including customers, suppliers, and supply-chain partners, understand what it takes to make outsourced projects succeed. The following is an overview of the five project elements required to achieve the fifth and final level or phase of integrated project management.

Figure 2-2

Integrated Project Management (IPM) Model

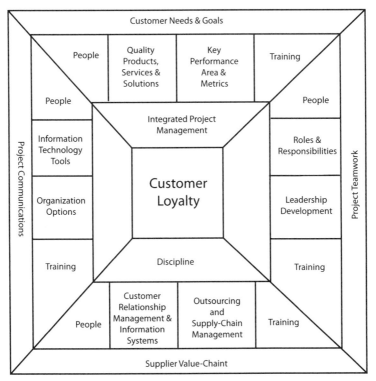

First Project Element: Customer Needs & Goals

In both the public and private sectors, listening to and understanding customers' needs and desires are critical to ultimate business success. Appropriate customer intimacy is a valuable and valued trait. Of course, in federal, state, and local government contracting there are many rules and regulations that govern appropriate behavior. U.S. government customers want suppliers who know what they really need, what they desire to achieve or their goals, the difference between their needs and goals, and how to accomplish both. Many U.S. government customers expect their business partners to become trusted advisors who help them meet or exceed their needs, thus achieving higher levels of performance enabling them to reach their goals (see Table 2-1).

TABLE 2-1
Customer Needs and Goals

• On-time delivery (to customer need date)	• High quality products, services, and
• Cost reduction (lower operations & support costs)	solutions
	• Supplier financing
• Short-cycle time (from request to delivery)	• End-customer/user satisfaction
• Best-value pricing	• Ongoing customer service
• Breakthrough technology	

Understanding Customer Needs

A fundamental mistake, which is all too common, especially when dealing with complex outsourced projects, is a lack of the true understanding of the customer's needs. Translating a U.S. government agency's general business needs into specific performance requirements is a formidable task. Further, translating specific U.S. government customer performance requirements into tailored business solutions, comprised of numerous products (hardware and software) and professional services, is a significant challenge requiring the effective use of the integrated project management discipline.

Translating Customer Needs into Projects

Today U.S. government agencies usually organize and plan their needs or requirements into specific projects. Often, customers have numerous related requirements, which involve delivering similar products or services to various locations, which are geographically diverse. U.S. government agencies typically group related projects into programs to facilitate the work and sharing of limited resources. Sometimes customers internally plan, schedule, and execute programs and their related projects using their own employees to achieve their needs. However, customers are increasingly outsourcing some or all of the work (products and/or services) that is required to meet their needs.

Four Major Inputs to Fulfill Customer Needs

(1) **People**.–To achieve U.S. government agency needs, the agency and prime contractor must assemble a small team of talented and experienced professionals to: (1) assess the real organizational needs, (2) distinguish between needs and desires, (3) establish appropriate performance-based requirements, and (4) then determine what efforts are best performed internally by the organization and which are best fulfilled using outsourcing.

(2) **Quality Products, Services, and Solutions**.–Ultimately what every customer wants are quality products, services, and/or solutions to meet or exceed their mission requirements at a fair market-based price.

(3) **Key Performance Areas and Metrics**.–In the past, most U.S. government customers described or defined the exact products and services they desired, often with detailed statements of work and rigid specifications. Today, more and more customers are creating performance-based requirements for their projects, both internally and externally (outsourced). As a result, U.S. government agencies should work closely with their prime contractors to ensure mutually agreeable or agreed-upon performance areas and related performance metrics, which are included in their project acceptance criteria. The use of performance-based contracts and related projects allows suppliers greater flexibility and, thus, the opportunity to be more innovative in meeting or exceeding the mutually agreed-upon performance requirements. Performance-based requirements must be clearly stated, challenging, measurable, realistically attainable, and most importantly mutually agreed to between customer and supplier. The most effective performance-based requirements are also linked to performance incentives, both positive and negative.

(4) **Training**.–U.S. government agencies should ensure their personnel involved with establishing organizational requirements/need statements are well educated and trained, including preparing performance-based requirements and statements of work, developing solicitation documents (e.g., requests for proposals and invitations to bid), and developing performance-based incentives, metrics, and acceptance criteria.

Integrating PM Discipline to Projects

The magic of making projects successful is really the blending of art and science. The secret to achieve customer needs is knowing what project management practices, tools, and techniques should be applied; when to apply them; and how to motivate others to do what needs to be done in a timely manner. Project leadership is imperative to ensure that project management discipline is consistently practiced and is vital to fulfilling customer needs, achieving customer goals, and ensuring customer loyalty.

Second Project Element: Supplier Value-Chain

For suppliers or prime contractors and subcontractors to survive and thrive in this increasingly competitive global marketplace they must be highly focused on their U.S. government agency end-customers' needs and goals. The prime contractor's leadership must instill a culture that is focused on helping customers achieve their goals and creating an ethical win-win professional business environment. The supplier's leadership must ensure it is providing value-based products, services, or solutions that help their customers solve their problems/challenges and maximize their opportunities.

More prime contractors are learning the importance of leveraging their supply-chain to add value to their customers, while also helping them reduce their own expenses and cycle time. As the use of outsourcing increases worldwide, the power of supply-chain management is significant and growing. Converting vendors or subcontractors into value-based business partners is critical to transforming the supply-chain into a supplier value-chain.

Making Projects Succeed via the Supplier Value-Chain

Most prime contractors translate customer needs into customer orders. Customer orders are then converted by suppliers into projects. Projects may involve products (hardware or software), professional services, or integrated business solutions, which typically contain a mix of the principal supplier's content and some degree of outsourced products and services from supply-chain partners.

TWO

Four Major Inputs to the Supplier Value-Chain

(1) **People.** Prime contractors must have a highly professional, well-educated, experienced employee-oriented and customer-focused leadership team. Too often supplier business leaders are too inwardly focused on short-term cost reduction and quick-fix productivity improvements by laying-off/firing some employees while forcing other employees to handle more work for the same or even less pay. Supplier leadership must be focused on achieving customer goals in a cost-effective and efficient manner by building strategic partnerships with their customers and their vendors, while supporting their employees and shareholders.

(2) **Customer Relationship Management and Information Systems.**–In order for a supplier to be successful, it must develop effective and efficient business processes. Suppliers must reduce or eliminate non-value-added work and ensure well-defined handoffs between their customers, their employees (functional operations), and their supply-chain partners. Information systems that provide suppliers with current, accurate, and timely data are extremely valuable assets that enable a supplier to maximize performance (i.e., reduce costs, reduce cycle time, and increase profitability). Increasingly suppliers are purchasing customer relationship management (CRM) software to help them standardize their business processes, increase their information accuracy, and improve their customer responsiveness.

(3) **Outsourcing and Supply-Chain Management.**–More and more organizations have come to realize the inherent value in closely managing the products and/or services that they outsource to other companies. The Institute of Supply Management (ISM), formerly the National Association of Purchasing Management (NAPM), has recognized the important evolution of simple commodity purchasing to the increasingly value-added role of supply-chain management. Likewise, more and more universities worldwide are transitioning their business school purchasing programs to teach the value of supply-chain management.

Simply stated, supply-chain management is about delivering value to customers as cost effectively as possible. Clearly, the concept of supply-chain management should evolve to a supplier value-chain.

(4) **Training**.—As the level of outsourcing grows and the need for effective supply-chain management increases so does the need for more people to be trained on a variety of related topics (e.g., purchasing, contract management, customer relationship management, supplier relationship management, capture management, and supply-chain management).

Integrating PM Discipline into Supplier-Value Chain

The project management (PM) discipline can serve as an essential integrator to suppliers' traditionally inwardly focused supply-chain organization, helping everyone stay focused on the customer's needs and goals. Again, the key to successfully integrating the PM discipline is to tailor the PM practices, tools, and techniques as appropriate to the respective projects. Another real value-added benefit to integrating PM into the supply-chain management organization is to allow the respective project managers to hold everyone accountable for what they are supposed to do, when they are supposed to do it, including customers, the supplier itself, and its supply-chain partners. When project managers hold everyone accountable, it often causes constructive tension, which is essential to drive the project(s) to a successful completion.

Third Project Element: Project Communications

Few actions are as important to the success of a project as how the parties involved communicate. Communication channels must be open, streamlined, and effective to ensure all the appropriate people involved with a project receive the right information at the right time in the right way. Project communications, which are vital to project success, include ensuring customer needs (requirements) and acceptance are well-defined criteria that are documented and mutually –agreed to; verifying that customer obligations are understood and properly performed; and establishing mutually agreed-to performance metrics for key areas of performance by the customer, supplier, and supply-chain partners, etc.

Making Project Communications Work

As George Bernard Shaw once said, "The greatest problem in communication is the illusion that it has been accomplished." Project success is heavily dependent on all of the involved parties' communicating effectively. Projects, by definition, provide a challenging environment for effective communication, because they typically bring together for a temporary period of time a group of individuals who were previously unknown to one another, each with different backgrounds and various personal agendas.

Four Major Inputs to Project Communications

(1) **People.**–As in all discussions of communication, the most important element or input is the people involved with the project. The most significant reason for the success or failure of any project is the human resources involved and the respective skills that they bring to the project. Effective oral and written communication skills are critical to project success. Communication skills are especially important for the project manager, whose job is to frequently communicate what needs to be done, by whom, and when to ensure that customer needs and goals are met or exceeded.

(2) **Information Technology Tools.**–Information technology has made it possible to conduct communications via a wide variety of media, which are continually evolving. When considering information technology tools for project communications, one needs to consider the communication flow. Communication flows fall into three basic types: (1) broadcast (i.e., one-way send), (2) exchange (i.e., send and receive), and (3) collection (i.e., one-way receive). Some information technology tools are more effective for certain communication flows than others. It is ironic that the root cause of many problems on project teams is still poor communication. As projects become larger and more complex, the number of team members increases, and with the addition of each new team member the channels of communication increase dramatically. Project communications must be taken seriously as an issue requiring advance planning and thought to be effective. The proper selection and use of information technology tools for each project is critical.[2]

(3) **Organization Options.**–One of the favorite activities of most new organizational leaders is to reorganize. Typically, organizational leaders reorganize to help them communicate or relate more effectively to the various functional or product/service-oriented departments within their span of control. Unfortunately, reorganizations often do not help improve the

flow of communications. There are a variety of organizational options that can be selected to staff a project team.

(4) **Training.**–To maximize the effectiveness of project communications all of the people involved with a project should receive timely team-based training to help facilitate effective project communications. Suggested project communications training should include oral and written communication skills, information technology tools, and diversity awareness.

Integrating PM Discipline into Project Communications

Clearly, effective project communication is fundamental to project success. Within the project management discipline there are numerous tools and techniques that are designed to improve project communications including:

- Work breakdown structure (WBS)
- Organizational breakdown structure (OBS)
- Responsibility assignment matrix (RAM)
- Master integrated schedule (MIS)
- Project communications plan
- Opportunity assessment
- Risk management plan
- Points-of- contact list
- Action item register
- Project status reports

All of the aforementioned PM tools and techniques are commonly used and appropriately tailored for the projects they support and to ensure that the PM discipline is well integrated into project communications.

Fourth Project Element: Project Teamwork

The involvement of groups of people into designated project teams is critical to making projects succeed. Teams should be the primary organizational structure to accomplish customer goals. Teams involve the internal organizational groups and include individuals from functional or product groups to form a multi-functional project team. Of course, the truly integrated project team includes individuals representing the customer, supplier, and supply-chain partners, as appropriate. The size of an integrated project team, individual skills, and physical location of team members often varies based on the needs of the customer and the specific project.

Developing Project Teamwork

Developing project teamwork initially involves three steps:

1. Agreeing on the project charter,
2. Defining roles and responsibilities, and
3. Creating a code of conduct

A project mission statement, often called a project charter, should provide a common focus on achieving customer goals.[3] An effective project charter should be clear, concise, customer-focused, and perceived by all team members as challenging but achievable. In addition, the project charter should be developed by the integrated project team with the support and commitment of their respective senior leadership. The project charter should include the following:

- Scope of project work (size, dollar amount, level of complexity, risk, etc.)
- Statement of project manager's level of authority
- Commitment of resources
- Specific key roles and responsibilities (level of empowerment)

After the integrated project team agrees on the project charter, the second step is to define roles and responsibilities. As part of the definition of roles and responsibilities, each team member must understand the following about his or her role and that of each team member:

- What each team member is generally expected to contribute
- Expected outputs of each team member
- Level of empowerment
- Key performance areas and metrics

Each project leader should spend time with each project team member to ensure his or her respective goals, objectives, and responsibilities are clearly defined, documented, challenging, measurable, specific, attainable, and customer-focused. Project leaders must ensure that team members' roles and responsibilities are updated as and when needed.

The third key step in developing teamwork is creating a code of conduct. The code of conduct provides some general guidelines for acceptable professional business practices, which all team members must follow.

Four Major Inputs to Project Teamwork

(1) **People** .–The most important aspect of every contract and related project is the people involved. Selection of the appropriate people for a specific project is often not carefully considered, resulting in frequent project failures. Just as in the case of sports teams, project teams take time to bond, gel, and evolve to a high-performance team. Individual chemistry, how people interact with one another, is vital to creating a successful team. Selection of the right person to serve as the project leader is critical to project success. Likewise failure of the project leader to resolve team member conflicts will negatively impact performance results and erode team morale. While all team members are important, they can all be replaced– and should be replaced if they are not working as a customer-focused integrated project team.

(2) **Leadership Development**.–Every member of an integrated project team is important, every team member needs to actively contribute to project success, and every team member must be supported to help him or her build leadership skills. There are numerous actions that can be taken to help team members build their leadership skills.

(3) **Roles and Responsibilities**.–As stated earlier, defining roles and responsibilities of team members is vital to building teamwork. Stated differently, when roles and responsibilities are not clearly defined, problems multiply, costs increase, productivity decreases, and projects often fail to meet customers' goals.

(4) **Training**.–Project teamwork is an important input to project success. Team-based training is an effective means of building teamwork in a project environment. Simply training individuals one-by-one does not allow the project team as a whole to understand the new tools and techniques, making the training less beneficial. Changes are more difficult to effectively implement when everyone is not singing off the same sheet of music. Project teamwork is enhanced when the training is customized

to real-world project scenarios that are based on the team's business environment.

Integrating PM Discipline into Project Teamwork

Clearly, project teamwork is essential for project success. Integrating the project management discipline, via PM practices, tools, and techniques performed by individual team members, is a proven-effective means of achieving customer goals. The use of project management (PM) tools such as responsibility assignment matrix (RAM), organizational breakdown structure (OBS), action-item register (AIR), master integrated schedule (MIS), and work breakdown structure (WBS), among others, help build teamwork and improve productivity.

Fifth Project Element: Integrated PM Discipline

The concept of an integrated project management discipline is based on the premise that for projects to be successful in an environment involving multiple parties–U.S. government agency, prime contractor, and subcontractors–everyone needs to be unified and focused on achieving customer goals. Moreover, the concept of integrated project management is based on the practice of rigid-flexibility. Rigid-flexibility for project management (PM) means ensuring that key PM practices are followed on every project, while realizing that how the PM practices are executed and what tools and techniques are most appropriate vary by project situation. Without truly integrating the PM discipline across all of the parties involved with a project and holding said parties accountable, it is nearly impossible to reach high-performance team results.

Integrated PM Essentials

There are four essentials to achieving an integrated project management (PM) discipline. They include the following:

- project practices
- project tools and techniques
- project training
- project leadership

(1) **Project Practices.**–Based upon the foremost professional association for the advancement of project management, the Project Management Institute (PMI), Project Management

Body of Knowledge (PMBOK), there are nine project management knowledge areas. Each of the nine project management knowledge areas contained within the PMBOK (see Figure 2-3) relates to one or more proven project practices.

Figure 2-3

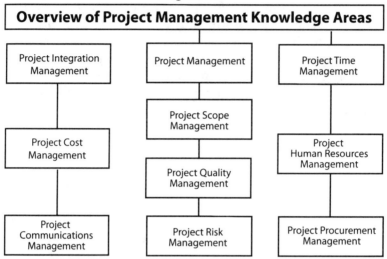

Overview of Project Management Knowledge Areas

| Project Integration Management | Project Management | Project Time Management |

| Project Cost Management | Project Scope Management | Project Human Resources Management |

| | Project Quality Management | |

| Project Communications Management | Project Risk Management | Project Procurement Management |

Source: PMI, Project Management Body of Knowledge

(2) **Project Tools and Techniques.**–For every project practice, there are one or more project tools and/or techniques available to help accomplish the work. A successful project manager is an individual who is very knowledgeable in all nine areas of the PMBOK, experienced in a variety of proven project practices, aware of the numerous project tools and techniques available, and knows when and how to apply specific project tools and techniques.

(3) **Project Training.**–There is a tremendous amount of project-oriented training available to help individuals and organizations improve their project performance. The best project management (PM) education and training is based on the Project Management Institute (PMI)'s Project Management Body of Knowledge (PMBOK) nine knowledge areas. The most effective PM training programs teach students to:

- Understand the nine knowledge areas of the PMBOK,
- know how to apply proven project practices to each of the nine areas of the PMBOK, and

- be able to successfully use project tools and techniques to accomplish each of the proven project practices.

Project training is available through many forms of media, including Web-based programs, CD-ROMS, audio tapes, videotapes, classroom instruction, coaching/mentoring, and various combinations of these. Optimal project results are can most likely be achieved by offering on-site, team-based training, which is then customized for the specific organization based on its business environment. Project management (PM) education and training is available from numerous providers. Below is a brief summary of some of the many excellent providers of PM competency-based educational programs.

College and University Project Management Graduate Degree Programs

- George Washington University – Master of Science in Project Management (www.sbpm.gwu.edu/mspm)
- University of Texas at Dallas – Master of Science in Project Management (http://som.utdallas.edu/project)
- University of Management and Technology Master of Science in Project Management (www.umtweb.edu)

Master's Certificate in Project Management Educational Programs (Non-degree)

- Stanford Advanced Project Management Program (http://apm.stanford.edu)
- International Institute of Learning – Project Management Master's Certificate (www.learning@iil.com)
- Boston University Project Management Master's Certificate Program (http://www.butrain.com/mdp)
- The Center of Systems Management Project Management Certificate Program (www.csm.com)

The above is not a complete list or an endorsement of the stated project management education and training providers; it is merely a sample of the many PMI registered education providers currently available.

(4) **Project Leadership.**–While each of the four essentials to achieve an integrated project management (PM) discipline are important, without real project leadership, projects usually fail.

Real project leadership skills are not learned in a classroom; rather they are learned and earned on-the-job managing real people, real money, in a real-world environment. Project leadership entails motivating or stimulating people to achieve higher levels of performance by working as an integrated project team. The most successful project leaders are usually people who are goal-oriented, strong communicators, with high-energy levels, who serve as a coach, teacher, or trusted advisor to their project team members. Likewise, successful project leaders hold their team members accountable for their actions and results.

SUMMARY

The IPM Life Cycle and Model are both designed and intended to serve as visual tools to guide thinking and action of all the parties involved with a U.S. government contract and related project. Using the IPM Model, in conjunction with a variety of opportunity and risk management tools discussed in Chapter 3, takes you beyond the basics to who, what, when, how, and why actions must be taken to consistently make complex U.S. government contracts and related projects succeed.

QUESTIONS TO CONSIDER

1. In which phase of the integrated project management (IPM) life cycle is your organization currently involved?

2. How effectively has your organization's senior executives created a culture that facilitates successful project management of complex U.S. government contracts and related projects?

3. Does your organization actively promote and support the project management discipline?

4. How well does your organization manage each of the five project elements of the integrated project management (IPM) Model?

ENDNOTES

1   Adapted from Garrett, G. A., & Bunnik, Ed. Creating a World-Class PM Organization. *PM Network Magazine*, September 2000.
2   Garrett, Gregory A. *World Class Contracting*. Chicago: CCH, 2001.
3   Kerzner, Harold. *In Search of Excellence in Project Management*. New York: Van Nostrand Reinhold, 1998.

CHAPTER  3

OPPORTUNITY AND RISK MANAGEMENT[1]

INTRODUCTION

It is the mission of the United States federal government to provide for our nation's defense, economy, homeland security, energy, education, transportation, and many other needs of our citizens. To meet these tremendous national challenges U.S. federal government agencies are increasingly required to successfully manage large, complex, high-technology contracts and projects, which integrate products, professional services, and software systems into solutions. These challenges involve varying degrees of risk—some to a high degree—all of which need to be managed accordingly. Said simply, the desired outcome for every project in both government and industry is to meet or exceed all contract and project performance requirements. But numerous Government Accountability Office (GAO) and inspector general (IG) findings purport that program managers do a poor job of managing their programs, projects, and contracts—and particularly of managing risk.

Managing a project within an organization is a formidable task. Managing a multi-sector workforce around a complex government project, meaning a project involving a customer (government agency), principal supplier (prime government contractor), and numerous supply-chain partners (vendors and subcontractors) with a combination of high-technology products and services, as illustrated in Figure 3-1, is a much greater challenge. This chapter provides a summary of the opportunity and risk management process that should be considered when managing complex government projects involving multiple parties and multiple functions.

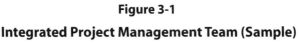

Figure 3-1
Integrated Project Management Team (Sample)

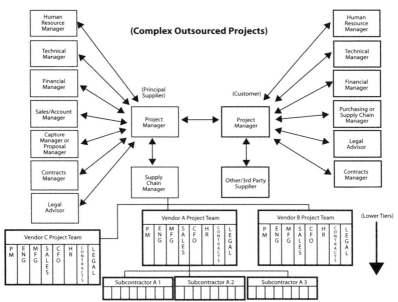

Managing opportunities and risks is an inherent part of everyone's life and a crucial aspect of every project, but many people, including project managers, assume risks without ever formally assessing or attempting to mitigate them. Because opportunity and risk management is an attempt to predict future outcomes based on current knowledge, it is not a precise science. However, it is possible to increase opportunities and reduce risks or prevent risk events from occurring by using a process approach to opportunity and risk management.

Opportunity and risk management is an important element of both contract management and project management because every project contains elements of uncertainty, such as varying amounts of funding, changes in contract delivery date(s), changes in technical requirements, and increases or decreases in quantity. Opportunity and risk management should be considered a part of the performance-based project management methodology.

What Is Opportunity?

Opportunity (a positive desired change) is the measure of the probability of an opportunity event's, occurring and the desired impact of that event.

What Is Risk?

Risk (an unwanted change) is the measure of the probability of a risk event's occurring and the associated effect of that event. In other words, risk consists of three components:

- A risk event (an unwanted change),
- the probability of occurrence (uncertainty), and
- the significance of the impact (the amount at stake).

How Do you Define Risk in the World of U.S. Federal Acquisition Management?

Risk is defined by the U.S. Department of Defense (DoD) as a measure of future uncertainties in achieving program performance goals and objectives within defined cost, schedule, and performance constraints. Specific areas of potential risk are provided in Table 3-1.

Table 3-1 DoD: Risk Areas, Definitions, & Examples		
Risk Area	**Definition**	**Significant Risks**
Threat	Sensitivity to uncertainty of threat description	• Uncertainty in threat accuracy • Sensitivity of design and technology to threat • Vulnerability of system to threat and threat countermeasures • Vulnerability of program to intelligence penetration
Requirements	Sensitivity to uncertainty in the system description and requirements	• Operational requirements vaguely stated or not properly established • Requirements not stable • Required operating environment not described • Requirements fail to address logistics and suitability • Requirements– identifying specific solutions that force high cost too constrictive

Design	Degree to which system design could change if the threat parameters change	• Design implications not sufficiently considered in concept exploration • System will not satisfy user requirements • Mismatch of user manpower or skill profiles with system design solution or human-machine interface problems • Increased skills or more training requirements identified late in the acquisition process • Design not cost effective • Design relies on immature technologies or "exotic" materials to achieve performance objectives • Software design, coding, and testing

Table 3-1
DoD: Risk Areas, Definitions, & Examples

Risk Area	Definition	Significant Risks
Modeling and Simulation (M&S)	Adequacy and capability of M&S to support all life-cycle phases	• Same risks contained in the significant risks for test and evaluation • M&S not verified, validated, or accredited for the intended purpose • Program lacks proper tools and M&S capability to assess alternatives
Technology	Degree to which technology has demonstrated maturity to meet program objectives	• Program depends on unproven technology for success with no alternatives • Program success depends on achieving advances in state-of-the-art technology • Potential advances in technology will result in less than optimally cost-effective system or make system components obsolete • Technology not demonstrated in required operating environment • Technology reliant on complex hardware, software, or integration designs
Logistics	Ability of the system configuration and documentation to achieve logistics objectives	• Inadequate supportability late in development or after fielding, resulting in need for engineering changes, increased costs, and/or schedule delays • Life-cycle costs not accurate because of poor logistics supportability analyses • Logistics analyses results not included in cost-performance trade-offs • Design trade studies lack supportability considerations

Table 3-1 DoD: Risk Areas, Definitions, & Examples		
Risk Area	**Definition**	**Significant Risks**
Production/ Facilities	Ability of the system configuration to achieve the program's production objectives	• Production implications not considered during concept exploration • Production not sufficiently considered during design • Inadequate planning for long lead items and vendor support • Production processes not proven • Prime contractors lack adequate plans for managing subcontractors • Sufficient facilities not readily available for cost-effective production • No contract incentives to modernize facilities or reduce cost
Concurrency	Sensitivity to uncertainty resulting from combining or overlapping phases or activities	• Immature or unproven technologies not adequately developed before production • Production funding available too early – before development effort has sufficiently matured • Concurrency established without clear understanding of risks
Industrial Capabilities	Abilities, experience, resources, and knowledge of provider to design, develop, manufacture, and support the system	• Developer has limited experience in specific type of development • Contractor has poor track record relative to costs and schedule • Contractor experiences loss of key personnel • Prime contractor relies excessively on subcontractors for major development efforts • Contractor requires significant capitalization to meet program requirements

Table 3-1
DoD: Risk Areas, Definitions, & Examples

Risk Area	Definition	Significant Risks
Cost	Ability of system to achieve life-cycle support objectives; includes effects on budgets, affordability, and effects of errors in cost estimating techniques	• Realistic cost objectives not established early • Marginal performance capabilities incorporated at excessive costs; satisfactory cost-performance trade-offs not done • Excessive life-cycle costs due to inadequate treatment of support requirements • Significant reliance on software • Funding profile does not match acquisition strategy • Funding profile not stable from budget cycle to budget cycle
Schedule	Sufficiency of time allocated for performing the defined acquisition tasks	• Schedule not considered in trade-off studies • Schedule does not reflect realistic acquisition planning • Acquisition program baseline schedule objectives not realistic and attainable • Resources not available to meet schedule

Table 3-1
DoD: Risk Areas, Definitions, & Examples

Risk Area	Definition	Significant Risks
Management	Degree to which program plans and strategies exist and are realistic and consistent	• Acquisition strategy fails to give adequate consideration to various essential elements, e.g., mission need, test and evaluation, technology, etc. • Subordinate strategies and plans not developed in a timely manner or based on the acquisition strategy • Proper mix (experience, skills, stability) of personnel not assigned to Program Management Office or contractor team • Effective risk assessments not performed or results not understood and acted on
External Factors	Availability of government resources external to the program office required to support the project, such as facilities, resources, personnel, government-furnished equipment, etc.	• External government resources unknown or uncertain • Little or no control over external resources • Changing external priorities threaten performance.

Budget	Sensitivity of program to budget changes and reductions	• Budget practices (releasing funds, quarterly or monthly) negatively affect long-term planning processes • Budget changes or reductions can negate contractual arrangements and continuity of operations
Earned Value Management (EVM) System	Adequacy of the contractors EVM process and realism of integration baseline	• Baseline proves unrealistic • Accurate and meaningful measures difficult to obtain • Contractor's EVM system fails to effectively support project tracking

Similarly, the U.S. federal government's Office of Management and Budget (OMB) Circular A-11 (Exhibit 300, capital planning documentation) identifies 19 different categories of risk to be addressed by government agencies. The OMB categories and the definitions used by the Department of Veterans Affairs are illustrated in Table 3-2.

Table 3-2 OMB: Risk Categories, Definitions, & Examples		
Risk Category	**Definition**	**Examples**
Schedule	The risk that the project will not meet all or part of its list of terminal elements with assigned start and finish dates, such as release(s), milestone(s), deliverable(s), or critical task(s)	• Project planning has the potential to become more complex than anticipated and could require significantly more time than estimated. • Implementation of the project is dependent on the completion of other projects; their delay would cause this project to be delayed.
Initial Cost	The risk that the quality of cost estimates and the ability to secure and manage budgetary resources for what is needed during the planning, preliminary engineering, and project design phases will be insufficient	• Estimates are based on interdependent projects that cannot be analyzed as a single entity, and project design and engineering is one of those interdependencies. • The project will use new and relatively unproven technologies for which there are no comparable VA or federal examples to benchmark preliminary design or engineering costs.
Life-Cycle Costs	The risk that there will be insufficient funds to take the project through the overall process of developing an information technology (IT) system from investigation of initial requirements through analysis, design, implementation, and maintenance	• Estimates are based on many questionable life-cycle cost assumptions (e.g., inflation rates). • Life-cycle costs can exceed estimates if the reliability of a system falls below projections. • Errors may exist in the cost-estimating technique used to derive the life-cycle costs.

Table 3-2 OMB: Risk Categories, Definitions, & Examples		
Risk Category	**Definition**	**Examples**
Technical Obsolescence	The risk that key technologies used in a project will lose value because a new, more functional product or technology has superseded the project's or the project's product(s) becomes less useful or useless due to changes before the project has completed its full functional life-cycle	• Strategies for avoiding the use of out-dated technical resources over the system life-cycle have not been incorporated into the project plan. • There is no plan for regular technology upgrades or refreshes.
Feasibility	The risk that a process design, procedure, or plan cannot be successfully accomplished in the required time frame as proposed	• The affected office(s) may not have the existing capability to successfully develop or implement the project within defined technical, scope, and schedule parameters. • There are no examples of successful implementation of the proposed approach, software, or hardware within public or private industry.
Reliability of Systems	The risk that the system, when operating under stated conditions, will not perform its intended function acceptably for a specified period of time	• The project may not have the ability to provide information about current or planned/desired system reliability. • The proposed system is new and no commercial or government installations are available to benchmark for actual reliability data.

Table 3-2 OMB: Risk Categories, Definitions, & Examples		
Risk Category	**Definition**	**Examples**
Dependencies and Interoperability between This System and Others	The risk that the project will fail because it depends on the successful completion of another system or the project will not be able to operate with other systems or products without an unplanned special effort	• The project relies on interoperability with other systems (existing or in development) within the department and/or across the federal government (e.g., technical interfaces, schedule dependencies). • The project is directly linked to the long-term success, implementation, or ongoing maintenance of other systems.

Surety (Asset Protection) Considerations	The risk associated with the ability of the project to meet its obligations or some public or private interest requires protection from the consequences of a contractor's default or a project's delinquency	• Loss or damage may result from a contractor's failing to deliver as promised. • There is the potential for substantial loss of capability of the project due to an unforeseen disaster and a lack of continuity of operations and/or disaster recovery plans.
Risk of Creating a Monopoly for Future Procurements	The risk associated with the use of closed or proprietary software/source code, as well as the dependence on a single vendor or product, which in turn creates a risk that in the future the contractor will be able to reap windfall profits by charging excessive costs or reducing service quality	• The customer cannot conduct open competition in the future due to a current or planned procurement. • The product uses non-open source code software. • The product cannot connect with existing or planned department systems without extensive customization.

Table 3-2 OMB: Risk Categories, Definitions, & Examples		
Risk Category	**Definition**	**Examples**
Capability of Agency to Manage the Investment	Risk associated with an inexperienced project owner and management team the lack of established OMB- approved management tools, or performance indicators that show that the contractor cannot deliver the project as promised	• Project manager(s) does not have a Project Management Professional or equivalent certification. • The contractor may lack an EVMS that meets OMB standards. • Earned value data show unexplained project cost and/or schedule variances greater than 10 percent. • Contractors do not use earned value reporting.
Overall Risk of Project Failure	Risk that there is an inherent project weakness, such as the project's missing a clear link with the organization's key strategic priorities, including agreed-on measures of success	• Veterans and health providers who are the customers for the project's deliverables may desire a different solution. • The project may be overtaken by activities being pursued outside the department (e.g., centralization of government functions into Centers of Excellence).

| Organizational and Change Management | Risk that activities involved in (1) defining and instilling new values, attitudes, norms, and behaviors within an organization to support new ways of doing work and overcome resistance to change; (2) building consensus among customers and stakeholders on specific changes designed to better meet their needs; and (3) planning, testing, and implementing all aspects of the transition from one organizational structure or business process to another will not be successful | • Organizational and/or departmental cultural resistance to proposed process change may be high.
 • Extensive employee training may be required to apply benefits of the project to existing or proposed process.
 • Initial operation of the new system demonstrates lack of use, improper use, or failure to fully use due to unchanged organizational structure or process. |

Table 3-2
OMB: Risk Categories, Definitions, & Examples

Risk Category	Definition	Examples
Business	Risk that the product will fail to achieve the expectations of the project's owners and customers	• The project's statements of support of department customers are not carried through in project outcomes. • Investment planning has little or no customer involvement.
Data/Information	Risk associated with data/ information loss or disruptions caused by natural disasters (hurricanes, tornadoes, floods, earthquakes, etc.) or by area-wide disruptions of communication or electric power or malicious attacks; also can include the inability of the contractor to obtain, store, produce, share, and manipulate data as planned	• No contingency plans exist to deal with the loss/misuse of data or information. • Project may not be able to access data from other sources (federal, state, and/or local agencies).
Technology	The risk of problems associated with the use of technologies new to the department, new software releases, or hardware new to the market	• Commercially available technology is immature. • Technical problems/failures are associated with the applications to be used. • The contractor is unable to provide the planned and desired technical functionality. • The application of software engineering theories, principles, and techniques will fail to yield the appropriate software product. • Final product will be overly expensive, delivered late, or otherwise unacceptable to the customer.

Table 3-2 OMB: Risk Categories, Definitions, & Examples		
Risk Category	**Definition**	**Examples**
Strategic	The risk of misalignment with department mission and strategic goals and/or the President's Management Agencies	• The investment fails to achieve those strategic goals it states it will support. • Project objectives are not clearly linked to the department's overall strategies or to government-wide policies and standards.
Security	The risk that the project does (or will) not conform to applicable department and/or federal security standards	• The project does not have a current security plan. • The systems associated with the project do not have current certification and accreditations (C&As). • The project's contractors are not in full compliance with department or federal security requirements. • Security training is not at 100-percent compliance.
Privacy	The risk of possible violations of the legal restrictions on the collection, use, maintenance, and release of information about individuals	• The project may feature a publicly accessible website with personal data links. • The project may involve a process that collects, manipulates, stores, or shares personally identifiable information. • The project may convert paper files with personal data to electronic files.

Table 3-2 OMB: Risk Categories, Definitions, & Examples		
Risk Category	**Definition**	**Examples**
Project Resources	The risk that assets available or anticipated, including people, equipment, facilities, and other things used to plan, implement, and maintain the project, will be insufficient.	• The scope of the project is not clear. • Necessary project resources are not clearly or completely specified. • No examples of a successful approach to problem-solving are provided in either the project description or in the discussion of alternatives.

What is Opportunity and Risk Management?

The primary goal of opportunity and risk management (ORM) is to continually seek ways to maximize opportunities and mitigate risks. ORM is an iterative process approach to managing those opportunities and risks that may occur during the course of business that could affect the success or failure of a project. Once identified, the probability of each event's occurrence and its potential effect on the project are analyzed and prioritized, or ranked from highest to lowest. Beginning with the highest prioritized events and working down, the project team determines what options or strategies are available and chooses the best strategy to maximize opportunities and reduce or prevent the identified risks from occurring. This information is the basis for the ORM plan, which should be continually referred to and updated during the project life cycle.

Some business managers rely solely on their intuitive reasoning (ability to guess correctly) as their basis for decision-making. But in today's complex systems environment, an astute business manager understands the importance of using a highly skilled project team to identify both opportunity and risk events, assess the possible effects, and develop appropriate strategies to increase opportunities and reduce risks. A project work breakdown structure (WBS) is an effective means of relating project tasks to possible opportunities and risks.

To integrate ORM into project management successfully, a project manager must ensure that ORM is included as part of the overall business management planning process. It is vital that ORM become a mindset for all business professionals, especially project managers and contract managers, both government and contractor.

Figure 3-2 lists the key inputs, numerous proven tools and techniques to increase business opportunities and mitigate project risks, and the desired outputs that should be considered when managing complex performance-based projects.

Figure 3-2

The Opportunity & Risk Management Process

Inputs	Tools & Techniques	Outputs
• People • Elements of Opportunity • Elements of Risk • Corporate Culture (Risk-Taking vs. Risk-Adverse) • Training	• ORM Model • Project Risk Management Plan Outline • Project Risk Mitigation Form • Project Doability Analysis Form	• Maximize Opportunities • Mitigate Risks • Deliver Successful Projects

INPUTS

The following items are all key inputs to the ORM process, which should be used when managing complex performance-based projects.

People

Given that multiple parties, usually consisting of people from numerous sectors and functional disciplines (project management, engineering, contracts, finance, manufacturing, purchasing/supply-chain management, quality, etc.), typically are involved in complex performance-based projects (see Figure 3-1), the need for effective opportunity and risk management is great.

Elements of Opportunity

Strategic alignment refers to how consistent a project opportunity is with the core mission, business, or corporate direction for new business. Companies have a much higher probability of winning and successfully delivering when a project opportunity is consistent with their core business and strategic direction. Agencies have a much higher probability of achieving mission success through strategic alignment of mission, project, and contract objectives.

Competitive environment refers to whether a company or its competitor is perceived by the customer as the product/service/solution leader and, thus, favored as the key supplier. Opportunities when the customer perceives a company as the leader and the favored supplier (for reasons other than price) are highly desirable. Customers may have this perception due to technology, reputation, past experience, industry commitment, and so on. For federal teams, performance-based competition can be managed to promote idea and price competition to support the agency's mission and achieve its objectives.

Project value refers to the dollar value of a project. The intent is to distinguish "small" from "large" revenue or value opportunities. Obviously, value needs to be assessed in the context of the size of a company or in relation to an agency's mission, budget, and rank ordering of projects.

Expected margin refers to the likely margins on the business, given the competitive environment and what it will take competitors to win.

Future business potential refers to degree to which a project will affect additional business beyond the scope of the specific opportunity. For example, the opportunity may be a means to win a new project. Consider the degree to which specific identifiable future business depends on winning and successfully delivering this particular project.

Probability of success refers to the likelihood that a project will succeed and, for competing contractors, that they will win the business as opposed to one of their competitors.

Collateral benefit refers to the degree to which pursuit of a project will improve the existing skill levels or develop new skills that will benefit other projects or future business.

Project importance refers to the overall need to deliver mission and program objectives, as assessed by the project manager–or to win the project, as assessed by the sales manager or key account manager. This should be based on consideration of all the opportunity elements, along with any other tangible or intangible aspects of the opportunity that are considered relevant.

Elements of Risk

Customer commitment refers to the degree to which the customer has demonstrated a solid commitment to implement the products/services/solution offered in the project. Typically, this commitment is demonstrated through either budgeting for the implementation in a current or future business plan or identifying and assigning resources to support the implementation.

Corporate competence refers to the company's past experience or core competencies in delivering the products/services/solution required in the project. The more past experience a company has in projects exactly like the project at hand, the lower the risk. Conversely, if the type of project has never been completed successfully by any company in the past, then there is a high risk.

External obstacles refers to the existence of roadblocks that are beyond the control of either an agency or a contractor. A good example of this would be if a customer were a regulated utility that must obtain approval from a state or federal authority before it can implement the project. Another example might be when a customer has yet to secure the budget needed to fund the implementation of a project during a period when capital is tightly constrained.

Opportunity engagement refers to the degree to which the contractor versus the contractor's competitors are involved or are likely to be involved or may have been involved in establishing the customer's requirements. Some contractors believe that if they do not help the customer develop—or inform the development of —its requirements, chances are one of their competitors will. While this is not necessarily the case, government teams should keep in mind that good acquisition planning and market research inform the agency in appropriate ways prior to the development of a requirement, often from multiple contractors' perspectives.

Solution lifecycle match refers to the degree to which a solution involves the use of existing mature products versus new products or leading-edge technology. If the solution involves mature products available today, the risk of the solution working is very low. On the other hand, if the solution involves many new products that have yet to be released or are based on leading-edge technology, there is a risk of encountering development delays or the products' not working as planned.

Period of performance refers to the length of a project. The longer a project the greater chance of significant changes. Personnel, customer environment, and business climate are a few examples of changes that can introduce risk affecting a project.

Delivery schedule refers to when delivery is required and who controls the schedule. From the contractor's viewpoint, the ideal situation is a flexible schedule that can be set by the company, which can than ensure adequate time to be successful. Conversely, if the government already has fixed the delivery schedule and also has identified penalties for missing schedules, the company will be assuming a risk associated with missing deliveries and may propose a higher price to mitigate risk.

Resource coordination refers to the number of internal and external groups that must be engaged to deliver a solution. The larger the number of internal groups required, the more coordination it will take to ensure successful delivery and the higher the risk of a disconnect and delivery problem. Coordination of outside suppliers or support groups typically introduces even greater risk, as there generally is more control over internal groups than external suppliers to resolve problems.

Non-performance penalties refers to the degree to which there are specified contract penalties for failure to deliver as promised. From the contractor's viewpoint, risk is mitigated if the customer has not specified penalties or there is an opportunity to negotiate them. If the customer has specified monetary or other penalties that are non-negotiable, this increases risk and may be mitigated by higher prices.

Overall feasibility refers to the degree of feasibility of a project as assessed by a knowledgeable representative of the groups accountable to deliver the solution. A major factor to consider in assessing feasibility is past experience in fulfilling obligations or addressing unforeseen problems equitably. If a project is extremely complex and the customer has a poor track record of supporting complex projects, there is a high risk that the project will not be implemented successfully.

Corporate culture refers to the tendency of an organization to either promote innovation and risk-taking or continue the status quo and avoid risk.

Training refers to the need of all individuals involved in managing complex performance-based projects to receive competency-based training on the opportunity and risk management process and the numerous related tools and techniques discussed in this chapter.

TOOLS AND TECHNIQUES

The following are a few of the many proven effective processes, tools, and techniques to help business professionals involved in complex government contracts and projects maximize the elements of opportunity and minimize or mitigate the elements of risk.

The Opportunity and Risk Management (ORM) Model

The ORM Model (Figure 3-3) is an ongoing process model that has two major parts: opportunity/risk assessment and opportunity/risk action plans. Opportunity/risk assessment is composed of three steps: (1) identifying opportunities and risks, (2) analyzing them, and (3) prioritizing them. Opportunity/risk action plans also are composed of three steps: (1) developing opportunity and risk action plans and strategies, (2) implementing opportunity and risk action plans within the project management plan, and (3) evaluating project results. Figure 3-3 illustrates the suggested six-step opportunity and risk management (ORM) model.

Figure 3-3
Opportunity and Risk Management Model (ORM)

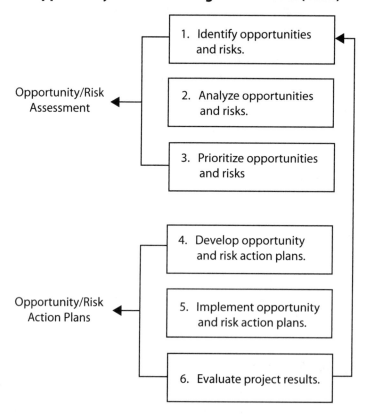

Project Risk Management Plan Outline

Use the following outline (figure 3-4) to prepare a comprehensive Project Risk Management Plan.

Figure 3-4
Project Risk Management Plan Outline

1.0 Project Scope

Insert the project scope statement or provide a brief summary of the project, including a description of the work to be accomplished, a description of the customer's goals and objectives for the project, a general description of how the project will be accomplished, and other pertinent information that will provide a good overview of the project.

2.0 Risk Event Descriptions

Identify any major risks involved in each element of the work breakdown structure (WBS). Complete risk event descriptions and risk event results. Reference or include a copy of the WBS in the section. The process is carried out as follows:

2.1 Identify Risks. For each element of the WBS, identify any major risks associated with that element. Ensure that each risk event refers to a specific WBS element.

2.2 Analyze Risks and Calculate the Weighted Cost Impact. In analyzing the risks, make the assumption that the risk event identified will occur. Think in terms of the remedial activity that will be needed to rectify the occurrence of the risk event.

Using the same guidelines employed in calculating the cost of the WBS elements, calculate the rectification cost (impact) without any form of "padding" or risk adjustment. Analyze the risk event and apply a weighting to the impact on a scale of 1 through 5 as follows:

- *Weight 1:* Has little potential to cause disruption of schedule, costs, or performance (quality). Increase the impact by 5%.

  Weight 2: May cause minor disruption of schedule, costs, or performance (quality). Increase the impact by 10%.

  Weight 3: May cause some disruption of schedule, costs, or performance (quality). Increase the impact by 15%.

  Weight 4: May cause major disruption of schedule, costs, or performance (quality). Increase the impact by 20%.

  Weight 5: Could cause significant serious disruption of schedule, costs, or performance (quality). Increase impact by 25%.

Finally, estimate the probability of the event occurring as a percentage (between 0.01 and 0.99) and calculate the weighted cost impact as follows:

(Cost Impact + Cost Impact Increase) x Probability of Occurrence = Weighted Cost Impact

Example: For a risk event with an estimated cost impact of $2,750, a weight of 4, and probability of occurrence at 85%:

$$(\$2,750 + \$550) \times 0.85 = \$2,805$$

Project Risk Management Plan Outline (cont.)

2.3   *Identify High-Risk Events*
If a specific risk event has greater than 75% probability and/or the weighted cost impact is greater than 10% of the total project cost, the risk event is by definition a high-risk event. For each high-risk event, create a separate and unique WBS element that identifies the work required and the weighted cost impact required to rectify the occurrence. This WBS element must be flagged as a high-risk event element as distinct from a normal WBS element.

2.4   *Develop Mitigation Strategies*
Determine potential strategies for mitigating the risk by either avoiding it, controlling it, or transferring it to another party. Assuming the risk consequences is also a potential mitigation strategy, but it is the least desirable. Evaluate the potential cost impact of the mitigation strategy and reflect that impact in the risk budget.

2.5   *Establish the Risk Budget*
Each high-risk event will become a line item in the risk budget. The other risk events should be accumulated and used to establish the managerial reserve. An amount for contingency, or those events and circumstances not anticipated in any way, should be calculated based on experience. These amounts together become the risk budget portion of the Project Budget. The risk budget should be margined at the same rate as the Project Budget to establish the budget at selling price. This then is presented to the customer in the proposal as the project price.

Project Risk Management Plan Outline (cont.)

3.0   Risk Reassessment Plan
Identify the major reassessment points for the project and ensure that they are identified in the Project Plan. At a minimum, high-risk events should be reassessed at the following times:

- Whenever major changes occur in the project or its environment
- Before major decision milestones
- Periodically, according to some predetermined schedule.

3.1   *Risk Management Timetable*
Indicate the timetable for risk management activities. Ensure that the key events are also reflected on the Project Schedule. Major milestones include the following:

- Completion of risk identification and analysis
- Risk prioritization
- Completion of mitigation strategy development
- Incorporation into Project Plans and WBS
- Key reassessment points
- Documentation of risk results.

Project Risk Mitigation Form

The following Form 3-1 provides a simple, yet proven effective, means of documenting possible project risk events, planned risk mitigation strategies, actual project results, and appropriate follow-up actions, if needed.

| Form 3-1 |
| Project Risk Mitigation Form |

Risk Event Results

Mitigation Strategy/Strategies Selected

Results of Mitigation Strategy/Strategies

Follow-Up Actions Required (if needed)

Project Doability Analysis

A number of successful companies and organizations worldwide have found it useful to summarize all of their project-related opportunities and risks in one simple document, often just a few pages in length, called a Project Doability Analysis. Form 3-2, a suggested Project Doability Analysis form, can be tailored and used by any organization to briefly summarize the opportunities and risks before or after an organization moves forward or bids on a project. Of course, it usually is better to conduct a doability analysis before an organization begins or bids on a project. It is important to know what your organization must do to achieve project success before it is contractually obligated to perform the work, especially on large, complex, performance-based projects.

Form 3-2	
Project Doability Analysis	

Project Manager Doability Assessment: Yes ☐   No ☐

Executive Summary

Project Name:	
Customer:	
Location(s):	Estimated Revenue in US$:
Start Date:	Completion Date:

Prepared by:	Phone #:
Fax:	e-mail:

I. Describe the project requirements/deliverables.

II. Evaluate the project technical requirements/availability/research & development.

III. Evaluate the feasibility of the project schedule (attach milestone schedule).

IV. Evaluate the reasonableness of the project financial commitments (attach the Project Business Case).

V. Conduct high-level risk assessment. Consider the following risks if appropriate: pricing, payment terms, acceptance, warranty, liability, R&D, implementation, environmental, etc. (attach the risk management plan).

VI. Describe significant assumptions implicit in the evaluation of the technical, scheduling, and financial commitments.

VII. Assess the skills of the selected project team members (experience, education, training, professional certifications, strengths, and weaknesses.)

VIII. Executive Assessment of Project

Doable: Yes ☐   No ☐

OUTPUT

By using the opportunity and risk management (ORM) six-step process and the numerous related proven processes, tools, and techniques discussed in this chapter it is possible to maximize opportunities, mitigate risks, and significantly improve project results. Clearly, the desired output of the ORM process and related tools and techniques is to achieve successful projects.

SUMMARY

This chapter provides a summary of the opportunity and risk management (ORM) process and a few related tools and techniques that should be considered when managing complex U.S. government contracts and projects. Too many organizations do not take the time and effort to thoroughly identify, assess, and prioritize business opportunities and risks or to develop action plans and implement them to maximize business opportunities and mitigate risks. In the next chapter, we will discuss the importance and value of contract changes management as a vital aspect of contract administration.

QUESTIONS TO CONSIDER

1. How well does your organization identify risk?

2. Has your organization developed an opportunity and risk management (ORM) process that is consistently used on all of your critical government contracts and projects?

3. How does your organization mitigate contract and project risks?

Endnotes

1 Adapted from The Capture Management Life-Cycle, by Gregory A. Garrett and Reginald J. Kipke, Chicago: CCH, 2003.

CHAPTER  4

CONTRACT CHANGES MANAGEMENT

THE CHALLENGE OF CONTRACT ADMINISTRATION

The contract administration phase of the contract management process represents the monitoring and control activities of contract management specifically and project management in general. It is during this phase that activities such as monitoring compliance with contract terms and conditions, monitoring and measuring contractor performance, processing contractor request for payments, and managing contract changes occur.

Effective contract administration is integral to successful project management. In projects that involve extensive procurement activities, that is, a contractor's or contractors' performing critical aspects of the project effort, the effectiveness of the contract administration process will determine the success of the project. As the contractor(s) performs the project effort, contract administration activities will be used to monitor the contractor's achievement of the project's cost, schedule, and performance objectives. Based on data and knowledge obtained during contracting administration activities (such as monitoring and measuring contractor performance), the project manager can then take preventive actions (in anticipation of possible problems) or corrective actions (when variances from the project plan are identified) to control the project effort's pursuit of cost, schedule, and performance objectives. Thus, contract administration activities put the teeth in project monitoring and control.

Managing and controlling contract changes is one of the major challenges of contract administration, requiring extensive process integration as well as communication among the project management team members. This chapter will focus specifically on managing and controlling the contract changes process aspect of contract administration. First, the need for a contract change control process will be discussed. The general types of contract changes will then be presented, along with a brief discussion of a Contract Changes clause. The contract change process is then discussed using the framework of the contract management process. Controlling contract changes and the dynamics involved are also discussed, and some essential elements of controlling contract changes are highlighted. Finally, best practices in contract changes management are presented. The goal of this chapter is to present contract changes management as a critical part of contract administration, contract management, and ultimately, project management.

The Need for a Contract Change Control Process

Change is inevitable in project management. Project plans are living documents that reflect the planned cost, schedule, and performance objectives of a project. As the project environment changes, impacting the project's cost, schedule, and performance requirements, the project plans are revised to reflect the new project requirements. Since contracts are integral parts of projects, contracts supporting projects must also evolve to reflect these changes in project cost, schedule, and performance requirements.

The basis for contract changes management, specifically contract change control, is the need for controlling all project-related activities. The Guide to the Project Management Body of Knowledge (PMBOK Guide) identifies integrated change control as part of the monitoring and control process group. The PMBOK Guide defines integrated change control as "the process of reviewing all change requests, approving changes, and managing changes to deliverables, organizational process assets, project documents, and the project management plan."[1] Contract changes management is essentially the application of the integrated change control concept to contracts. Just as the contract administration phase of contract management is one of the monitoring and control activities in project management, controlling contract changes is a key aspect of contract administration, reflecting the concept of integrated change control.

Types of Contract Changes

Either the buyer or the seller may propose a modification to a contract at any time during the contract's period of performance. In addition, contracts frequently require changes due to various reasons during the project period, including a change in administrative requirements, such as a change in paying office or funding data, or any other administration issues. Contract changes could also result from significant revisions to the project plan, such as the contract statement of work (SOW), specifications, or other contractual requirements documents. A major part of contract changes management activities is focused on managing the contract changes process, which will reflect the specific type of contract change.

Any change to a contract should be executed through a formal contract modification process and be documented appropriately. Using a formal contract changes process ensures proper communication and coordination with all project stakeholders in planning and executing the contract change. In government contracting, changes to the contract are typically referred to as modifications, while changes to solicitations are typically referred to as amendments.

Two general types of contract modifications are bilateral and unilateral modifications. A bilateral modification is used to make changes to contracts that require agreement from both the buyer and seller. These types of changes include negotiated equitable adjustments resulting from the issuance of a change order; definitized letter contracts; and other agreements of the parties modifying the terms and conditions of the contract.[2] Bilateral modifications are signed by both the seller and the buyer. An engineering change proposal (ECP) or formal contract change proposal (CCP) that requires negotiated agreement of contract terms and conditions are examples of bilateral contract modifications.

A unilateral modification does not need the agreement of both parties; thus, it is signed only by the buyer's contract manager. These types of modifications are used to make administrative changes and issue change orders.[3] Many contracts include a Changes Clause that authorizes the buyer to direct the seller to conform with certain changes made at the buyer's discretion. An example of a Changes Clause for ABC Company is provided below:

Changes

ABC Company reserves the right at anytime to make changes in the specifications, drawings, samples, or other descriptions to which the products are to conform, in the methods of shipment and packaging, or in the time or place of delivery. In such event, any claim for an adjustment shall be mutually satisfactory to ABC Company and Seller, but any claim by Seller for an adjustment shall be deemed waived unless notice of a claim is made in writing within thirty (30) days following Seller's receipt of such changes. Price increases or extensions of time shall not be binding upon ABC Company unless evidenced by a purchase order change issued by ABC Company. No substitutions of materials or accessories may be made without ABC Company's written consent. No

> charges for extras will be allowed unless such extras
> have been ordered in writing by ABC Company and
> the price agreed upon.[4]

It should be emphasized that this Changes Clause only authorizes the buyer to make unilaterally directed changes specifically to specifications, drawings, samples, or other descriptions to which the products are to conform, in the methods of shipment and packaging, or in the time or place of delivery. Thus, a change to the contract directed at contract requirements outside of these areas would not be an authorized change notice in accordance with this clause. Additionally, for government contracts, directed changes under the Changes Clause must be within the scope of the contract. Changes outside the scope of the Changes Clause are considered Cardinal Changes and are considered a breach of contract.[5]

As stated in the above clause, the Changes Clause requires the seller to submit a notice of a claim for an equitable adjustment in writing within thirty (30) days following the seller's receipt of such changes. Furthermore, the equitable adjustment resulting from the change will be mutually satisfactory to both ABC Company and the seller.

The mechanics of the contract Changes Clause is a good illustration of a unilateral contract modification as well as a bilateral contract modification. The buyer directing a change to a contract specification, for example, under the authority of the Changes Clause and through the use of a Change Order is an example of a unilateral contract modification. However, the negotiation of the equitable adjustment resulting from the changed contract would be an example of a bilateral contract modification.

Contract changes can also be categorized as definitized or undefinitized contract actions. Depending on the urgency of the proposed contract change, the contract change may be incorporated into the contract prior to the parties' fully agreeing to the contract terms, specifications, or price of the change. These types of contract changes are called undefinitized contractual actions (UCAs).[6] UCAs are used to allow the seller to begin performance of the changed work prior to completing negotiations on the cost, schedule, or performance of the changed work. Although UCAs are valuable tools for meeting urgent and critical contract requirements, buyers should understand the increased cost risk of these types of changes. Appropriate justifications and management controls of UCAs should be part of the contract changes process. Management of UCAs should include a limit on funding paid to the seller with the initial award of the UCA contract modification, a time line for the negotiation (definitization) of the contract change, and additional oversight of the seller performing the changed contract effort.

As previously stated, any change to a contract should be executed through a formal contract modification process and documented appropriately.

The Contract Changes Process

A modification to a contract formally changes the contract terms, conditions, and responsibilities of the contracting parties. Thus, the result of the changed contract is a new contract documenting the changed relationship between the parties. Although changes to a contract occur during the contract administration phase, the process used to manage contract changes is similar to the process used to manage the basic contract. Thus, the contract changes process can be considered a microcosm of the contract management process. Just as the initial basic contract is managed using the six phases of the contract management process (procurement planning, solicitation planning, solicitation, source selection, contract administration, and contract closeout), contract changes are also managed using these same six phases, with slight differences. This contract changes process is discussed below.

Procurement Planning –

Procurement planning is the process of identifying which business needs can be best met by procuring products or services outside the organization. This process involves determining whether to procure, how to procure, what to procure, how much to procure, and when to procure.[7] In terms of the contract changes process, procurement planning occurs when the need for a contract change is first identified. This need may arise from the discovery of a defective specification, a buyer-requested change to the performance requirement of the supply or service being procured, a need to accelerate the project schedule, or a reduction in the project budget, to name just a few reasons. Thus, the procurement planning phase of the contract changes process is focused on identifying the need for the contract change and deciding how to accomplish the change. Some examples of contract changes include correcting a specification, incorporating a revised performance requirement, applying additional resources to crash the project, or proposing options to de-scope the project to meet a new budget.

Solicitation Planning–

Solicitation planning is the process of preparing the documents needed to support the solicitation. This process involves documenting program requirements and identifying potential sources.[8] In the case of contract changes, solicitation planning involves preparing the documents needed to incorporate the proposed change to the contract. These documents may include revised specifications, statements of work (SOW), or revised product/service descriptions. Solicitation planning would also include developing the documents that relate to new or revised contract clauses, incentives, or even contract line items. Since changes to the contract may be initiated by either party, some of these documents may be developed by either the buyer or the seller.

Solicitation–

Solicitation is the process of obtaining information (bids and proposals) from the prospective sellers on how project needs can be met.[9] For contract changes purposes, solicitation involves communicating the revised contract requirements, as reflected in the documents developed during the solicitation planning phase, to the seller for the purpose of incorporating the changed work into the project effort. For proposed contract changes that will result in a change to contract cost, the solicitation phase directs the contractor to prepare a proposal for negotiating the cost of the changes into the contract.

Source Selection–

Source Selection is the process of receiving bids or proposals and applying the proposal evaluation criteria to select a supplier.[10] The source selection process includes an evaluation of offers and proposals and contract negotiations between the buyer and the seller in attempting to come to agreement on all aspects of the contract—including cost, schedule, performance, terms and conditions, and anything else related to the contracted effort. In terms of the contract changes process, source selection, or in this situation, specifically contract negotiations since the contractor has already been selected, involves the buyer and the seller negotiating and coming to agreement on the terms and conditions (cost, schedule, and performance requirements) of the changed project effort.

Contract Administration–

Contract administration is the process of ensuring that each party's performance meets the contractual requirements.[11] Activities include monitoring the contractor's performance and ensuring that it complies with the contractual technical and quality requirements. For the contract changes process, the contract administration phase ensures that the new effort reflected in the contract change is performed by the contractor in accordance with the contract requirements. Contract changes could result in the deletion of work, the incorporation of additional work, or the modification of work currently on contract. The effort resulted from the contract change is now part of the formal contract and is included in the buyer's and the seller's contract administration activities.

Contract Closeout–

Contract closeout is the process of verifying that all administrative matters are concluded on a contract that is otherwise physically complete.[12] This process includes activities such as the disposition of government property, final acceptance of products or services, final contractor payments, and documentation of the contractor's final past-performance report. The contract closeout process for the basic contract is the same as for the work resulting from the contract change. As the contract effort, including the effort resulting from the contract change, is completed and accepted by the buyer, the contract closeout activities will be performed to administratively close out the physically completed contract.

As noted in the above discussion, the basic contract management process can be used as the foundation for managing contract changes. A formal contract change process based on the contract management phases discussed above is essential for effective contract administration. Contracts and related documents should be continuously conformed to reflect the implementation of approved contract modifications. In addition, the contract modification documentation should provide a concise audit trail

FOUR

of all approved contract changes. Formal contract management processes and documentation are essential elements of controlling contract changes.

Controlling Contract Changes

As noted, managing and controlling contract changes requires extensive process integration as well as communication among the various project management team members. Projects, and the contracts that support projects, are managed using project teams. These project teams consist of specialists from the various functional disciplines that are involved in a project effort. In addition, the project team members include employees of both the buying organization as well as the selling organization. These functional specialists should be in constant communication with each other while performing project activities, including monitoring and measuring the work performed by the contractor and comparing actual results with planned results. It is during these monitoring and measuring activities that potential changes to the contract are identified, planned, and implemented using the contract changes process described above. The dynamics of project team members' coordinating, communicating, and interacting among themselves in performing project activities may have the potential to result in an unorganized, ad hoc, or even chaotic approach to contract changes. This may also result in a possible risk of allowing unauthorized changes to the contract. Following are some essential components to controlling contract changes during contract administration.

Contract Change Authority

Organizations typically control the authority to bind themselves legally in contractual obligations. Only specifically designated individuals within an organization, often referred to as contracts managers, have the authority to award, administer, and terminate contracts and make any related contractual decisions. This is especially true in government agencies where only designated contracting officers have this authority. Controlling contracting authority is how organizations ensure that contracts are crafted to ensure compliance with business and financial requirements, organizational policies, and legal constraints.

Just as the authority for awarding, administering, and terminating contracts is controlled in specifically designated individuals, the authority for awarding contract changes should also be similarly controlled by specific individuals. A controlled and centralized contract change authority keeps the contract from being informally modified by multiple members of the project team. Without a controlled and centralized contract change authority during contract administration, an organization runs the risk of becoming legally bound to less-than-favorable contracts. In addition, without a controlled and centralized contract change authority, project managers run the risk of losing control of the project's cost, schedule, and performance requirements, as well as losing control of the direction of the project's effort. Just as the project manager is concerned with controlling the cost, schedule, and performance requirements of the project, the contracts manager is concerned with controlling the cost, schedule, and performance requirements of the contract.

Depending on the complexities and uncertainties of project activities, centralizing the contract change authority in the contracts manager often results in the need for integrated contract management processes. Research shows that integrated processes are one facet of contract management process maturity. Organizations with contract management processes integrated throughout all functional areas of the organization typically have high contract management process capability and maturity. [13] The lack of contract management process integration in an organization will result in convoluted contract management processes. Due to ill-defined requirements or inaccurate cost and schedule estimates, projects may require numerous contract changes. When the contract changes must be negotiated and awarded by the contracts manager, the contracts manager will often be viewed as an obstacle to the progress of the project effort. As project activities are performed, and changes to statement of work (SOW) requirements, technical specifications, or quality specifications are identified, it is typically the contracts manager who insists on ensuring that all contract changes be in compliance with organizational policies, business and financial requirements, and legal constraints. This insistence by the contracts manager is usually an annoyance to the project manager and other members of the project team. This may explain the reason why a contracts manager typically has the reputation of being the most "unpopular player on the project team."[14] Of course, the contracts manager's due diligence in ensuring that contracts maintain compliance with organizational policies, business and financial requirements, and legal constraints will ultimately be one of the determining factors in the project's as well as the organization's success.

As noted in the discussion on contract change authority, the management of contract changes requires extensive communication and coordination among project team members and integration of project management and contract management processes. It should be noted that, although the contracts manager is the *authorizing* official for contract changes (that is, the individual authorized to modify the contract), this does not mean that the contracts manager is the *approving* official for proposed contract changes. The project manager is responsible for ensuring the project meets its cost, schedule, and performance requirements and has the responsibility and authority for approving any changes to the project's requirements. Thus, the project manager needs to ensure that any proposed changes are properly coordinated and communicated among the project team members, customers, and other stakeholders, as appropriate. One method available to the project manager for coordinating and communicating proposed project, and ultimately contract, changes is through the use of a Change Control Board (CCB).

Change Control Board (CCB)

Integrated change control is part of project monitoring and control and occurs during the contract administration phase of the contract management process. Included within integrated change control is the concept of the Change Control Board (CCB), which is responsible for "meeting and reviewing the change requests and approving or rejecting those change requests."[15] The project manager should establish a CCB for reviewing and approving all proposed changes to the project plan and to document and communicate those changes to all involved stakeholders. Any changes to the project plan approved by the CCB that result in a change to the contract would then be processed by the contracts manager through the contract changes process. Thus, the contracts manager should look to the CCB for decision authority to proceed with implementing the contract change process for approved changes.

Since proposed changes to a project may originate from many different sources and affect many different aspects of a project, it is important that the CCB fully consider all implications of a proposed change. Thus, CCB membership should include the various representatives from the functional areas involved in the project. This would include senior project team members from the technical, schedule, cost, and contracts areas. The CCB may also include senior project team members from systems engineering, software development, test/evaluation, manufacturing/production, logistics, and any other major project area. These members of the CCB are responsible for reviewing the proposed project change requests within each of their functional areas (technical, schedule, cost, contracts, etc.) and then approving or rejecting those change requests.

If the proposed change is approved, each of the CCB functional representatives would then be responsible for developing the project change documentation (specifications, schedules, budgets and funding documents, and related contract documents) as required in the contract change process. These project change documents would then be used by the contracts manager for executing the contract change and for the audit trail supporting the project and contract change. Figure 4-1 illustrates the contract change process and the role of the Change Control Board (CCB).

Figure 4-1

Change Control Board Process

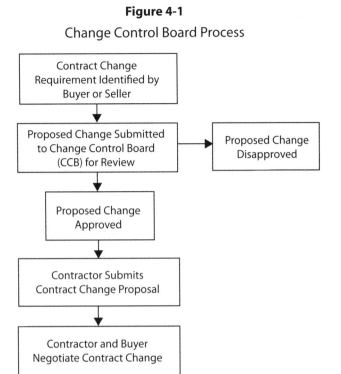

Changes to the project and associated contracts should be controlled and executed by authorized designated individuals. In addition, these project and contract changes should be, when applicable, formally reviewed by the project manager and senior project team members to fully consider the change effects on technical, schedule, cost, and contractual areas, as well as other project areas. The CCB is typically the forum for these change request reviews. Formally approved changes to the project should be in writing and properly documented and communicated to all concerned stakeholders. Finally, changes to the contract should be executed through a formal contract modification, and not through simple contract correspondence or letters to the contractor.

There may be situations during project performance and contract administration where the contractor may correspond with the buyer's contracts manager for the purpose of requesting clarification on specific aspects of the contract. In these situations, the contracts manager may communicate to the contractor through formal letter correspondence.

Contracts Manager's Letter

Managing the contract change process is an important aspect of contract administration and project management. It is through the monitoring and control of project activities that the project manager ensures achievement of the project cost, schedule, and performance objectives. And it is through the control of contract changes and the award of formal contract modifications that the contracts manager ensures that the contract supports the project objectives.

Another aspect of the day-to-day activities of contract administration is the formal communication between the purchasing organization and the contractor. This formal, written communication is sent pursuant to the terms of the contract to enforce, interpret, or clarify contractual terms and conditions or to provide direction consistent with the contract terms and conditions. Formal communication interpreting or clarifying contract terms and conditions typically involves the contractor's formally requesting clarification on contractual requirements (such as technical specifications and/ or statement of work (SOW) language) to the contracts manager. The contracts manager's formal responses to the contractor should also be submitted in the form of a formal letter. However, it is important that the contractor does not interpret the contracts manager's response as a change to the contract requirements. The contracts manager should take all precautions necessary to ensure that the response to the contractor is not misconstrued as a formal direction to change the contract. A proven method for ensuring that there is no misinterpretation of contracts manager's letters is to include a disclaimer in the letter. A sample disclaimer for this purpose is provided below:

DISCLAIMER

This contractual clarification and/or direction is issued with the understanding that it does not result in any change to the contractual requirements that would warrant a change in contract price (estimated cost and/or fee) and/or a change of delivery schedule or time of performance. If (Contractor's Name) is not in agreement with such understanding, and a change in contract price (estimated cost and/or fee) and/or change of schedule or time of performance is considered to be warranted, this direction shall be automatically null and void. If applicable, written notice of non-concurrence shall be furnished to the contracts manager within seven (7) days after receipt hereof. Failure to notify as herein provided shall constitute (Contractor's Name) concurrence and agreement to comply herewith.

This disclaimer illustrates some important points. First, the contracts manager's letter does not result in a change to the cost, schedule, or technical requirements of the contract. Second, if the contractor does not concur and believes that the contracts manager's letter does in fact result in a change to the contract requirements, the clarification or direction in the letter is without effect. Finally, the contractor must provide written notice of non-concurrence to the contracts manager within seven days after receipt of the letter, and failure to provide such notification constitutes concurrence and agreement. The time limit for contractor written notice may be revised depending on the complexity and urgency of the situation. However, it should be noted that excessive time limits result in increased risk to the buyer and should be avoided.

This disclaimer is intended for use when the contracts manager is concerned that the contractor will interpret the clarification as a direction to change the contract's requirements. The use of the disclaimer in formal communications to the contractor will help in controlling unintentional contract changes. A contracts manager's letters to the contractor, especially letters containing the disclaimer, should be controlled, numbered, and traceable by the contracts office.

Therefore, the essence of contract changes management is monitoring and controlling the changes to the contract. It was previously stated that all changes to a contract should be managed using formal, written contract modifications processed through the contract changes process..

Advance Change Adjustment Agreement

One of the challenges in following a formal contract change methodology is the administrative cost and time involved in issuing large numbers of low-cost contract modifications. One method for resolving this challenge is through the use of an advance change adjustment agreement.

It is common in large dollar value development contracts to negotiate in the basic contract price a lump sum amount to cover all subsequent low dollar value contract changes. In addition to this negotiated lump sum, an advanced change adjustment agreement clause (sometimes called a "swing clause") may also be incorporated into the contract. This clause includes a dollar amount threshold that determines if a change will be incorporated into the contract without contract price adjustments. Under this clause the buyer and the contractor agree that, if any contract change is estimated at less than the "swing clause" amount and the proposed change does not affect contract delivery or performance schedules, it can be contractually incorporated into the contract through a no-cost modification. The advance change adjustment agreement clause specifies the maximum dollar amount of proposed changes that would be incorporated into the contract using a no-cost modification. An example of an advance change adjustment agreement clause is shown below:

Advance Change Adjustment Agreement

This clause establishes a procedure by which the parties agree to change this contract according to the Changes clause of this contract without an equitable adjustment to the contract price as specified in this subparagraph. The parties agree that each change not exceeding (insert dollar amount), which also does not affect the contract delivery or performance schedules or any other contract provision, shall be a change having no effect on the contract price. For cost contracts, there will be no fee adjustment for each change not exceeding (insert dollar amount) which does not affect contract delivery or performance, or any contract provision.

When it is proposed to make a change under the Changes clause and both parties agree that such a change will require no equitable adjustment as contemplated by this clause, the Contractor shall submit a written proposal or offer to accomplish the proposed change without an equitable adjustment. If the buyer determines no adjustment is necessary, the Contractor's proposal may be accepted by issuing a formal contract modification. The modification shall (i) be issued under the Changes clause; (ii) cite this clause; (iii) reference the Contractor's proposal or offer; and (iv) direct the changes to be made. The issuance of the modification shall constitute acceptance of the Contractor's proposal or offer, shall be binding on both parties, and shall be a full, complete and final settlement for the directed changes.

Controlling contract changes is a critical part of contract changes management and a major challenge during contract administration. Through the use of centralized contract change authority, a contract change control board (CCB), contracts manager's letters and disclaimer, and advanced change adjustment agreements, the contracts manager can provide effective control of the contract, thus providing the project manager with control of project activities.

Best Practices in Contract Changes Management

Effective contract changes management requires extensive process integration as well as communication among the various project management team members. Both the project manager and contracts manager have important roles and responsibilities in terms of managing changes to the project and, ultimately, the contract. Some best practices in managing contract changes include the following:

- Develop and use a formal and disciplined contract management methodology.
- Develop and use a formal and disciplined contract change process as part of the organization's contract management methodology.
- Provide training to all project team members on the formal contract management methodology and contract change process.
- Formally appoint individuals authorized to negotiate and award contract modifications. Reflect this appointment in the contract.

- Document and execute all contract changes through formal modifications to the contract.
- Provide copies of the basic contract and all contract modifications to all affected organizations.
- Maintain an electronic copy of the conformed contract accessible to all project team members.
- Implement a Change Control Board (CCB) to review proposed contract changes.
- Properly use contracts manager's letters and associated disclaimers.
- Periodically assess your organization's contract management process maturity.

SUMMARY

Contract administration is where the "rubber meets the road" in project management. It is during this phase of project management that the project effort is performed by the contractor, and this actual performance is then compared to planned performance to identify any cost, schedule, or performance variances. These variances are then used to identify any corrective actions or preventive actions required to ensure that the project meets its goals. It is also during this phase of the project that some of the project plans, such as statements of work (SOW), work breakdown structures (WBS), specifications, technical procedures, budgets, and schedules have to be changed to reflect the actual project environment and effort already accomplished. Managing and controlling these changes to the project, as reflected in the project contract, is a critical and important activity of contract administration. The contract reflects the agreement between a buyer and a seller on all aspects of a project, and thus, its currency and accuracy is of the utmost importance. It is paramount that both parties to a contract maintain a formal, disciplined, and methodical process for managing contract changes. Both the buyer and the seller should ensure that only authorized individuals are able to initiate, process, and approve contract changes. In addition, it is essential that all changes to the contract be documented and processed as a formal modification to the contract document.

Chapter 5 reviews the use of contract financing, payments, and profitability, which are so vital to effective contract administration and contract execution.

Endnotes

1   Project Management Institute. *A Guide to the Project Management Body of Knowledge* (PMBOK Guide) 61. Newtown Square, PA , 2009.

2   Nash, Jr., R.C., Schooner, S.L., O'Brien-DeBakey. *The Government Contracts Reference Book: A Comprehensive Guide to the Language of Procurement*, 3rd ed. Chicago: CCH, 2007.

3   Ibid.

4   Garrett, Gregory A., *World Class Contracting*, 4th ed. Chicago: CCH, 2007.

5   Ibid., n. 2.

6   Ibid.

7   Ibid., n. 4.

8   Ibid.

9   Ibid.

10 Ibid.

11 Ibid.

12 Ibid.

13 Garrett, Gregory A., & Rendon, R. G. *Contract Management Organizational Assessment Tools.* McLean, Va.: National Contract Management Association, 2005.

14 Hirsch, W. J. *The Contracts Management Deskbook*, rev. ed. New York: American Management Association, 1986.

15 PMI at 94.

CHAPTER

CONTRACT FINANCING, PAYMENTS, AND PROFITABILITY

INTRODUCTION

In the world of business cash flow is king! Thus, the topic of contract financing, payments, and profitability are vital to all contractors and subcontractors to ensure they both survive and thrive. Likewise, payment is critical to U.S. government agencies to ensure that they have a viable supplier base to provide them the products, services, systems, and solutions they require to support the needs of our nation. In this chapter, we will briefly review (1) how U.S. government agencies often provide money via payments to contractors prior to the completion of work to assist contractors in financing a contract; (2) how and when payments are made by government agencies to contractors; and (3) the tools and techniques that contractors or government agencies typically use to evaluate contract or contractor profitability.

CONTRACT FINANCING TECHNIQUES

In some situations, U.S. government agencies will provide payments to a prime contractor, which are unrelated to completion or delivery of contract work, in order to assist the contractor in financing the performance of the work. The major types of U.S. government contract financing techniques are (1) U.S. government grants and loans; (2) advance payments; (3) provisional payments; and (4) progress payments.

Grants and Loans

U.S. government agencies provide grants and government-backed loans via the Small Business Administration (SBA) and other agencies to assist a wide range of small businesses to both compete and execute U.S. government contracts. Grants are based on specified criteria in appropriate authorization bills that are passed by the U.S. Congress and signed into law by the U.S. President. Grant payments may be provided either as a form of financing or for the payment of specific work. Grant funding does not have to be repaid to the government. U.S.-backed or guaranteed loans are provided expressly to businesses that need a short-term influx of cash to sustain the business until the completion of work when final payments are typically provided. Loans typically have to be repaid over an extended period of time, which varies based upon the situation.

Advance Payments

Said simply, advance payments by U.S. government agencies to contractors are very seldom used as a means of contract financing. As is to be expected there are numerous U.S. government restrictions on agencies' paying contractors prior to the contractor's incurrence of costs and/or performance of work. Advance payments differ fundamentally from progress payments and partial payments, which are payments made by government agencies to contractors based on a contractor's completion of work, measured performance progress, or actual cost of performance.

Advance payments are expressly authorized by 10 United States Code (U.S.C.) Section 2307, which permits the head of a defense agency to approve the use of advance payments up to the unpaid contract price if the contractor gives adequate security and the head of the agency determines that the advance payments would be in the public interest. Likewise, 41 U.S.C. Section 255 permits advance payments to be used in a similar manner by civilian agencies. Further, in 31 U.S.C. Section 3324(d), advance payments are permitted for all types of publications. Further, the Federal Acquisition Streamlining Act (FASA) of 1994 (Public Law No. 103-355) added a provision in 10 U.S.C. Section 2307 providing for advance payments for commercial items, not to exceed 15 percent of the contract price.[1]

FAR 32.403 describes the appropriate uses of advance payments. If advance payments are not expressly permitted by statute, they are usually held to be invalid. If a contractor believes there is a valid justification for advance payments, then the contractor should request them via the appropriate government contracting officer for review and approval by the head of the agency.

Provisional Payments

Provisional payments are a contract financing technique, which is not provided for by the standard U.S. government acquisition regulations, and their use is restricted to unusual circumstances where they are deemed necessary to enable a contractor to continue contract performance.[2] The need for provisional payments typically arises when a U.S. government contracting officer issues a unilateral contract change order, pursuant to the Changes Clause FAR 52.243-1, and the contractor is required to perform the work directed in the change order, but can not bill or invoice for the work until the contract is modified via a supplemental agreement to add the negotiated equitable adjustment to the contract price. A problem often arises when the government agency rejects an invoice that includes the value of changed work and the contractor claims interest under the Prompt Payment Act. Although the FAR is silent regarding the use of provisional payments on undefinitized contractual actions (UCAs), contractors performing a significant amount of work on UCAs that cannot be priced in a timely manner, may request contract modifications permitting provisional payments for such work.[3]

Further, FAR 16.603-2 provides that:

- a letter contract may be used when (1) the Government's interests
- Demand that the contractor be given a binding commitment so that work can start immediately and (2) negotiating a definitive contract is not possible in sufficient time to meet the requirement.

A negotiating and definitization schedule is required in UCAs calling for definitization and payment within 180 days after the date of issuance of a UCA. However, this requirement can be waived. FAR 32.102(e) (2) provides that payment "may not exceed 80 percent of the eligible costs of work accomplished on undefinitized contract actions." Other government agency FAR supplements provide further restrictions on the use and level of funding of provisional payments.

Progress Payments

Cost-based progress payments are considered to be a common form of contract financing on U.S. government contracts. They apply when the work is for six months or longer for large businesses or four months or longer for small businesses and the contract value is over $1,000,000 for large businesses or over $100,000 for small businesses. Cost-based progress payments are made on the basis of contractor requests for payments, which are subject to audit by the government per clause FAR 52.232-16. The Progress Payments clause at FAR 52-232-16 provides that payment will be made when requested by the contractor "as the work progresses but not more frequently than monthly."

FIVE

The length of time that a U.S. government agency has to make a progress payment to a contractor depends on agency policy. FAR 32.906 permits agencies to set the time for payment not earlier than 7 days, nor later than 30 days after receipt of a proper request.

TYPES OF PAYMENT

Fundamentally, there are two major types of payment under Government contracts: (1) payment of the contract price for completed items of work and (2) progress payments based on costs incurred or a percentage of completion of the work. The earlier forms of payment discussed are considered contract financing techniques. In U.S. government contracts, payment of the contract price is typically due upon completion of the work and submission of appropriate invoices unless otherwise agreed to by the parties.[4] The payments clause for supply and service contracts, FAR 52.232-1, states:

- The Government shall pay the Contractor, upon submission of proper invoices or vouchers, the prices stipulated in this contract for supplies delivered and accepted or services rendered and accepted, less any deductions provided in this contract.
- Partial payments are encouraged for supplies and services pursuant to FAR 32.102(d) which states:
- Partial payments for accepted supplies and services that are only a part of the contract requirements are authorized...Although partial payments are generally treated as a method of payment and not used as a method of contract financing, using partial payments can assist contractors to participate in Government contracts without, or with minimal, contract financing. When appropriate, agencies shall use this payment method.

Progress payments based on costs are considered contract financing, as discussed earlier, while those based on completion of the work are not. FAR 32.102 provides that progress payments based on a percentage or stage of completion "may be used as a payment method under agency procedures."

The Federal Acquisition Streamlining Act of 1994, P.L. 103-355, amended 10 U.S.C. 2307(b) and 41 U.S.C. 255(b) to add new standards for progress payments. These provisions require "performance-based" payments "whenever practicable" using any of the following bases:

1. Performance measured by objective, quantifiable methods such as delivery of acceptable items, work measurement, or statistical process controls.
2. Accomplishment of events defined in the program management plan.
3. Other quantifiable measures of results.

Since 1981, the Department of Defense has authorized so-called "flexible progress payments" based upon rates determined through application of a computer model, "CASH," which considers key cash flow factors in a contractor's operations. This alternative approach, which contracting officers have discretion to authorize for fixed-price contracts in excess of $1 million dollars where cost or pricing data is submitted, was instituted because customary progress payments based on a fixed percent of incurred costs were deemed to be "insensitive" to numerous factors affecting a contractor's actual investment in work-in-progress inventory. DFARS 232.502-1-71(b) states that DOD may change the uniform progress payment rate and/or the minimum contractor investment rate. In order to avoid frequent revision , "the program is designed to permit use of either a particular model (CASH-II, CASH-V, etc.) or a program option to input the equivalent uniform progress payment rate and minimum contractor investment rate (90%/5%, 80%/20%)."[5]

Prompt Payment

The U.S. government contracting payment process begins with the contractor's submission of a request for payment. The request for payment is typically made via a contractor's submission of a proper invoice or voucher. The invoice or voucher is then reviewed by the government and either accepted or rejected. If the invoice or voucher is rejected by the government, it is then returned to the contractor for possible corrections and resubmission. If the invoice or voucher is accepted, then payment is made pursuant to the terms of the contract. Under the Prompt Payment Act, 31 U.S.C. Section 3902(a), the contractor is entitled to interest for delayed payments when proper invoices are submitted for each "complete delivered item of property or service."

The contractor must submit a "proper invoice" to obtain interest for a delayed payment. The Prompt Payment Act, 31 U.S.C. 3901 (a)(3), states that a 'proper invoice' is an invoice containing or accompanied by substantiating documentation the Director of the Office of Management and budget may require by regulation and the head of the appropriate agency may require by regulation or contract." OMB Circular A-125, Section 5(b) contains detailed guidance concerning the required content of contractor invoices. To constitute a proper invoice, a contractor must submit the following information:

1. Name of contractor and invoice date (contractors are encouraged to date invoices as close as possible to the date of mailing or transmission)
2. Contract number or other authorization for delivery of property or services (assignment of an invoice number by the contractor is recommended)
3. Description, price, and quantity of property and services actually delivered or rendered
4. Shipping and payment terms
5. Other substantiating documentation or information as required by the contract
6. Name (where practicable), title, telephone number, and complete mailing address of responsible official to whom payment is to be sent

In addition to these requirements, FAR 32-905(e) (7) requires the "name (where practicable), title, phone number, and mailing address of person to be notified in event of a defective invoice." The voucher must also include an accounting classification, the amount to be disbursed, the method of disbursement, and the payee.[6]

Fast Payment

FAR 13.4 establishes a "fast payment" procedure that allows expedited payment for small purchases. FAR 13.402 states that "the fast payment procedure may be used, provided that use of the procedure is consistent with the other conditions of the purchase." The conditions for use of the fast payment procedure are as follows:

a. Individual purchasing instruments do not exceed $30,000, except that executive agencies may permit higher dollar limitations for specified activities or items on a case-by-case basis.
b. Deliveries of supplies are to occur at locations where there is both a geographical separation and a lack of adequate communications facilities between Government receiving and disbursing activities that will make it impractical to make

timely payment based on evidence of Government acceptance. [Use of the fast payment procedure would not be indicated, for example, for small purchases by an activity if material being purchased is destined for use at that activity and contract administration will be performed by the purchasing office at that activity.]

c. Title to the supplies passes to the Government (1) upon delivery to a post office or common carrier for mailing or shipment to destination; or (2) upon receipt by the Government if the shipment is by means other than Postal Service or common carrier.

d. The supplier agrees to replace, repair, or correct supplies not received at destination, damaged in transit, or not conforming to purchase requirements.

e. The purchasing instrument is a firm-fixed price contract, a purchase order, or a delivery order for supplies.

f. A system is in place to ensure (1) documentation of evidence of contractor performance under fast payment purchases; (2) timely feedback to the contracting officer in case of contractor deficiencies; and (3) identification of suppliers that have a current history of abusing the fast payment procedure.

Under this procedure, payment is processed upon the agency's receipt of the invoice without the need to wait for inspection and formal acceptance of the goods. In return, the contractor is required to represent that it has delivered the goods and will replace repair, or correct any damaged or nonconforming items.[7]

Profit Analysis

Profit analysis is extremely important to stakeholders who have different perspectives of profit. For example, stockholders have a great interest in profit analysis since they receive revenue in the form of dividends from the corporations in which they invest. Creditors find profit analysis of vital importance since profits are a source from which debt is paid. Furthermore, since profits help finance the operations of a business, managers use profit analysis to measure the income or operating performance of a business.[8] In addition, competitors are interested in profit analysis for comparison purposes in the performance and efficiency of businesses that are operating in the same industry.[9]

Without profit, it would be difficult for a business to purchase updated equipment, construct or acquire buildings, or obtain additional working capital through either loans or the sale of stock. However, an unhealthy emphasis on profit that does not consider risk could jeopardize a business' potential for continued existence. When analyzing a prospective investment, managers must consider possible risk associated with the prospective profit.[10]

In attempting to determine the appropriate rate of return or profitability for goods or services, it is important to consider the four principles for profit analysis set forth by the Department of Defense (DoD). The principles were set forth by acquisition regulations in order to encourage effective and economical contract performance and to draw exemplary contractors to defense contracting.[11] The four principles of profit analysis are as follow:

1. Motivate contractors to undertake more difficult work requiring higher skills and reward those who do so.
2. Allow the contractor an opportunity to earn profits commensurate with the extent of the cost risk he is willing to assume.
3. Motivate contractors to provide their own facilities and financing and establish their competence through development work undertaken at their own risk and reward those who do so.
4. Reward contractors for productivity increases.[12]

In government, contracting officers conducting a profit analysis should acknowledge efficient and effective contractor effort and the risk that the contractor is willing to take in a particular contract. In efforts to meet the goal of motivating effective contractor performance, contracting officers should not focus merely on the negotiation of the lowest possible profit, especially if it is based solely on applying a randomly determined percentage to the total product cost. Of course, the higher the potential profits, the higher will be the risk involved. Businesses that choose to accept the higher risk will do so in hopes of reaping the reward of potentially higher profits.[13]

Profitability

It is important to distinguish between profit and profitability. The profit or earnings of a business are found on the income statement of a business. If the income is greater than expenditures, the business is considered to have a profit. If the income is less than expenditures, the business is considered to have a loss for that particular operating period.

For government contracts, the Contract Pricing Reference Guides provide guidelines for profit/fee ceilings. When preparing the profit/fee calculations, contracting officers must take into consideration the distinctive conditions of each individual negotiation. In addition, the contract fee must not exceed the statutory limits that apply to cost-plus-fixed-fee contracts as illustrated in the following Figure 5-1.[14]

Figure 5-1

Statutory Limits on Contract Fee	
Type of Contract	Statutory Fee Limitation
Experimental, developmental, or research work performed under a cost-plus-fixed-fee contract	15% of estimated contract cost
All other cost-plus-fixed-fee contracts	10% of estimated contract cost

Profitability, on the other hand, is measured by utilizing ratios that incorporate profit or earnings with a minimum of one other number from the financial statements, such as the income statement or the balance sheet.[15] In essence, profitability is the capability of a business to offer its investors a certain rate of return on their investment.[16] Additionally, profitability ratios evaluate the operating or income performance of a business.[17] A few profitability ratios will be discussed below.

In order to firmly grasp the concept of profitability, the ability to differentiate between absolute and relative profitability is necessary. Absolute profitability assesses the effect on the overall earnings or profits of a business of adding or dropping a certain business segment or product with no additional changes. Relative profitability, on the other hand, deals with the ranking of products and other business segments to establish which segment or product should be prioritized. Relative profitability is particularly useful if a business has several profitable opportunities that cannot be pursued all at once.[18]

Usually, the relative profitability of projects or segments can be evaluated using the profitability index. The profitability index, a variation of the net present value, is a viable approach to capital budgeting. The profitability index can be computed as follows:[19]

Profitability Index = Present Value of Cash Inflows/Present Value of Cash Outflows

For a project to be acceptable, a profitability index of 1 or greater is required. When a business does not have the available resources to fund all of the potential projects that have a positive net present value, the profitability index can bring some helpful insights into the decision-making process.[20]

MEASURES OF PROFITABILITY

In government contracting, financial analysis is comprised of evaluating the financial capability of potential contractors, analyzing the consequences that government financing decisions could have on the financial management of contractors, and reviewing the necessity for government protection due to performance problems stemming from the financial problems of contractors.[21]

The starting point for assessing and measuring profitability is generally the annual report of a business, which includes the financial statements such as the income statement and the balance sheet. The income statement shows all of the sales and service revenues earned by a business during a specific period of time as well as all of the expenses or costs incurred to produce that particular revenue. A balance sheet is a snapshot of a business that portrays the financial position of the company at a specific point in time and is comprised of assets, liabilities, and stockholders' (owners') equity.[22] Assets are considered to be the economic resources owned by a business that provide future benefits by helping to generate revenues. Liabilities are the claims by external creditors against the assets of a business. Owners' (stockholders') equity is an owner's financial claim against the assets of a business.[23]

When conducting financial analysis, the contracting officer has the responsibility of determining whether poor finances could possibly hinder future contract performance. In order to properly conduct a financial analysis, contracting officers must comprehend the relationship between assets, liabilities, and owners' equity, which are shown on the balance sheet of a business. The relationship is illustrated when reviewing the following accounting equation, which should always balance:[24]

Assets = Liabilities + Owners' (Stockholders') Equity

An in-depth analysis of the financial strength of a business generally involves various comparisons including comparisons within the same business over a period of years to identify trends, comparisons with other businesses in the same industry, and comparisons against the industry itself. It is also important to remember that different types of businesses will have different financial structures.[25]

Overall, financial ratio analysis assists managers in evaluating a business's past performance as well as estimating its future performance. [26] The following sections will illustrate some of the many ratios available for use in analyzing the performance of a business.

Return on Investment (ROI)

The return on investment (ROI) evaluates the earnings performance of a business. It measures the income earned on the capital invested by the business and how well the business uses its assets or investments.[27] In its simplest form, ROI is calculated by merely dividing income by the invested capital.[28]

ROI = Income/Invested Capital

However, depending on how the ROI measure is intended to be used, there could be different definitions of income and invested capital. For example, income could be only the income provided by the particular investment, gross profit, net income, operating income, or earnings before interest and taxes. Invested capital could be only the amount of the particular investment, stockholders' equity, or in other cases, total assets, which includes the total capital provided by both sources of financing, debt and equity.[29]

The rate of return quantifies a business' return on investment. Contracting officers generally use the following formula for calculating the rate of return.[30]

$$\text{Rate of Return} = \frac{\text{Gross Profit}}{\text{Fixed Assets} + \text{Net Working Capital}}$$

Gross profit is calculated by subtracting the cost of selling the products or services (also known as the cost of goods sold) from the sales or service revenue (the amount that a business earns for the goods it sells or the services it provides).[31]

Revenue – Cost of Goods Sold = Gross Profit

Fixed assets are generally the long-term assets of a business such as buildings and equipment while net working capital, a measure of liquidity, is calculated by subtracting current liabilities from current assets. Current assets refer to cash, accounts receivable, and inventories whereas current liabilities include debt that is due within a year, such as accounts payable and short-term notes payable.

The rate of return is normally used to evaluate potential investments within a business where a higher ratio could signify a comparatively better and more profitable use of the business' assets or investments.[32] If the calculated ROI exceeds the predetermined required rate of return (also known as cost of capital rate or hurdle rate) of a business, then the investment or project should be considered for acceptance.[33] Because ROI is sometimes considered to be a type of return on capital, it tends to measure the ability of a business to reward providers of long-term finances as well as to draw providers of future potentially needed funds.[34]

Two types of risk that businesses need to address and that are associated with potential investments include business risk and financial risk. Whereas business risk deals with the inability of a business to remain competitive and sustain stability and earnings growth, financial risk refers to the inability of a business to meet its liability or debt obligations as they come due.[35]

When analyzing a contractor's proposal, the facilities investment cost of money is considered because it has an influence on profit.[36] Whenever managers assess potential new investments or projects, they will approximate the amount of possible revenue that could be made from the investment as well as the probable costs associated with earning that particular revenue.[37] Successful managers want to make sure that investments will be worthwhile and profitable for the business.

While there are several methods of calculating the ROI, one frequently used measurement for ROI is profit margin multiplied by the asset turnover rate, also known as return on assets (ROA), which will be discussed in the next section.

Return on Assets (ROA)

Generally, a business acquires assets in efforts to create potential income, which in turn produces a profit.[38] A ratio that is useful in analyzing the overall profit performance of a business is the return on assets (ROA).[39] ROA is also referred to as return on invested capital. Invested capital includes total financing, which is comprised of both owner (equity) and non-owner (debt) financing.[40]

The total assets, as shown on the balance sheet, represent the total amount of physical and financial resources or assets that a business had available for use during the operating period to create the profit shown on the income statement.[41] ROA measures how well a business is utilizing its resources or assets to create earnings.[42]

Return on assets (investment) can be calculated in two different ways:

1. Return on Assets = Net Income/Average Total Assets
2. Return on Assets = Profit margin X Asset Turnover

$$\text{Profit Margin} = \text{Net Income/Sales}$$

$$\text{Asset Turnover} = \text{Sales/Average Total Assets}$$

The first method is the most basic form of the ROA calculation. The second method is referred to as the DuPont measurement system of analysis, which was first developed by DuPont's managers to assist business managers in the decision-making process. A high profit margin, an income statement ratio, indicates the business is adequately controlling its costs.[43] In calculating average total assets, beginning total assets are added to ending total assets and divided by two. A higher asset turnover indicates more sales dollars are being created by each asset dollar, indicating that the business is operating in a more efficient manner.[44]

The DuPont analysis method offers managers more detailed analyses that could provide insights regarding areas of the operations of a business needing management attention and improvement, which in turn could lead to efforts to enhance the competitive advantages of a business.[45] It is important to note that the DuPont analysis system is widely applied to both ROI and ROA, which are sometimes used interchangeably.

The DuPont measurement system of financial control concentrates on the return on investment or assets by focusing on two components, which include a measurement to evaluate efficiency and a turnover measurement that analyzes the productivity of a business. The profit margin, a ratio of income to sales (also called return on sales or sales margin), measures efficiency. It represents the ability of a business to control its costs at a particular level of sales. The asset turnover, a ratio of sales to total assets (investment) (also called asset turnover), measures productivity and shows the capability of a business to produce sales from a certain level of investment (assets).[46] For example, when analyzing the efficiency ratio of operating income to sales, the different cost elements, such as manufacturing, selling, and administration, and their relationship to sales can be easily examined. Ordinarily, industry competition, economic circumstances, debt financing usage, and other business operating attributes can cause the profit margin to differ within as well as between industries.[47] Figure 5-2 illustrates the ROA DuPont method:[4]

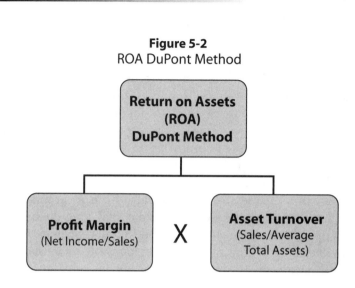

Figure 5-2
ROA DuPont Method

In evaluating the productivity ratio of sales to total assets (investment), managers can monitor the turnover measures, which include working capital elements such as inventory, accounts receivable, and cash, as well as long-term or permanent asset (investment) elements such as equipment and buildings The ability to evaluate these different elements can assist managers in their decision-making process to pinpoint where improvements may be necessary.[49]

Since a business may spend over half of its total dollars in purchasing, this fact has a high significance in the profit-making prospects of the purchasing and supply function of a business. Purchasing costs can contribute to the ROI (or ROA) of a business by increasing both the profit margin and the asset turnover rate. In other words, each dollar saved in purchasing is equal to a new dollar of profit. However, because expenses are deducted from sales to arrive at a profit, it is essential to understand that an additional dollar of income from sales is not necessarily a new dollar of profit.[50]

Generally, higher efficiency signifies higher profitability as well as a business' ability to turn its resources or assets into cash to meet current liabilities or debt. It is vitally important to analyze a contractor's trends over a period of time. If a contractor becomes less efficient in utilizing its resources and assets, it may be an indication that the contractor is experiencing decreasing profits and in turn increasing its dependence on borrowing as a source of funds to sustain its operations.[51] Even though there are several variations of ROA, it is considered one of the most widely used financial ratios.

Internal Rate of Return (IRR)

The internal rate of return (IRR), expressed as a percentage, is an approach widely used in capital budgeting to evaluate capital investment proposals. The essential assessment issue in dealing with a capital investment or a long-term asset is whether or not the investment's future benefits warrant its initial cost.

When the IRR is used to analyze an investment or project, it is compared with a predetermined hurdle rate, which is the minimum rate of return that management is willing to accept. As illustrated in Figure 5-3, if the IRR is higher than the hurdle rate, the project is accepted; if the IRR is lower than the hurdle rate, the project is rejected. The selection of the hurdle rate is subjective in nature and is the decision of the management of a business in analyzing different potential capital investments. In addition, the hurdle rate is usually different for various individual projects depending on the risk that management is willing to take.[52]

Figure 5-3
Internal Rate of Retrn

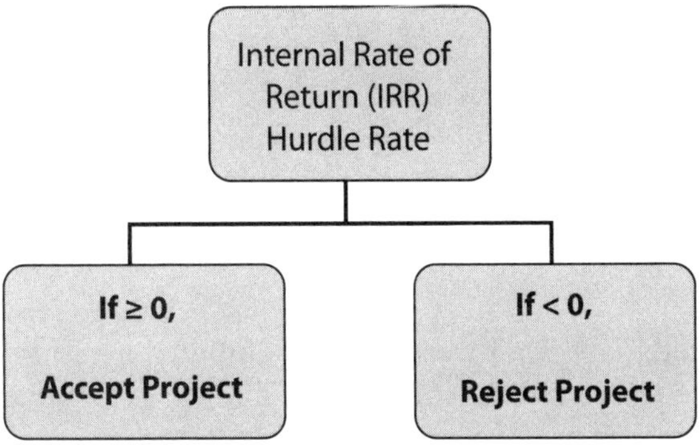

The IRR is the discount rate that makes the investment's net present value equal to zero and is the actual rate of return projected from an investment.[53] There are two main methods that can be used to compute the IRR. The first method involves the use of a present value table. The IRR is calculated by first computing the present value factor of the investment or project.

Present Value Factor = Required Initial Investment/Annual Net Cash Inflows

Next, the IRR calculation involves finding the present value factor in the present value of an annuity of a table, which may fall between two factors on the table. Once the calculated present value factor is found in the table for the number of periods of the project life, the IRR can be approximated. The second method of calculating the IRR is by using a financial calculator, which would provide a more precise figure.

However, the IRR has a few disadvantages. First, the IRR makes the erroneous assumption that a business will reinvest a project's cash flows at the project's internal rate of return. Secondly, the IRR can produce vague results, especially when analyzing opposing projects in circumstances where lack of sufficient funds keeps the business from investing in all of the potential projects with a positive net present value.[54] Third, another limitation of the IRR is that it ignores the varying risks over the life of a project.[55]

The tax effect on capital budgeting decisions includes the fact that a business must pay taxes on any net benefits generated by the investment in long-term assets. In addition, a business can use the depreciation related to a capital investment to decrease its taxable income and offset part of the taxes. The method of depreciation that tax laws allow a business to depreciate acquisition costs of its long-term assets as tax-deductible expenses may differ from business to business.[56]

Overall, the IRR is an excellent profitability measurement that reflects the time value of money and allows for comparisons between dissimilar projects or investments.[57]

Measured Operating Income (MOI)

In measuring profitability, it is vitally important to be able to measure operating income and the earning power of a business. Core operating income includes sales and service revenue less the cost of goods sold and less selling, general, and administrative expenses, also referred to as operating expenses.[58] In other words, operating income includes revenue and expenses from the ordinary operations of a business and excludes items such as other revenue (losses), extraordinary items, and income from discontinued operations.[59]

Earning power is the capability of a business to create profits and increase its future assets.[60]

Operating income is also called operating profit or income from operations. A multi-step income statement usually lists operating expenses, which relate to the ongoing operations of a business and offset the related operating income. For measurement purposes when analyzing income trends, it is important to compare the operating income over time or between businesses in order to concentrate on the factors of selling the product or service and controlling the related costs. For example, if a business includes revenue from the sale of a business segment, which is not considered revenue from the day-to-day operations of the business, to offset ordinary operating expenses, it would in essence be showing a deceptive or misleading operating income amount. Therefore, it is important for a business to show its non-operating income and expenses in a separate section of the income statement.[61]

Accrual-based accounting refers to the recognition of revenue when it is earned and the recognition of expenses when they are incurred to earn that revenue, regardless of the timing of the cash receipt or payment. Under Generally Accepted Accounting Principles (GAAP), this matching principle requires that expenses be recognized, or shown on the income statement, in the same period as the revenue that the expenses helped create.[62] Accrual accounting is considered to better match economic benefit with economic effort, which in turn yields a measure of operating performance (accrual earnings) that gives a practical and realistic picture of past economic transactions. However, it is imperative to recognize that reported accrual accounting income may not always paint an accurate picture of the underlying economic performance of a business for a particular period of time due to various reasons, including the issue of income recognition.[63]

In a competitive environment, the amount of profit realized by a business will depend on its capability of controlling and reducing its costs. Government buyers are usually concerned with obtaining a fair and reasonable price based on sufficient market competition. On the other hand, when there is no competitive market, the market constraints placed on cost and profit are not present; therefore, cost analysis and profit analysis are absolutely critical. [64]

Operating income or operating profit can be calculated as follows:[65]

Gross Profit – Operating Expenses = Operating Income or Profit

Measuring operating income is one of the key factors of performance measurement of a business in order to succeed financially from the financial perspective of the balanced scorecard, which is an integrated set of performance measurements organized around four distinctive perspectives, which include financial, customer, internal, and innovation and learning.[66] At the organizational level, MOI is a measure that is used to quantify the value that has been produced or lost from the ongoing operations of a business.

Days of Sales Outstanding (DSO)

Accounts receivable, a current asset shown on the balance sheet, is the business account that includes the sales of products and services sold to clients or customers on credit or on account.[67] For better cash flow, a business must convert its accounts receivables into cash. The days of sales outstanding (DSO) (also known as days' sales in receivables or collection period) indicates how many days' sales remain in accounts receivables waiting to be collected.[68]

There are different methods of calculating DSO. One widely used method of computing DSO is as follows:[69]

Average net accounts receivables/ (net sales/365 days) = Days of Sales
Outstanding (DSO)

Overall, DSO measures how long, on average, it takes a business to collect its accounts receivables. Generally, outstanding receivables should not be allowed to exceed credit terms by 10-15 days.[70]

Another method of computing DSO is by dividing 365 by the accounts receivable turnover, which is net credit sales divided by average accounts receivable. The accounts receivable turnover reflects the number of times that receivables turn over within a year. The DSO is a good indicator for analyzing customer payment patterns. [71]

It is essential to understand that profit is not the same as cash. The profit shown on an income statement is not necessarily represented by cash at the end of the operating and reporting period. When using the accrual basis of accounting, if a business shows a profit in the income statement, it does not necessarily mean that the cash has been collected and is available for use by the business. Sales revenue on an income statement usually includes both cash and credit sales. When a business offers its clients or customers credit terms, the business is actually making a loan to its customers until payment is received from those customers sometime in the future. Consequently, when a sale is made, it is included in the income statement for the operating period; however, cash related to that sale may not have been received yet. The timing difference between the recognition of an economic event or transaction and the related cash receipt can have critical and important implications for a business.[72]

Depending on the credit terms, a high DSO may indicate that a business is encountering difficulties in collecting cash from its clients or customers. If this is a recurring and consistent problem, a business may be facing a going concern issue, which means that it may not be able to sustain its operations to remain in business.[73]

Weighted Guidelines Method (WGM)

Since 1963 when the Department of Defense (DoD) initially issued the weighted guidelines method (WGM) to be used in establishing profit objectives, there have been changes to the profit policy. The WGM, similar to the commercial marketplace, offers the promise of various degrees of rewards based on the cost risks assumed by a contractor, a contractor's performance, and other factors unique to the contract.[74]

Effective April 26, 2002, the new profit policy changes had the effect of reducing the weight on facilities investment, adding general and administrative expenses to the cost base utilized in arriving at the profit objectives, increasing the importance of performance risk, and encouraging contractors in cost reduction efforts. The contracting officer has flexibility in determining the best method of evaluating a contractor's efforts to reduce costs that benefit the contract and may increase the pre-negotiation profit objective to reward a contractor's efforts.[75]

Over the past years, the current DoD weighted guidelines method of profit policy has undergone many studies resulting in differing outcomes as to the effectiveness of this profit policy and measurement analysis within DoD. Overall, when appropriately used, the WGM will reward contractors with profits proportionate to the risks assumed and the unique conditions of each contract. In general, the WGM provides a guide for properly documenting the profit objective and makes sure that a contractor's effort, risk assumed, facility investment, and other unique factors particular to a contract are considered in the profit/fee determination.[76]

It is mandatory for DoD contracting officers to use the structured WGM for profit/fee analysis when cost analysis is used in determining the reasonableness of price in a contract. The WGM outlines a structure for profit/fee analysis that involves the designation of ranges for objective values and norm values that can be tailored to fit the unique conditions of a particular contract. Form 5-1 illustrates the Weighted Guidelines Form (DD Form 1547) which provides the structure for DoD profit/fee analysis and reporting.[77]

Form 5-1
DD Form 1547

Record Of Weighted Guidelines Application							Report Control Symbol Dd-A&T(Q)1751	
1. Report No.	2. Basic Procurement Instrument Identification No.					3. Spiin	4. Date Of Action	
	A. Purchasing Office		B. Fy	C. Type Proc Inst Code	D. Prisn		A. Year	B.
5. Contracting Office Code			Item	Cost Category			Objective	
6. Name Of Contractor			13.	Material				
			14.	Subcontracts				
7. Duns Number	8. Federal Supply Code		15.	Direct Labor				
			16.	Indirect Expenses				
9. Dod Claimant Program	10. Contract Type Code		17.	Other Direct Charges				
			18.	Subtotal Costs (13 Thru 17)				
11. Type Effort	12. Use Code		19.	General And Administrative				
			20.	Total Costs (18+19)				

	Weighted Guidelines Profit Factors						
Item	Contractor Risk Factors	Assigned Weighting	Assigned Value	Base (Item 20)		Profit Objective	
21.	Technical	%					
22.	Management/Cost Control	%					
23.	Performance Risk (Composite)						

24.	Contract Type Risk					
25.	Working Capital	Costs Financed	Length Factor	Interest Rate		▮
				%		
	Contractor Facilities Capital Employed		Assigned Value	Amount Employed		▮
26.	Land		▮			▮
27.	Buildings		▮			▮
28.	Equipment					▮
29.	Cost Efficiency Factor		Assigned Value	Base (Item 20)		▮
30.	Total Profit Objective					

	Negotiated Summary			
		Proposed	Objective	Negotiated
31.	Total Costs			
32.	Facilities Capital Cost Of Money (Dd Form 1861)			
33.	Profit			
34.	Total Price (Line 31 + 32 + 33)			
35.	Markup Rate (Line 32 + 33 Divided By 31)	%	%	%

	Contracting Officer Approval		
36. Typed/Printed Name Of Contracting Officer (Last, First, Middle Initial)	37. Signature Of Contracting Officer	38. Telephone No.	39. Date Submitted (Yyyymmdd)

	Optional Use		
96.	97.	98.	99.

DD FORM 1547, JUL 2002   PREVIOUS EDITION IS OBSOLETE.

As illustrated in Table 5-1, for profit/fee analysis, the factors for performance of risk analysis include technical and management/cost control. Items 21-23 of the DD Form 1547 are intended to reward contractors who assume more performance risk in the contracts that they accept. In order to evaluate performance risk, contracting officers need to analyze the risk associated with satisfying the requirements of the contract. The following Figure 5-5 outlines factors that should be taken into consideration when analyzing each type of risk:[78]

Table 5-1

Factors for Performance of Risk Analysis	
Risk Type	**Examples of Factors to Be Considered**
Technical	• Technology being applied or developed by the contractor • Technical complexity • Program maturity • Performance specifications and tolerances • Delivery schedule • Extent of warranty or guarantee
Management/Cost Control	• Contractor's management and internal control systems • Management involvement expected under the contract • Resources applied and value added by the contractor • Contractor support for federal socioeconomic programs • Expected reliability of cost estimates • Adequacy of management's approach to controlling cost and schedule • Other factors affecting contractor's ability to meet cost targets

As illustrated in the DD Form 1547, risk analysis involves different evaluation factors and can be complex. The actual detailed steps and instructions for completing the DD Form 1547 are beyond the scope of this work. Overall, the form is divided into five parts to include contractor effort, contractor risk, facilities investment, special factors, and cost of money offset. Different profit weight ranges are assigned to each profit/fee factor. It is important to note that fixed-price contracts with financing usually have lower profit/fee ranges than fixed-price contracts with no financing. When the government provides financing, the contractor would be likely to assume less financial risk. When assigning values, the contracting officer should assign a profit/fee value consistent with the value for performance risk. The contracting officer signs and dates the DD Form 1547 after the completion of the negotiation.[79]

Earnings Before Interest, Taxes, Depreciation & Amortization (EBITDA)

One measure of profitability currently being utilized is that of earnings before interest, taxation, depreciation, and amortization (EBITDA). The main argument for using this measure is that it eliminates all of the minor items in order to focus on the true profitability of a business without being influenced by capital structures, tax systems, or methods of depreciation. While EBITDA can be very useful as part of a detailed analysis of a business, it is important to note that EBITDA ignores the cost of fixed assets used in a business as well as depreciation, interest, and taxes. For example, a business showing an after-tax loss from a large investment in fixed assets that were financed by equal amounts of debt could look rather healthy on an EBITDA basis.[80] Therefore, a careful evaluation of a business using EBITDA should be made in the total profitability analysis. The calculation for EBITDA is as follows:[81]

Net Income – (Interest expense + Tax expense + Depreciation expense + Amortization) = EBITDA

In the 1980s, EBITDA superseded EBIT (earnings before interest and taxes) as a financial yardstick for measuring the cash flow of a business. EBITDA removes depreciation and amortization from the profit calculation, which are non-cash items comprising a majority of the expenses for many businesses. Those in favor of using EBITDA believe that it is an accurate measure of cash flow. On the other hand, those who criticize the use of EBITDA, disagree that it measures cash flow because it ignores the working capital growth cash requirements as well as cash necessary for replacement of outdated assets such as obsolete equipment. In addition, since EBITDA does not consider whether operating revenues and expenses directly affect cash, the quality of the earnings is not properly reflected, which can result in the possible manipulation of earnings through aggressive accounting policies relating to both revenue and expenses. Furthermore, non-GAAP earnings like EBITDA overlook certain business expenses or costs, such as depreciation, which can result in a faulty representation of the profitability of a business.[82]

SUMMARY

While financial ratios are a powerful tool for analyzing the performance and profitability of a business, it is important to keep in mind that there is no one correct method of computing financial ratios. For various reasons, companies may include or exclude certain numbers or use different numbers in their calculations to arrive at the ratios. Since companies may use different terminology for the same item on financial statements, it is important to understand exactly how the numbers are derived. While financial ratios can assist managers in asking the right questions, they cannot provide the answers. Ratio analyses help shed light on the overwhelming amount of information and data found on financial statements. In addition, it is wise to be cautious of accounting discrepancies or distortions that could obscure the interpretation of financial ratios.[83]

As part of the decision-making process in evaluating new prospects or investments, profitability measures are indeed useful and appropriate tools. Ratio analyses assist managers by giving meaning and significance to the numbers on financial statements.[84] For example, for profitability analysis, ROA is broken down into meaningful components using the DuPont system of financial analysis.

It is important to analyze a business using various methods not limited to only the financial aspects of the business, but also to review the non-financial features of the business as a whole. Over the years, financial ratio analysis has become more popular; however, it is important to make sure that the ratios utilized in profit analysis are meaningful and can contribute to the analysis and evaluation of the performance of a business as well as to the overall long-term financial health of the business.

The following Table 5-2 summarizes the various measures of profitability discussed in this chapter:

Table 5-2
Summary of Analytical Measures of Profitability

Ratio or Other Measure	Method of Calculation	Implication
Profitability Index	Present Value of Cash Inflows/ Present Value of Cash Outflows	Capital budgeting method for evaluating projects. PI of 1 or better is required.
Return on Investment (ROI)	Income/Invested Capital	It measures the income earned on the capital invested.
Return on Assets (ROA)	Income/Average Total Assets OR Profit margin X Asset Turnover	It measures return on total investment in a business. It measures both the efficiency and the productivity of assets.
Internal Rate of Return (IRR)	Method 1: Use of PV Table: Present Value Factor = Required Initial Investment/Annual Net Cash Inflows Method 2: Use of Financial Calculator	An approach that is used in capital budgeting to evaluate capital investment proposals.
Measured Operating Income (MOI)	Gross Profit – Operating Expenses	Measures the profitability of a business' basic business activities.
Days of Sales Outstanding (DSO)	Average net accounts receivable/(net sales/365 days)	It measures how long, on average, it takes a business to collect its accounts receivable.
Weighted Guidelines Method (WGM)	DD Form 1547	DoD method for determining the profit objectives of a contract.
Earnings Before Interest, Taxes, Depreciation & Amortization (EBITDA)	Net Income – (Interest Expense + Tax Expense + Depreciation Expense + Amortization)	It measures the cash flow of a business.

RECOMMENDATIONS

To fully evaluate the effectiveness and operating performance of a business, contracting officers need to look beyond the mere numbers on financial statements such as sales revenue, profits, and total assets. They must possess the ability to understand how the numbers on the financial statements can be useful for evaluating and measuring performance, especially profitability. When used in conjunction with other business assessment processes, comparative ratio analysis is a powerful method that can help tremendously to assist in identifying and quantifying the strengths and weaknesses of a business, in analyzing the profitability of a business, in reviewing the financial position of a business, and in considering and understanding the impending risks that a business may be assuming.[85]

In evaluating a business for profitability purposes, two major issues must be addressed. First, the capability of the business to produce a profit from its operations must be analyzed. The profit margin, part of ROA, is a good indicator of the profitability level of the operations of a business. Secondly, the utilization of available assets and capital to produce a profit needs to be assessed. The major reason for a business to maintain assets is to sustain its operations and aid in the production of current and future profits. When making comparisons, three to five years of financial data should be used.[86]

Because of differing accounting policies and the flexibility given to businesses in the preparation of their financial statements, a financial analysis needs to take into consideration various GAAP limitations, the business environment, competitive issues, and business strategies. The notes to financial statements usually disclose other valuable information to assist in evaluating and measuring the profit performance of a business.

Chapter 6 discusses how contract claims are handled on U.S. government contracts and the various means to resolve contract disputes.

QUESTIONS TO CONSIDER

1. Which contract financing techniques does your organization typically use when executing government contracts?

2. Does your organization provide specific guidance on preparing and reviewing invoices, vouchers, and making payments?

3. Is your organization actively monitoring its profitability over the years and making comparisons with industry averages?

4. Does your organization offer or support any training on contract financing, payments, and profit analysis tools and techniques?

ENDNOTES

1. Nash, Ralph C., and Cibinic, John. Government Contract Administration, 4th ed. Chicago: CCH, 2001.
2. Ibid.
3. Ibid.
4. Ibid.
5. Ibid.
6. Ibid.
7. Ibid.
8. Gibson, Charles H. Financial Reporting & Analysis: Using Financial Accounting Information, 10th ed. Mason, OH: Thomson South-Western, 2007.
9. Vause, Bob. Guide to Analyzing Companies. London, England: The Economist Newspaper Ltd., 2007.
10. Brittelli, Joseph L., Lynch, Patrick J., and Emmelhainz, Peggy Principles of Contract Pricing. 4th ed. Course number 6610018383. Extension Course Institute, Air University. Wright-Patterson AFB, OH: School of Systems and Logistics, AFIT, 1983.
11. Ibid.
12. Ibid. at 85.
13. Ibid.
14. Analyzing Profit or Fee: DOD Weighted Guidelines Method (2005, August 26). DOD Defense Procurement and Acquisition Policy. Contract Pricing Reference Guides. Retrieved January 6, 2007, from http://www.acq.osd.mil/dpap/contractpricing/vol3chap11.htm; FAR 15.404-4(a)(3) and 15.404-4(c)(4).
15. Ibid., note 9.
16. Horngren, Charles T., Sundem, Gary L., Elliott, John A., and Philbrick, Donna R. Introduction to Financial Accounting, 9th ed. Upper Saddle River, NJ: Pearson Education, Inc., 2006.
17. Reimers, Jane L. Financial Accounting. Upper Saddle River, New Jersey: Pearson Education, Inc., 2007.
18. Garrison, R. H., Noreen, E. W., & Brewer, P. C. Managerial Accounting, 11th ed. New York: McGraw-Hill Irwin, 2006.
19. Atkinson, Anthony A., Kaplan, Robert S., Matsumura, Ella Mae, and Young, S. Mark. Management Accounting, 5th ed. Upper Saddle River, NJ: Pearson, 2007.
20. Ibid.
21. Ibid., note 14; FAR 9.104-1, 28.103-2(3), and 32.006-4(d)(3).
22. Ibid., note 17.
23. Ibid., note 14.
24. Ibid.
25. Ibid.
26. Ibid., note 17.
27. Ibid., note 8.
28. Ibid., note 16.
29. Ibid., note 14.
30. Ibid., note 17.
31. Ibid., note 14.
32. Werner, Michael L., and Jones, Kumen H. Introduction to Accounting: A User Perspective, 2nd ed. Upper Saddle River, NJ: Pearson Education, Inc., 2004.
33. Ibid., note 8.
34. Block, Stanley B., & Hirt, Geoffrey A. Foundations of Financial Management, 11th ed. New York: McGraw-Hill/Irwin, 2005.
35. Ibid., note 10..
36. Ibid., note 17.
37. Ibid.
38. Ibid., note 9.
39. Dyckman, Thomas R., Easton, Peter D., & Pfeiffer, Glenn M. Financial Accounting. Cambridge Business Publishers, LLC, 2007.
40. Ibid., note 9.
41. Ibid., note 17.
42. Ibid., note 34.
43. Ibid., note 14. http://www.acq.osd.mil/dpap/contractpricing/vol4chap9.htm

44. Ibid., note 39.
45. Ibid., note 18..
46. Ibid., note 8.
47. Ibid., note 39..
48. Ibid., note 8.
49. Dobler, Donald W., & Burt, David N. Purchasing and Supply Management: Text and Cases. New York: The McGraw Hill Companies, 1996)
50. Performing Financial Analyses, Contract Pricing Reference Guides.
51. Larson, Kermit D., Wild, John J., & Chiappetta, Barbara Fundamental Accounting Principles, 15th ed. New York: McGraw-Hill Companies, Inc., 1999.
52. Ibid., note 8.
53. Ibid.
54. Ibid., note 51.
55. Ibid., note 8.
56. Ibid., note 51.
57. Ibid., note 39.
58. Analyzing Your Financial Ratios. (n.d.) Retrieved December 27, 2006, from http://www.va-interactive.com/inbusiness/editorial/finance/ibt/ratio_analysis.html#4.
59. Ibid., note 17.
60. Ibid., note 16.
61. Ibid., note 17.
62. Revsine, Lawrence, Collins, Daniel W., & Johnson, W. Bruce. Financial Reporting and Analysis, 3rd ed. Upper Saddle River, NJ: Pearson Education, Inc., 2005.
63. Ibid., note 10.
64. Ibid., note 17.
65. Ibid., note 32.
66. Ibid., note 58.
67. Harrison, Walter T., & Horngren, Charles T., Financial Accounting, 6th ed. Upper Saddle River, NJ: Pearson Education, Inc., 2006.
68. Ibid. at 622.
69. Ibid., note 58.http://www.va-interactive.com/inbusiness/editorial/finance/ibt/ratio_analysis.html#4
70. Ibid., note 62.
71. Ibid., note 9..
72. Ingram, Robert W., and Albright, Thomas L., Financial Accounting: A Bridge to Decision-Making, 6th ed. Mason, OH: Thomson South-Western, 2007.
73. Truger, Paul M. Defense Contract Profits: Weighted Guidelines Method. Journal of Accountancy. Volume 119, Issue 2, pp. 45-50 (1965, February). Retrieved January 6, 2007, from EBSCO database.
74. Defense Federal Acquisition Regulation Supplement: Changes to Profit Policy (2002, April 26). Retrieved January 13, 2007, from http://www.acq.osd.mil/dpap/dars/dfars/changenotice/docs/2000d018f.pdf
75. Ibid., note 10.
76. Ibid., note 14; FAR 15.404-4(a)(3) and 15.404-4(c)(4); DFARS 215.404-4(b), 215.404-71-2(c), and 215.404-71-4(c).
77. Ibid.; DFARS 215.404-71-2.
78. Ibid.
79. Ibid., note 9.
80. Ibid., note 62.
81. Ibid.
82. Ibid.
83. Ibid., note 16.
84. Ibid., note 58.
85. Ibid., note 9.
86. Ibid., note 39.

CHAPTER  **6**

CONTRACT CLAIMS AND DISPUTE RESOLUTION

INTRODUCTION

A contractor may make a claim when its request for equitable adjustment (REA) has failed, either in whole or in part. Of course, there is no requirement for a contractor to submit a REA prior to submitting its claim, but most do. In the communications and discussions with contracting officers about an unsuccessful REA, contractors may learn the government's position in some detail. This process generally narrows the factual and/or legal differences between the parties, and for that reason it is usually worthwhile for contractors to make the effort to negotiate a REA with a contracting officer before making a claim.

A request for equitable adjustment is a proposal, but a claim is a demand. One aspect of claims under government contracts that differ from claims under commercial contracts is that a claim under a government contract must be founded on a relief-granting clause. In this regard, long experience has shown that the vast majority of government contract claims arise under the Changes clause.

The claims process begins with the contractor forwarding a claim to the contracting officer, along with a brief statement explaining why the contractor believes the government is liable. The contracting officer must then render a final decision on the claim. The final decision must be issued within 60 days for claims under $100,000. For claims greater than $100,000, FAR 33.211(c) provides that the contractor must be told within 60 days when a final decision may be expected, and thereafter the final decision must be issued within a "reasonable time." Should the contracting officer's final decision deny the claim, either in whole or in part, the contractor may then file an appeal. Under the Contract Disputes Act a contractor's appeal also has time limits.

Appeals of a final decision may be bifurcated, i.e., divided into two phases. The first phase is entitlement, in which the question for resolution is whether the government breached the contract. Only if it is determined that the government breached the contract do the parties then address quantum, which is the second phase of a claim. Quantum concerns how the contractor's damages are to be measured.

SIX

ENTITLEMENT

Contract Disputes Act of 1978 (41 U.S. C. §§601-613)

Contractor Claims

A contractor must base its claim on a relief-granting clause in the contract. This is important because some FAR clauses vary the recovery that a contractor may receive. For example, the Termination for Convenience clause (FAR 52.249-2) provides that a contractor may receive payment for (1) its unpaid costs up to the date of termination; (2) its settlement costs; and (3) an "allowance for profit" (an undefined term). On the other hand, the only relief a contractor may receive under the Differing Site Conditions clause (FAR 52.236-2) is that "an equitable adjustment shall be made" to the contract, and only if the contractor notified the government of the condition "promptly."

Regardless of the basis, a contractor's claim must first be submitted to the contracting officer for a final decision. If the contractor's claim is denied, either in whole or in part, the contractor may then appeal that denial. Under the Contract Disputes Act, government contractors do not have direct access to the courts. All claims are first subject to a contracting officer's final decision.

One problem area for contractors is with claims by subcontractors. Because subcontractors do not have a contract with the government, they do not have a right to file a contract claim against the government (in government contract law, this is known as a lack of privity). In order for a subcontractor to have its claim presented to a contracting officer it must first have its prime contractor exercise its right to file a claim against the government. Then the contractor must forward the claim to the contracting officer on behalf of the subcontractor. Subcontractor claims are sometimes called sponsored claims, because the prime contractor essentially sponsors its subcontractor's claim. All of the requirements applicable to a prime contractor's claim are equally applicable to a subcontractor's claim.

Government Claims

While infrequent, a claim may be made by the government against a contractor and these are referred to as affirmative claims. A government claim may be made directly against a contractor (in which case the government is the plaintiff), or it may arise as a counter-claim where the government is the defendant. In either event, the Contract Disputes Act requires any government claim also to be subject to a contracting officer's final decision.

Other Claims

Certain types of claims may arise in particular circumstances, which may make these claims different. For example, government construction contracts over $100,000 require the prime contractor to provide a performance and a payment bond. These bonds are required under the Miller Act (40 U.S.C. §3131 *et seq.*). The prime contractor may only purchase such bonds from surety companies approved by the U.S. Treasury. Should the prime contractor fail to perform the contract (i.e., be terminated for default), the contracting officer tasks the surety to complete performance. Also, suppliers or subcontractors on a project who were unpaid by the prime contractor may recover from the surety.

> Miller Act claims are a specialized kind of government contract claim, with unique procedural requirements related to the rights of sureties. Individuals working on these claims need to have a thorough understanding of the litigation requirements associated with federal construction contracts.

FINAL DECISIONS

All claims arising under a government contract must first be considered by a contracting officer. As stated above, a claim may be made after an unsuccessful request for equitable adjustment (although the submission of a REA is not required).

The requirements applicable to a claim are found in FAR Part 33.2. One requirement is that claims over $100,000 must be certified as follows:

> I certify that the claim is made in good faith; that the supporting data are accurate and complete to the best of my knowledge and belief; that the amount requested accurately reflects the contract adjustment for which the contractor believes the Government is

liable; and that I am duly authorized to certify the claim on behalf of the contractor.

Legal interest starts on the day the contracting officer receives the claim (*see* FAR 33.208(a)(1)) and continues until the claim is paid. Unlike a request for equitable adjustment, estimates of costs may not be used because the Contract Disputes Act requires a claim to be for a "sum certain."

After a contractor submits a claim, a contracting officer's typical first move is to have the claim audited. Of course, an audit only considers the quantum portion of a contractor's claim, not entitlement, and this area is considered in greater detail below.

Appeal of a Final Decision

When a contractor's claim is denied, in whole or in part, by a contracting officer's final decision, the contractor may appeal that decision to either an agency board of contract appeals or the U.S. Court of Federal Claims. If the contractor chooses to make an appeal to an agency board of contract appeals, it must file an appeal within 90 days after receiving the contracting officer's final decision.

Agency Boards of Contract Appeals

There are several agency boards of contract appeals: the Armed Services Board of Contract Appeals (ASBCA); the Civilian Agency Board of Contract Appeals (CBCA); the Postal Service Board of Contract Appeals (PSBCA), and the TVA Board of Contract Appeals (TVABCA). Of these, the ASBCA is the largest and has the greatest number of cases.

Expedited Appeals

An expedited appeal, arising under Section 608 of the Contract Disputes Act, is for claims of $50,000 or less ($150,000 for small businesses). Expedited appeals are decided by one judge (and concurred in by a vice-chairman) and must be decided within 120 days from the date of a contractor's appeal. The election to have an appeal heard using the expedited procedure is at the sole discretion of the contractor.

Accelerated Appeals

Pursuant to the rules of the agency board, accelerated appeals are for claims of $100,000 or less. These appeals are heard by three judges and are decided within 180 days from the date of a contractor's appeal. Here as well, only the contractor can decide whether to avail itself of the accelerated procedures.

Regular Appeals

All other appeals are decided by a majority of the judges on a panel. Because there are five judges on a panel, three judges must agree on the result. However, if one of the three judges does not concur with the judge who heard the case, then the case is decided by the full five-judge panel.

Not surprisingly, most discovery occurs with non-expedited and non-accelerated appeals. The term "discovery" refers to the process whereby one party is permitted to learn about the evidence held by the other party. This process may involve written requests for admissions, interrogatories, requests for production of documents, or depositions of witnesses. Depending on the dollar amount involved and the complexity of the case, discovery may be a time-consuming and expensive process for contractors.

Record Submissions

Sometimes, it is not necessary to have a hearing because testimonial evidence is not required to resolve a dispute. As a simple illustration of this, assume a contractor and a contracting officer disagree only about how particular wording in a clause should be interpreted. They understand each other's positions, but do not agree on which interpretation is legally correct. In this situation, the appeal could be via a record submission (under ASBCA Rule 11, this procedure is called a Submission without a Hearing and all other agency boards have a similar rule). Essentially, each side is allowed to submit whatever documentation it deems appropriate for the board to consider. The appeal would be decided only on the documentary evidence.

Alternative Dispute Resolution

Alternative dispute resolution (ADR) is a relatively recent development in the government contracts arena. Essentially, ADR is a process that avoids the time and cost of litigation by providing an informal mechanism for resolving disagreement(s) between the parties. There are two kinds of ADR: mediation and arbitration. Participation in ADR is voluntary to both sides.

Mediation

There are occasions where the cause of a dispute relates to the fact that the parties are simply unable to communicate with one another. In such circumstances, a mediator may be the solution to the problem. The process begins when a knowledgeable, neutral third-party is chosen by both sides. The mediator has no authority over the parties whatsoever, so neither side can be compelled to produce documents, attend a hearing, or do anything it does not want to do. Rather, the mediator is an individual who meets informally with each side (usually in their own respective offices) and asks each side what outcome they are seeking. After hearing the positions of both sides (and reviewing their evidence), the mediator makes recommendations for a settlement. In dealing with the parties, the mediator travels back and forth and communicates the positions of each side. This process continues until either a settlement is reached, or it becomes clear that a settlement is unlikely. When mediation fails, litigation becomes the only alternative.

In resolving government contract claims, mediation is available through agency boards of contract appeals. The process starts when a BCA judge is chosen by the parties to act as a mediator. If the mediation process fails and the parties decide the resort to litigation, the case is transferred to a different BCA judge.

Arbitration

Mediation and arbitration are similar in that the arbitrator is a qualified, neutral third-party chosen by both sides. However, they are significantly dissimilar because an arbitrator is empowered to decide a dispute. Qualified arbitrators may be selected from rosters maintained by professional organizations, the largest of which is the American Arbitration Association.

After hearing a case (usually in a conference room), the arbitrator takes the matter under advisement. Thereafter, each side may submit a post-hearing and a reply brief. Within a month or so after the briefing schedule has concluded, the arbitrator issues a decision.

Non-binding Arbitration

In non-binding arbitration, an arbitrator conducts the arbitration process as necessary but the arbitrator's decision is treated by both sides as advisory only. Because the arbitrator's decision is merely advisory, some might wonder what value there would be in non-binding arbitration. The answer is that each side gets to present its case without the restrictions of the Federal Rules of Evidence (FRE) and the Federal Rules of Civil Procedure, so literally everything a party wants to present is considered. If a party loses its case in non-binding arbitration after presenting all the evidence it possibly can, that's a strong indication that it would also lose its case in court. Accordingly, non-binding arbitration is a means whereby a losing party may avoid the time and expense of litigation *in addition to* absorbing losses associated with its case.

Binding Arbitration

In binding arbitration, an arbitrator's decision equates to a judgment of the case. Also, it is extremely difficult to win an appeal of an arbitration decision, largely because the decisions themselves are so laconic. For example, a typical arbitration decision reads as follows:

> In the arbitration matter of A versus B, judgment in favor of A in the amount of X dollars.

Obviously, there's not much there to appeal! So arbitration is an inexpensive but limited form of alternate dispute resolution.

Under the Alternate Dispute Resolution Act, an agency's policy for binding arbitration must first be submitted for approval to the Department of Justice, and few have done so. For that reason, most federal agencies cannot submit their government contract disputes to binding arbitration (one exception is that the Navy has recently issued its policy in this area). For this reason, binding arbitration in government contracts cases applies almost entirely to disputes either between prime contractors and their subcontractors or between subcontractors.

U.S. Court of Federal Claims

Instead of appealing a contracting officer's final decision to an agency board of contract appeals, a contractor may appeal the final decision to the U.S. Court of Federal Claims (COFC). This decision is known as a contractor's choice of forum. If a contractor elects to have its appeal heard by the COFC, it must file its appeal within one year of receiving the final decision.

U.S. Court of Federal Appeals

A party losing its case at either an agency board of contract appeals or the COFC may appeal to the U.S. Court of Appeals for the Federal Circuit (CAFC). In the judicial hierarchy, the CAFC is just below the U.S. Supreme Court. A party losing its case at the CAFC may try to appeal to the U.S. Supreme Court, but appeals to the Supreme Court are not automatic. To the contrary, only those appeals that obtain a writ of certiorari may be appealed to the Supreme Court, and only a small fraction of cases that apply for such writs receive one. Because government contract cases almost never receive a writ of certiorari, the CAFC is the *de facto* supreme court on matters of government contract law.

The CAFC issues few government contract decisions each year, as one might expect. As noted, government contract cases are appeals of decisions made by an agency board of contract appeals or the U.S. Court of Federal Claims (COFC). While most appeals to the CAFC are made by contractors disappointed with the decision made by the COFC or agency board of contract appeals, some appeals are made by the government. In these cases, the government is represented by attorneys with the Civil Division of the U.S. Department of Justice (DOJ).

QUANTUM

Methods of Proving Damages

At one time, there were three methods for contractors to prove their damages (or quantum) under a government contract: the total cost method; the modified total cost method; and the actual damages method. While each of these methodologies will be briefly reviewed, for reasons set forth below the actual damages methodology is the only one currently available.

Total Cost Method

To compute damages using the total cost method, a contractor would need to demonstrate the following:

- that the actual costs are impossible to determine;
- that its bid was realistic;
- that its incurred costs were reasonable; and
- that the government was responsible for the contractor's increased costs.

Even when its use was permitted, the total cost method was always the least-favored method of computing damages by the courts and boards, and was only applicable in situations where the contractor's damages could not be determined by either actual cost data or the modified total cost method.

Modified Total Cost Method

The modified total cost method was essentially the same as the total cost method, except that adjustments were made to accommodate minor shortcomings in the contractor's evidence in satisfying the requirements of the total cost method. The adjustments made varied depending on the nature and degree of evidentiary deficiencies in the case.

Actual Cost Method

As its name indicates, in the actual cost method a contractor documents its claim using actual cost data. A contractor should be able to prove its actual costs if its accounting system has the ability to track increased costs related to the work. More specifically, the contractor should be able to identify and separately accumulate specific costs incurred under a contract, particularly if the changed work is separately identifiable. For many years, all off-the-shelf accounting software provided the capability to amass costs into discrete groupings, so inadequacies in an accounting system could not be used to excuse a contractor from using the actual cost method. Accordingly, contractors that did not use the actual cost method typically alleged that the changed work could not be differentiated from the underlying contract work.

Jury Verdict Method

The jury verdict method is merely a name generally given to damages calculations arrived at by a judge based on the available evidence. There is no specific method of computation. The circumstances of the case are usually such that there is considerable uncertainty concerning the amount of the contractor's damages, although there is no uncertainty that the contractor has been damaged. In such cases, the courts have concluded that the risk of that uncertainty should not be placed on the injured party, and an approximation of the damages is based on what the court believes a jury verdict would be. In government contract claims, the jury verdict method has been applied almost exclusively in breach-of-contract cases, which explains why jury verdict damages are infrequent.

Propellex v. United States

Because of the long-standing reluctance of the courts and boards to accept claims computed with the total cost method, it has been infrequently used. In fact, as a result of the decision by the Court of Appeals for the Federal Circuit in the *Propellex* case, circumstances justifying the use of either the total cost method or modified total cost method should almost never arise (*Propellex Corp. v. Brownlee*, CAFC, 342 F3d 1335, September 9, 2003).

In *Propellex*, the contracting officer ultimately conceded on the issue of entitlement because the facts showed that the government had wrongly rejected conforming shipments of gun primers. Propellex used the modified total cost method to compute its claim. Propellex, an experienced government contractor, could have accumulated its actual additional costs of performance but failed to do so. Because Propellex failed to show how it could not have used the actual cost methodology, its modified total cost claim was denied by the contracting officer. Propellex appealed, but the ASBCA affirmed the contracting officer's decision. When Propellex appealed the ASBCA decision to the Court of Appeals for the Federal Circuit (CAFC), the decision of the ASBCA was affirmed. Essentially, *Propellex* stands for the proposition that contractors will be required to prove their claims by the actual cost method, or prove why they can not do so. Because sophisticated accounting software is inexpensive and user friendly, there will almost never be a case where a contractor could not employ the actual cost methodology.

Grumman Aerospace

The CAFC's holding in *Propellex* was reinforced by the decision of the Armed Services Board of Contract Appeals (ASBCA) in *Grumman Aerospace Corp.*, ASBCA No. 48006, February 28, 2006.

In *Grumman*, the contractor's original claim was approximately $66 million. After winning entitlement on some of the issues, the parties could not settle on the amount due and eventually there was a quantum appeal. To support its position, Grumman submitted a report by a "Big Four" accounting firm. Using the modified total cost method, the accounting firm's report concluded that Grumman's damages amounted to $50.4 million. The ASBCA, however, was unswayed by this report. In its decision, the ASBCA determined that Grumman had not met three of the four requirements for the modified total cost method, and on that basis the accounting firm's report was completely rejected. Using the available documents in the record (some of which had been introduced by the government), the ASBCA determined Grumman's damages to be approximately $387,000.

The significance of the *Propellex* and *Grumman* decisions lie beyond the matters disputed between the parties. In short, the decisions were a painful reminder to contractors that they will be expected to prove their quantum through the actual cost methodology, or be able to prove why they could not. After *Propellex* and *Grumman*, it should be a rare case indeed when a contractor meets the criteria for applying either the total cost or the modified total cost methodology.

Even when actual cost data is not available, there are various techniques accountants may resort to in establishing reasonably reliable data that may be used in lieu of actual data. Many of these techniques were developed by disaster recovery experts, which is a specialized field of accounting. Briefly stated, even in the absence of any records whatsoever, accountants can ascertain with a high degree of confidence what a contractor's actual costs were. This is essentially accomplished by using collateral sources of information and "reverse engineering" a path to the actual cost figures.

DISCOVERY

Testimonial Evidence: Expert Witnesses

The acceptance of someone as an expert in court requires that the individual meet the *Daubert* test (*Daubert v. Merrill Dow Pharmaceuticals, Inc.*, 509 S.Ct. 579, 1993). The four-part *Daubert* test, based on Federal Rule of Evidence (FRE) 702, established the following criteria for an expert witness:

- Is the witness an expert in the sense of having credentials or experience?
- Does the expert's testimony have a basis in fact?
- Is the expert's testimony relevant and reliable?
- Are there any other factors that bear upon the question of admissibility?

A crucial threshold question concerns the expert's credentials or experience. This has been construed to mean that the expert must demonstrate that his or her expertise is recognized by others in the expert's field. For an accounting expert, this means more than merely being a certified public accountant. Activities that are normally associated with being an accounting expert include authoring articles and textbooks, teaching in a scholarly setting (not just in-house lunchtime learning sessions), speaking at meetings of professional or trade associations, receiving professional awards, and so on.

The *Daubert* test is routinely applied in civil litigation in federal courts. Moreover, to assist litigators in dealing with experts, there is a *Daubert* website that maintains a record of expert testimony in all reported federal and state cases, as well as many unreported cases (www.dauberttracker.com). The website helps attorneys with cases involving expert witness testimony by

- detailing how individual courts and judges regarded an expert's testimony;
- assisting in preparing an expert for rebuttal testimony;
- providing information useful in challenging an opposing expert;
- identifying new methodologies for testimony;
- providing information to defend against potential challenges to an expert's methodologies and opinions; and
- providing the court documents and briefs that contain the arguments attorneys have used for and against the exclusion of an expert's testimony.

For whatever reason, in government contract disputes before boards and arbitration panels, the *Daubert* test is generally not applied. As a result, individuals who would otherwise not meet the requirements to be an expert witness are permitted to participate in the proceedings as if they were. When *Daubert* objections are raised in government contract litigation, triers of fact typically respond that the objections go to the weight and not to the admissibility of the expert's testimony. Indeed, it has not been uncommon in board or arbitration proceedings for testimony to be admitted by accounting "experts" who were not CPAs, had never been published, had no experience with government contract claims, and did not even have a degree in accounting. Notwithstanding this, it is a matter of trial strategy for an attorney to decide in a given case whether to raise or ignore the opposing expert's lack of qualifications.

Perhaps the biggest tactical difference regarding experts between government trial attorneys and attorneys who represent contractors is that government trial attorneys rarely retain a non-testifying expert. Contractor attorneys frequently do, particularly where the amount in dispute justifies the additional cost. Of course, having a non-testifying expert may accord the contractor attorney a tactical advantage in discovery matters (depositions, document requests, and so on).

Documentary Evidence

Government contract claims are invariably voluminous because the documentary evidence consists of all records in the contract file. This evidence may be supplemented by both sides, and in this process the appeal record may grow substantially to include maps, charts, photographs, blueprints, payroll records or any other kind of documentation.

Where quantum is concerned, government auditors seek to obtain and review the source documents related to a contractor's claim. It is not unusual for the auditor to learn that a contractor's records are not available or are inadequate because documents were not retained or needed information was not recorded at the time. When archival data must be retrieved, factors that hamper contractor organizations include frequent personnel turnover, multiple mergers and acquisitions, perennial corporate reorganizations, installation of new accounting systems, and the pressure to meet current goals (i.e., little attention is focused on past events that gave rise to the contractor's claims).

Disputes over access to contractor records are infrequent. In the discovery process, the objective for the government is to ensure that all aspects of a contractor's claim are appropriately documented, and where costs are not appropriately documented or supported, those dollars are challenged. On occasion, contractors are hard pressed to document costs from archived records or discontinued accounting systems.

An audit of documents related to entitlement is rare. The process used by an auditor in reviewing quantum is a straightforward procedure. Starting with the contractor's claim, the auditor progresses backward through a series of interconnected documents in the contractor's accounting system to the supporting documentation. This process is sometimes referred to as "drilling down." Where the contractor's records substantiate the claimed amounts, few quantum issues are presented. On the other hand, where a contractor's records are undecipherable, unavailable, unclear or even contradictory, the contractor's costs are subject to challenge.

In this area, an emerging field concerns discovery of electronic records, or e-discovery. The American Bar Association's Law Practice Management Section has fielded a new publication, "The Electronic Evidence and Discovery Handbook: Forms, Checklists and Guidelines." Also, there are seminars and articles on e-discovery topics, although they tend to concentrate on the discovery of emails and management meeting materials, not on contract records.

Finally, trend analyses and statistical evaluations are uncommon in government contract litigation and are a tool almost universally unused by government trial attorneys. However, there are powerful mathematical tools that can be used, in appropriate settings, to refute all or part of a contractor's quantum presentation. For example, there are software programs that can perform sophisticated statistical evaluations on large bodies of data. These evaluations can reveal data anomalies, trends, cost element relationships, and other important information that may contradict a contractor's claim.

TYPES OF CLAIMS

Now that both the entitlement and quantum aspects of a claim have been discussed, it is worthwhile to consider the attributes of the different types of claims. On this point, claims under government contracts may be categorized by the relief-granting clause under which they are made. As mentioned earlier, claims under the Changes clause are the most frequent. (Claims for extraordinary relief under P.L. 85-804 are not claims under the Contract Disputes Act, and in any event lie beyond the scope of this work.)

Changes Clause Claims - Change Order Accounting

There are two types of changes to a government contract: actual and constructive. Actual changes occur by direction of the contracting officer, usually in the form of a unilateral modification to the contract. On the other hand, constructive changes occur whenever circumstances beyond the contractor's control alter the terms and conditions that affect the performance of the contract. For example, a constructive change may arise when an overzealous government inspector wrongfully rejects conforming goods, or where a government engineer provides defective site maps. To recover under the Changes clause (FAR 52.243-4), a contractor adversely affected by a constructive change relies on its accounting system for the information necessary to attain full recovery of its additional costs of performance (*see* FAR Subpart 43.2).

The Changes clause provides for damages to be determined through an equitable adjustment (" . . . the Contracting Officer shall make an equitable adjustment and modify the contract in writing."). However, no guidance on the measurement of damages is provided. Even the Change Order Accounting clause (FAR 52.243-6) calls only for the contractor to accumulate the pertinent cost data:

The contracting officer *may* require change order accounting whenever the estimated cost of a change or series of related changes *exceeds $100,000*. The contractor, for each change or series of related changes, shall maintain separate accounts, by job order or other suitable accounting procedure, of all incurred, segregable direct costs (less allocable credits) of work, both changed and not changed, allocable to the change. The contractor shall maintain such accounts until the parties agree to an equitable adjustment for the changes ordered by the contracting officer or the matter is conclusively disposed of in accordance with the Disputes clause. [Emphasis added.]

Note that the contracting officer "may" require change order accounting; it is not compulsory. That said, it is always advisable, whenever possible, for a contractor to identify and separately accumulate its costs related to changed work. This is because the contractor bears the burden of proving its costs, either to the contracting officer or on appeal under the Disputes clause. To the extent that a contractor commingles its change order costs with its contract costs or otherwise fails to appropriately track its costs, it increases the likelihood of cost duplication in its claim, unwisely places a heavier burden of proof on itself, and accords government trial attorneys a significant tactical advantage (*Defense Supply Systems, Inc.*, ASBCA No. 54494, 05-2 BCA ¶33,031). However, there are some situations where even change order accounting cannot provide the needed cost data, and damages are determined using the jury verdict method (*Service Engineering Company*, ASBCA No. 40274, 93-2 BCA ¶25,885).

When calculating the quantum, it is necessary to both subtract the costs of deleted work and add the increased costs of changed work (*Precision Dynamics, Inc.*, ASBCA No. 50519, 05-2 BCA ¶33,071). Of course, contractors will be required to prove their additional costs through the actual cost method or show why that is not possible (*TPS, Inc.*, ASBCA No. 52421, 04-1 BCA ¶32,570). Where the actual cost data is available, a contractor may recover both its damages and profit for additional work under Change orders (*Stewart & Stevenson Services, Inc.*, ASBCA No. 43631, 97-2 BCA ¶29,252).

The DCAA guidance for Changes clause claims is found in Section 12-700 of the Contract Audit Manual (CAM), but much of that guidance relates to the discredited total cost and modified total cost methodologies. Moreover, DCAA auditors will not make profit recommendations, which is in the sole discretion of the contracting officer.

Unabsorbed Overhead Claims

Unabsorbed overhead is sometimes a source of confusion among non-accountants, but the concept is really quite simple. When a contractor prepares its bid, a portion of its proposed costs relate to overhead. Many of the overhead expenses that a contractor expects to incur operate as a function of time, particularly the fixed and semi-variable costs. For this reason, the contract term relates directly to the amount of overhead. When the contract term is extended for reasons attributable to the government (such as a stop work order), the contract term becomes protracted. The contractor is now working for a longer period of time than anticipated when the cost proposal was formulated. The additional time means the contractor will experience additional overhead costs that were not included in (or absorbed by) its bid. In other words, the additional overhead is "unabsorbed."

The *Eichleay* formula is the only methodology used to measure unabsorbed overhead. (*See Libby Corp.*, ASBCA Nos. 40765 and 42553, 96-1 BCA ¶28,255, *aff'd without opinion*, CAFC 96-1351, Fed. Cir.1997). There are three steps to the *Eichleay* formula. First, the overhead allocable to the contract ("A") is calculated as follows:

(Contract billings/Total billings)(Total overhead for the contract period) = A

Second, the daily overhead rate for the contract ("B") is determined:

A / Days of performance = B

Finally, the unabsorbed overhead ("C") is:

(B)(Number of days delayed) = C

To illustrate using a DCAA example, assume that a contractor receives three contracts (contract X, contract Y, and contract Z) in a two-year period. Assume further that contract Y was a one-year contract to be performed in its entirety coincident with FY 2001, but was delayed for a full year so that performance was not completed until the end of FY 2002. Continuing with this example, assume that contract Z was also performed in FY 2001 and contract X was performed in FY 2002. If the contractor's fixed annual overhead each year was $110,000, contract Y (i.e., the delayed contract) had revenues of $598,400, and the contractor's other revenues totaled $726,000 in FY 2001 and $671,000 in FY 2002. Applying the *Eichleay* formula to these facts, the unabsorbed overhead is computed as follows:

(1) Compute the fixed overhead allocable to the contract ("A"):

From the facts given the total revenues may be determined as follows:

FY 2001 Revenues:	$726,000
FY 2002 Revenues:	$671,000
Total	$1,397,000

A = (Contract revenues / Total revenues) (Total fixed overhead)

= ($598,400 / $1,397,000)($110,000 + $110,000)

= (43%) ($220,000)

= **$94,600**

(2) Compute the daily overhead rate for the contract ("B"):

B = A / Total days of performance

= $94,600 / (FY 2001 + FY 2002)

= $94,600 / (365 + 365)

= $94,600 / 730

= **$130**

(3) Compute the unabsorbed overhead ("C"):

C = B (Number of days delayed)

= $130 (365)

= **$47,450**

In its audit guidance in this area, DCAA uses the expression "fixed overhead," but does not define what is meant by that term. While overhead costs have fixed and variable cost components (as mentioned earlier), how costs are so categorized is not stated anywhere in the FAR, in any FAR Supplement, or even in the CAM. In decisions dealing with unabsorbed overhead claims, the contractor's accounting system is what it is, and costs are either fixed or not, depending on whether they respond to variances in work volume. Consequently, these are factual questions not requiring the assistance of an expert.

The CAM presents the applicable guidance for this type of claim in Sections 12-803 through 12-806.

Termination Claims

There are two types of contract terminations under a government contract: a termination for default (FAR 52.249-8) and termination for convenience (FAR 52.249-2). It is widely understood that a termination for default is part of a contractor's performance record and will adversely affect its ability to compete for future government contracts. What is not as widely known is that in construction contracts, a termination for default will assuredly increase a contractor's bond premiums.

A termination for convenience equates to the government's buying its way out of the contract, and there are no negative consequences on the contractor's performance record.

When a contract is terminated for the convenience of the government, the contractor is entitled to compensation (1) for work already performed; (2) for commitments made; and (3) for its costs of settlement. For the work performed, the contractor is also entitled to a "reasonable profit" (a term nowhere defined), unless the government can demonstrate that the contractor would have incurred a loss had the contract been completed (*see Boeing Defense & Space Group*, ASBCA No. 50048, 98-2 BCA ¶29,927). Because the contractor is entitled to compensation (which may be substantial but cannot exceed the original contract price), it is important that all allowable costs be included in the contractor's termination settlement proposal, which may include legal and accounting fees (*see* FAR 52.249-2(g)(3)(i)).

There are many different forms for submitting termination settlement proposals, depending on the type of property involved and the valuation methodology used, including the following:

Form	Title
SF 1423*	Inventory Verification Survey
SF 1424	Inventory Disposal Report
SF 1426*	Inventory Schedule A (Metals in Mill Product Form)
SF 1427	Inventory Schedule A (Metals in Mill Product Form) - Continuation Sheet
SF 1428*	Inventory Schedule B
SF 1429	Inventory Schedule B - Continuation Sheet
SF 1430*	Inventory Schedule C (Work in Process)
SF 1431	Inventory Schedule C (Work in Process) - Continuation Sheet
SF 1432*	Inventory Schedule D (Special Tooling and Special Test Equipment)
SF 1433	Inventory Schedule D - Continuation Sheet

SF 1434*   Inventory Schedule E (Short Form for use with SF
           1438 only)
SF 1435   Settlement Proposal (Inventory Basis)
SF 1436   Settlement Proposal (Total Cost Basis)
SF 1437   Settlement Proposal for Cost Reimbursement
           Contracts
SF 1438   Settlement Proposal (Short Form)
SF 1439   Schedule of Accounting Information

These forms can be found in FAR Part 53. The forms above marked with an asterisk were revised in March 1998 to eliminate duplicative certifications.

Few contractors have the capability to handle the complexity and nuances of these forms, nor do contractor personnel generally have either the time or the interest. Hence, accounting firms are frequently brought in to do so. After the termination settlement proposal is audited, the contractor enters into settlement negotiations with the termination contracting officer (TCO). Litigation ensues if these negotiations fail.

Although litigation related to a termination for convenience is infrequent, such cases do not usually involve accounting issues, but, rather, questions of valuation and/or utilization. Specifically, the government may believe that equipment on a termination settlement proposal is either overvalued or can be used commercially. In some instances, considerable disagreement about termination-for-convenience issues arises among various government agencies, and in litigation these differences are typically resolved in the contractor's favor (*see Raytheon Company*, ASBCA Nos. 51652, 53509, 03-2 BCA ¶32,337).

Under a default termination, the contractor may be obligated to compensate the government for any additional costs it incurs in procuring similar products or services from another supplier (called excess reprocurement costs). This obligation arises under the terms of the termination-for-default clause itself, which provides in pertinent part:

> If the Government terminates this contract, in whole
> or in part, it may acquire, under the terms and in the

manner the Contracting Officer considers appropriate, supplies or services similar to those terminated, and *the contractor will be liable to the Government for any excess costs for those supplies or services.* However, the contractor shall continue the work not terminated. [Emphasis added.]

Here also, properly accounting for the government's reprocurement costs is important for the accurate determination of the defaulted contractor's liability (*see Specialty Transportation, Inc. v. United States,* COFC, 57 Fed. Cl. 1, May 2, 2003). Documentation from the reprocurement contract file is usually, but not always, sufficient for the government's claim to be upheld.

For additional reference material, DCAA guidance may be found in Sections 12-100 through 12-400 of the Contract Audit Manual (CAM).

Delay and Disruption Claims

One significant difference between delay and disruption claims and other types of claims is that while the governing clause does not address damages determinations, an allowance for profit is permitted (*see* FAR 52.242-15 (Stop Work Order), FAR 52.236-2 (Differing Site Condition), and FAR 52.243 (Changes)(discussed above)). The Stop Work Order clause, found in supply, service, and R&D contracts, provides for damages simply by stating that there will be an equitable adjustment ("The Contracting Officer shall make an equitable adjustment in the delivery schedule or the contract price, or both, and the contract shall be modified, in writing, accordingly . . . "). The equitable adjustment may include profit, but the clause is silent on how either the damages or the profit should be ascertained. Similarly, no guidance is provided in the Differing Site Conditions clause about how an affected contractor's damages or profit is to be measured.

When performance is impaired, the easiest methodology for the contractor to follow is to retain its current accounting practices and only supplement its record keeping as necessary. For direct labor costs, an increase is indicated when employees spend more hours accomplishing various aspects of the work (although an increase in direct labor rates can also be the cause of increased costs, it is not as common as increased hours). For increased indirect costs, a contractor is required to use its normal methods for calculating the amounts involved.

While delay and disruption claims can arise out of widely varying factual backgrounds, sometimes several different relief-granting clauses may apply. Regardless of the cause of the delay, the effect is the same: the contractor must show that its costs of performance increased. Here too, the burden is on the contractor to show the facts substantiating the alleged delay or disruption, as well as the costs affected and to what extent (*The Clark Construction Group, Inc.,* JCL-BCA, 05-1 BCA ¶32,843; *Callozo Contractors, Inc.,* ASBCA No. 53925, 05-2 BCA ¶33,035).

In its audit, the government will also examine the contractor's proposal to compare its indirect and profit rates with the claimed rates. If the contractor departs in its claim from the rates used in its proposal, it will need to justify the difference.

Cost Overrun Claims

Notwithstanding the fact that cost reimbursement contracts emphasize that contractors exceed the cost ceiling at their own risk, when contractors go over their cost ceilings they are disposed to file a claim against the government for the excess. Cost overrun claims are made every year without fail, and (surprisingly) even by knowledgeable, experienced contractors.

The courts have been generally unsympathetic to cost overrun claims. However, they have held that such claims are recoverable where the costs involved could not have been foreseen. Whether certain costs were or were not foreseeable is by and large a fact-based question, so these appeals do not turn on differing views of applicable accounting requirements. Where the facts demonstrate that a cost overrun could not have been foreseen, even with an adequate accounting system, appeals have been successful (*Johnson Controls World Services, Inc. v. United States,* 48 Fed. Cl. 479, Jan. 26, 2001; *Optical E.T.C., Inc.,* ASBCA No. 53350, 04-1 BCA ¶32,608).

An illustrative case involving a discussion of the issues typically raised in a cost overrun claim is *American Electronic Laboratories, Inc.,* ASBCA, 84-2 BCA ¶17,468. The courts interpret the LOC/LOF clauses strictly, and constructive changes will not be construed to increase the cost ceiling (*Ceramics Process Systems Corp.,* ASBCA No.

49432, 97-2 BCA ¶29,134), nor will mere notice to the contracting officer of an impending cost overrun serve to increase the funding (*Connell-Beach Associates International, Inc.,* ASBCA No. 45318, 97-1 BCA ¶28,753).

Loss of Efficiency Claims

Loss of efficiency claims are relatively rare and generally arise from very large supply or construction contracts. The theory underlying such claims is that government action precluded cost savings attained from learning curve efficiencies. In order to prove such claims, a contractor may use either a total cost methodology or (more commonly) a should-cost analysis. In a should-cost analysis, a contractor uses its performance data occurring before the complained-of action to establish a baseline. A theoretical learning curve is then applied to demonstrate where the same performance levels should be under that contract if no impediment had been encountered. Then an overlay of the actual performance data is applied for the same period of time. The differences between the theoretical learning curve level and the actual performance level for each reporting period are the contractor's claim. In addition, the contractor may support its claim with expert testimony (accounting and/or technical), industry guides, and similar collateral information.

Obviously, a loss of efficiency claim requires large volumes of data. Moreover, that data must be discrete, i.e., both the baseline and actual performance level data must be free of other influences or events that could distort the results. Finally, the theoretical or technical basis on which the learning curve itself is derived is sometimes tenuous at best or speculative at worst. Because the assumptions on which loss of efficiency claims are based are so vulnerable to criticism, such claims are infrequently persuasive. For example, in the following diverse board cases the contractors' loss of efficiency claims were unsuccessful on evidentiary grounds: *Herman B. Taylor Construction Co.,* GSBCA No. 15421, 03-2 BCA ¶32,320; *Bay Construction Co.,* VABCA No. V662C-1439, 02-1 BCA ¶31,795; *B.R. Services, Inc.,* ASBCA Nos. 47673, 48249, 48257, 99-2 BCA ¶30,397; *Gottfried Corp.,* ASBCA No. 51041, 98-2 BCA ¶30,063; *Roberts J.R. Corp.,* DOT BCA No. 2499, 98-1 BCA ¶29,680; and *Moore Overseas Construction Co.,* ENG BCA No. PCC-125, 98-1 BCA ¶29,682. Loss of efficiency claims have had a similar unsuccessful track record in court. *See Southern Comfort*

Builders, Inc. v. U.S., 67 Fed. Cl. 124, No. 00-542C (July 29, 2005); and *Sunshine Construction & Engineering, Inc. v. U.S.,* 64 Fed. Cl. 346, No. 02-250C (March 4, 2005).

Section 12-808 of the CAM discusses the audit guidance related to loss of efficiency claims. That section warns auditors, *inter alia*, to be wary of duplicative claims, i.e., the same costs being claimed for loss of efficiency as well as unabsorbed overhead.

A contractor presenting a loss of efficiency claim would almost certainly require the services of an expert witness, so an expert witness also would likely be needed by the government to analyze and rebut such a claim.

Loss of Profits Claims

Because loss of profits claims are so speculative, it is rare indeed for a contractor to recover for lost profits, although it has happened. Moreover, profit is specifically unallowable for claims arising under the Suspension of Work clause (FAR 52.242-14) and Government Delay of Work clause (FAR 52.242-17).

The few cases where lost profits were recovered by contractors involved circumstances where the courts found a government breach of the contract (*see S&W Tire Services, Inc.,* GSBCA No. 6,376, 82-2 BCA ¶ 16,048; *Ronald A. Torncello and Soledad Enterprises, Inc. v. United States,* 231 Ct. Cl. 20, 681 F.2d 756, 1982). This is a high legal standard often alleged by contractors but infrequently supported by the facts.

If a contractor wins on entitlement to lost profits, the quantum issue presented concerns the appropriate rate. Some might think the contractor would merely receive additional profit at the same rate used in its proposal, but this assumption is incorrect. In fact, there have been wide variances by the courts, even going as high as 25% (*see Apex International Management Services, Inc.,* ASBCA No. 38087, 94-2 BCA ¶ 26,842; *Department of Defense Cable Television Franchise Agreements,* COFC No. 96-133X, 35 Fed. Cl. 171, July 11, 1996; *AJT & Associates, Inc.,* ASBCA No. 50240, 97-1 BCA ¶ 28,823).

Given the growing use of outsourcing by government prime contractors, managing subcontracts is becoming a key aspect of successful government contract administration. Chapter 7 provides a practical discussion of the challenges and best practices of government subcontract management.

CHAPTER  7

MANAGING
SUBCONTRACTS:
CHALLENGES
AND BEST
PRACTICES

INTRODUCTION

In 2008, the U.S. federal government awarded more than 7 million contracts valued at over $531 billion[1] to acquire needed products, services, systems, and integrated solutions from thousands of government contractors, also referred to as prime contractors. Serving as a prime contractor is not an easy business, because the U.S. federal government is very demanding. U.S. federal government prime contractors often must select and manage multiple subcontractors and comply with a tremendous number of complex laws, regulations, policies, standards, and specifications and face an increasing assortment of government oversight-audits, reviews, and investigations. This chapter provides a detailed discussion of the critical challenges and proven best practices of U.S. federal government prime contractors in managing their respective supply chains to not only comply with all the government's laws, regulations, policies, etc., but also to achieve on-time delivery of quality products and/or services within budget, which meet or exceed the customer's requirements.

U.S. GOVERNMENT PRIME CONTRACTORS' SUPPLY CHAIN CHALLENGES

Table 7-1 provides a list of ten critical challenges that U.S. federal government prime contractors often encounter in building and managing their respective supply chains with their customers and subcontractors. Following Table 7-1 is a brief discussion of each of the stated ten critical supply chain challenges.

Table 7-1

Ten Critical Supply Chain Challenges Faced by U.S. Government Prime Contractors
1. Financial pressures, due to global economic downturn, affecting prime contractors and subcontractors
2. Poor demand planning and requirements' determination by U.S. federal government agencies
3. Insufficient government contracting and supply chain management team competencies
4. Lack of supplier leverage
5. Demanding U.S. government small business subcontracting goals
6. Excessive U.S. government mandatory flow-down of terms and conditions to subcontractors
7. Lack of competition in supplier selection
8. Increased government cost reduction demands
9. Excessive government detailed requirements
10. Increased U.S. government oversight-audits, reviews, and investigations

1. Financial Pressures, Due to Global Economic Downturn, Affecting Prime Contractors and Subcontractors

The global economic downturn continues to manifest itself in many ways, and certainly one of them is the risk that many companies are facing because some of their suppliers are under significant financial pressure. Many companies in both domestic and international markets are under growing financial pressure, but this is especially true of smaller companies that are not well capitalized. A key factor in the current financial struggles of many subcontractors in both the public and private sectors is that their customers often pay even more slowly than usual, while prime contractors face their own economic challenges.[2]

Cash flow is the heart of business. Financially strapped prime contractors and subcontractors may be late paying their suppliers as a result of their financial difficulties in finding available loans, securing credit, paying higher interest rates, and receiving late payments from some of their customers.

A recent survey by *CPO Agenda* magazine found that more than three quarters of procurement executives said they were facing great pressure to reduce costs—and we're surprised the number isn't higher (see Figure 7-1).[3]

Figure 7-1

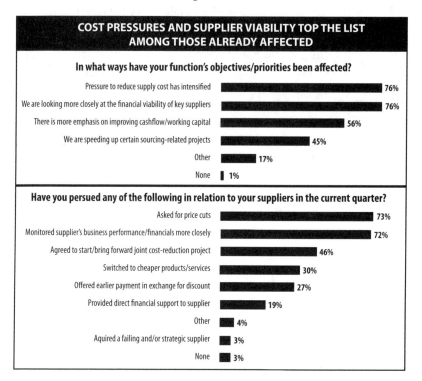

COST PRESSURES AND SUPPLIER VIABILITY TOP THE LIST AMONG THOSE ALREADY AFFECTED

In what ways have your function's objectives/priorities been affected?

Pressure to reduce supply cost has intensified	76%
We are looking more closely at the financial viability of key suppliers	76%
There is more emphasis on improving cashflow/working capital	56%
We are speeding up certain sourcing-related projects	45%
Other	17%
None	1%

Have you persued any of the following in relation to your suppliers in the current quarter?

Asked for price cuts	73%
Monitored supplier's business performance/financials more closely	72%
Agreed to start/bring forward joint cost-reduction project	46%
Switched to cheaper products/services	30%
Offered earlier payment in exchange for discount	27%
Provided direct financial support to supplier	19%
Other	4%
Aquired a failing and/or strategic supplier	3%
None	3%

2. Poor Demand Planning and Requirements' Determination by U.S. Federal Government Agencies

It may startle some business professionals, but one of the biggest challenges government prime contractors and subcontractors encounter is that U.S. federal government agencies do not always know what they want, when they need it, and/or how many they will need! Of course, one of the golden rules for creating a cost-effective and efficient supply chain is to have an accurate demand plan/forecast of the quantity of products and/or services that the customer needs and a time line as to when they are required. For a variety of reasons, U.S. federal government agencies have histori-cally been unable to   accurately align their stated needs with their congressionally authorized and appropriated department budgets. As a result, government prime contractors and subcontractors often become frustrated by the inaccuracy of the government's requirements and the frequent changes to the quantity, quality, and delivery schedule.

3. Insufficient Government Contracting and Supply Chain Management Team Competencies

Many U.S. government prime contractors and subcontractors do not have a sufficient number of highly-skilled, well-educated, well-trained, and experienced professionals who fully understand the laws, regulations, and best practices of U.S. government contracts and supply chain management. As a result, numerous U.S. government prime contractors and subcontractors struggle to truly optimize their supply chain. Frequent company reorganizations, downsizing, and changing company policies, processes, and practices further complicate companies' ability to enhance both organizational and individual competencies in U.S. government contracting and supply chain management.

4. Lack of Supplier Leverage

One of the hallmarks of world class supply chain management companies, such as Wal-Mart, Proctor & Gamble, and IBM, is their ability to effectively leverage suppliers. Leveraging suppliers is a company's ability to negotiate discounts, obtain preferred contract terms and conditions (i.e., payment terms, cycle-time, delivery schedule, extended warranties, etc.), and form mutually successful business partnerships.[4] Unfortunately, for a variety of reasons many government prime contractors and subcontractors often struggle to form meaningful supplier relationships, which prohibits them from being able to effectively leverage their suppliers.

5. Demanding U.S. Government Small Business Subcontracting Goals

In accordance with Federal Acquisition Regulation (FAR) Part 19, Small Business Contracting, every U.S. federal government agency is required to establish goals to award a certain percentage of their acquisition budget to U.S. small businesses. In addition, FAR Part 19 mandates that government contracting officers require large businesses awarded specified government contracts valued above $500,000 to create a small business contracting plan to achieve stated goals. Further, FAR Part 19 establishes numerous specific categories of small businesses, including small disadvantaged businesses, women-owned small businesses, veteran-owned small businesses, HUB-zoned small businesses, and Alaskan and Native American–owned small businesses. Often, U.S. federal government agencies establish an overall contract goal for prime contractors–for example, a requirement that 20% of the value of the contract be subcontracted to small businesses–frequently with specific subcontracting targets for each specific small business category. Achieving these contract- specific small business category targets and overall small business subcontracting goals can prove very challenging in some product and service areas.

6. Excessive U.S. Government Mandatory Flow-Down of Contract Terms and Conditions to Subcontractors

As the old saying goes, "What the big print giveth, the little print taketh away." Clearly, in the realm of U.S. government contracts the above statement is true as pertains to the vast number of complex, detailed, and one-sided mandatory contract clauses, often called terms and conditions (Ts & Cs), which are required by government laws, regulations, and policies. Of course, as one of the biggest buyers of products and services in the world, the U.S. federal government has a right to leverage their suppliers and protect its interest. However, the U.S. federal government has extended its leverage beyond the rule of contract privity to the prime contractor's subcontractors via mandatory flow-down contract clauses.

Stated differently, U.S. federal government agencies are required by FAR to ensure the mandatory flow-down of numerous (in most cases over 50) government contract clauses to subcontractors. Further, each government department or agency has developed a list of additional terms and conditions, or contract clauses, that must be flowed-down to subcontractors at all levels below the prime contract. For example, a U.S. Department of Defense (DOD) prime contractor who has received a contract above $500,000 may be required to flow-down over 50 Federal Acquisition Regulation (FAR) contract clauses and another 50-plus Department of Defense Federal Acquisition Regulation Supplement (DFARS) contract clauses to their subcontractors. This results in more than 100 detailed, complex, and often expensive-to-implement subcontract requirements above and beyond what it normally takes to deliver the products and/or services specified.

7. Lack of Competition in Supplier Selection

Given the numerous obstacles to successful entry into the U.S. federal government marketplace, including   the complexity of requirements, entrenched incumbent competitors, unstable funding, changing requirements, numerous delays, government politics and bureaucracy, and increased government oversight-reviews, audits, and investigations, competition in supplier selections is often difficult to. At both the prime contract level and subcontract level(s) it can prove very challenging to maintain two or more viable suppliers, especially for some of the highly complex systems and integrated solutions required by the U.S. government agencies.

8. Increased Government Cost Reduction Demands

As the global economic downturn affects governments and industry worldwide, more U.S. government funding is being directed to support failing industries and financial institutions. Thus, it is widely expected that many U.S. government departments and agencies will receive less funding for their key contracts and major programs. Clearly, the focus of the Obama administration is on healthcare, house, energy, transportation, and the environment. Therefore, the U.S. federal government departments of Health and Human Services (HHS), Veteran Affairs (VA), Housing and Urban Development (HUD), Transportation, Energy, and the Environmental Protection Agency (EPA) are all expected to receive increased acquisition funding from the U.S. Congress with the support and approval of President Obama. Likewise, it is widely expected that the Department of Defense (DOD), Department of Homeland Security (DHS), and the National Aeronautics and Space Administration (NASA) will receive less funding than in previous years. Consequently, it is expected that DOD, DHS, and NASA will be highly focused on controlling expenses, especially on the design, production, and operation of major acquisition programs.[5] Government contractors will increasingly be contractually required to reduce their costs by any and all means possible within the realm of business ethics.

9. Excessive Government Detailed How-to-Do-It Requirements

For more than 40 years, U.S. federal government agencies, especially the U.S. Department of Defense (DOD), have developed highly detailed designs, specifications, and standards to ensure they get what they want, how they want it. Unfortunately, this highly detailed and prescriptive government requirements process has often resulted in high costs, over budget, behind schedule, and sometimes poor performing products, services, systems, and integrated solutions. Further, the U.S. government's detailed specification-oriented and statement of work-driven task documents are sometimes inaccurate and/or outdated. Finally, the U.S. government's traditional detailed "how-to-do-it" requirements process does not allow for much flexibility, innovation, or cost efficiencies to be considered or implemented by industry.

10. Increased U.S. Government Oversight-Audits, Reviews, and Investigations

Today, we live in a world of mistrust or, stated simply, a lack of trust in government contracting. As a result of some violations of U.S. government laws, regulations, and policies by some government prime contractors and subcontractors, industry is often perceived by the U.S. Congress and the public to be crooks. Because of this fundamental lack of trust, U.S. government prime contractors are forced to endure numerous government audits, reviews, and investigations, many of which include civil and/or criminal penalties for non-compliance. Unfortunately, because of the wrongdoings of a relatively small percentage of government prime contractors, the industry as a whole is forced to endure an unprecedented level of government oversight lead by the Government Accountability Office (GAO), Department Inspector General (IG) offices, Defense Contract Audit Agency (DCAA), Defense Contract Management Agency (DCMA), and many others.

U.S. GOVERNMENT PRIME CONTRACTORS SUPPLY CHAIN— BEST PRACTICES

Table 7-2 provides a list of ten proven effective supply chain best practices as implemented by industry in either the public and/or private sector. Following Table 7-2 is a brief discussion of the supply chain best practices.

Table 7-2

Ten Supply Chain Best Practices for U.S. Government Prime Contractors
1. Enhance cash-flow and financial management of suppliers
2. Understand government needs and contract requirements
3. Implement a supply chain management professional development program and Center of Excellence
4. Conduct strategic sourcing and spend analysis
5. Implement supplier relationship improvement programs
6. Expand the use of commercial item acquisitions
7. Enhance market research for supplier sourcing
8. Implement price-benchmarking clauses
9. Expand use of performance-based contracts
10. Benchmark supply chain management processes and performance metrics

1. Enhance Cash-Flow and Financial Management of Suppliers

Many suppliers in both the public and private sectors, are facing cash-flow issues and growing financial pressures. U.S. government prime contractors must effectively manage their invoice, payment, and cost-flow process with their government agency customers, appropriately requesting loans, advance payment, milestone-based payments for results achieved (also known as. progress payments or cost reimbursement for allowable and allocable expenses incurred), depending on the financial situation and the pricing arrangement agreed to in the contract. Similarly, prime contractors must do all they can afford to do to help their selected subcontractors via contract financing such as collateralized loans, improved payment terms, faster payments, progress payments, and operational assistance when necessary and appropriate. A good supplier is hard to find and if helping suppliers through a tough financial time will most likely create a strong prime-subcontractor business relationship.

2. Understand Customer Needs and Contract Requirements

In order to become a successful U.S. government prime contractor, it is vital to understand both the government customer's needs and its stated contract requirements. At times government agencies do not properly develop their contract requirements; thus it is possible for a prime contractor to provide the government with the product and services that they contractually required, yet still not meet the government's real needs. The goal of a business seller is to meet or exceed their customer/buyer's needs while achieving their company performance goals. Thus, it is essential for a prime contractor to understand the government customer's needs and align those needs with the actual contract requirements.

A tool designed to help prime contractors and subcontractors alike ensure that they understand the customer's needs and the key contract/subcontract requirements is the Customer Requirements/ Deliverable Matrix (CR/DM). The CR/DM is a simple matrix jointly developed by a buyer and a seller that clearly lists all the critical customer needs and products, services, or systems that will be developed and/or delivered to meet or exceed each contract requirement. Further, top supply chain companies ensure that each contract requirement is tracked via a Work Breakdown Structure (WBS), which is linked to a Responsibility Assignment Matrix (RAM) for assigning work to specific individuals; and time-phased via a Master Integrated Schedule (MIS), with a budget established for each contract deliverable, project, and program.

3. Implement a Supply Chain Management Professional Development Program and Center of Excellence

World-class companies like IBM, Dell, and Toyota, among others, have focused on not only creating effective supply chain processes, systems, and performance metrics, but have also invested in their most important asset, their people. Specifically, many of the leading global companies like Toyota have made significant investments in supply chain management education, training, and cross-functional work experience for their team members. In addition, a few organizations in both the public and private sectors have established a supply chain management Center of Excellence to facilitate processes, tools, training, coaching/mentoring, lessons learned, and best practices using a coordinated and integrated Knowledge Management Center. Many government agencies and companies also are using numerous supply chain management education and training courses available from colleges and universities worldwide. Today, supply chain management education is offered in classroom-based instruction, computer-based instruction, and interactive online programs like the Supply Chain Management Master's Certificate Program offered by the University of San Francisco through the University Alliance online program.

4. Conduct Strategic Sourcing and Spend Analysis

Leading purchasing organizations worldwide have learned the value and power of conducting spend analysis as a vital element of strategic sourcing. Simply stated, a buying/purchasing organization should know how it is spending its money, with whom it is spending the money-byproduct or service, and the quality of the products and services it is receiving. Strategic sourcing is a process approach for effectively analyzing the supply chain to reduce cycle-time, reduce costs, and improve product and service performance results. Many companies and government agencies have created commodity councils to aggregate their demand planning for specific commercially available raw materials, products, and/or services. Improving demand planning or product/services forecasting is an important first step for procurement organizations to more effectively leverage their suppliers through economic-order-quantity buying practices.

5. Implement Supplier Relationship Improvement Programs

Numerous world-class companies like Wal-Mart, IBM, and Honda have created, implemented, and maintained highly successful supplier relationship improvement programs. Wal-Mart works to help its suppliers improve the quality and marketability of their products. Honda provides all of their suppliers with performance goals/targets and monthly supplier "report cards." Additionally, Honda helps its suppliers improve their manufacturing processes and find innovative way to reduce cycle-times and expenses.[6] IBM categorizes its suppliers based on performance and instituted a supplier inventive/rewards program. The U.S. Department of Defense (DOD) developed and implemented the DOD Pilot Mentor-Protégé program years ago, which has helped improve the performance of many small businesses working in partnership with a successful major defense prime contractor.

6. Expand the Use of Commercial Item Acquisitions

U.S. federal government agencies have tried to increase their use of commercial contracting practices by implementing Federal Acquisition Regulation (FAR) Part 12, Commercial-Item Acquisition. FAR Part 12 provides significant process and contractual streamlining compared to the typical federal contracting process. The use of the Commercial-Item Acquisition process saves significant time and money for subcontractors, prime contractors, government agencies, and U.S. taxpayers. U.S. government agencies must embrace and require the use of more commercially available products and services, rather than creating unique detailed government requirements.

7. Enhance Market Research for Supplier Sourcing

Many prime contractors and U.S. federal government agencies are subject to the "incumbent contractor syndrome," which can be either positive or negative depending on the performance of the selected contractor. Continually purchasing products and/or services from a selected contractor over an extended period of time can prove successful if the incumbent contractor continually improves its personnel, processes, and performance. However, incumbent contractors have a tendency to become complacent, seeking higher revenues and profits without improving their people, processes, products, and/or pricing. To combat the incumbent contractor syndrome, use market research to identify and select the best suppliers.

Market research can be accomplished by numerous methods, including (1) hiring a professional market research firm (i.e., Dunn & Bradstreet, The Gartner Group, The Hackett Group, or Forrester Research), (2) conducting one-on-one market focus-group meetings with leading suppliers, (3) developing and conducting web-based market surveys, (4) conducting Internet-based searches of available suppliers, (5) contacting industry trade associations for lists of available product and/or service providers, (6) reviewing industry/trade magazine and catalogs, and (7) attending industry/trade association conferences and exhibitions.

8. Implement Price-Benchmarking Clauses

A benchmarking clause is used in an outsourcing contract as a check against significant price "drift" over time. This type drift is of particular concern in longer-term contracts where major discrepancies can occur between contract prices and market pricing. Most outsourcing projects, especially longer-term ones, have complex mechanisms in place for changing contract prices. These mechanisms are the primary drivers of micro-price adjustment and include year-on-year productivity improvements, inflation adjustments, and adjustments for changes in required service volumes. The underlying commercial basis for including a benchmarking clause is not to treat it as a supplement to these mechanisms, which would cause it to become just another tool to enable an additional micro-price adjustment.[7]

9. Expand Use of Performance-Based Contracts

In simple terms, a Performance-Based Contract (PBC) contains the following essential elements:

- Performance Work Statement (PWS) or Statement of Objectives (SOO),
- Performance standards, measures, and metrics,
- Performance incentives (positive and negative),
- Quality Assurance Surveillance Plan (QASP), and
- Appropriate pricing arrangement(s).

Without all of these essential elements, a contract lacks the means to truly empower and motivate a supplier to achieve the art of the possible. Today, too many U.S. government agencies and prime contractors still rely on outdated, overly legalistic, highly prescriptive, and overly complex contracts containing detailed designs, specifications, and lengthy task-oriented statements of work, which often drive-up costs, extend the acquisition cycle-time, and result in poor performance results. When effectively structured and intelligently implemented, PBCs can achieve superior performance results for all of the parties involved.

10. Benchmark Supply Chain Management Processes and Key Performance Indicators

Establishing and reporting on key performance indicators (KPIs) is critical to the success of any contract. According to the recent 2007 cross-industry benchmarking studies conducted by the Center for Advanced Purchasing Studies (CAPS) research, the most popular commercial procurement KPIs include:

- Purchase spend as a percentage of sales dollars,
- Purchasing operating expense as a percentage of sales dollars,
- Purchasing operating expense as a percentage of purchase spend,
- Purchasing operating expense per purchasing employee,
- Purchasing employees as a percentage of company employees,

- Purchase spend per purchasing employee,
- Managed spend per purchasing employee,
- Percentage of purchase spend managed/controlled by purchasing,
- Percentage of companies that reported outsourcing some of their procurement activities,
- Percentage of managed spend outsourced,
- Percentage of purchase spend offshore,
- Percentage of purchase spend onshore,
- Average annual spend on training per purchasing employees,
- Cost avoidance savings as a percentage of total purchase spend,
- Cost reduction savings as a percentage of total purchase spend,
- Percentage of active suppliers accounting for 80 percent of purchase spend,
- Percentage of purchase spend with diversity suppliers, and
- Percentage of active suppliers who are e-procurement enabled.

Most organizations understand the importance and value of conducting benchmarking of their procurement practices and performance metrics or key performance indicators. Today, many senior procurement executives, in both government and industry, are assessing how their organization adds value to the mission determining their value proposition. The Hackett Group, a world-class benchmarking firm, has developed a five-stage model for procurement's evolving proposition (see Table 7-3).[8]

Table 7-3

Supply Management		Customer Management		
Stage	1 Supply Assurance	2 Price	3 Total Cost Of Ownership	4 Demand Management	5 Value Management
Goal	Right goods and services at the right time at the right price	Right goods and services AND at the right price	Shift from lowest price to lowest total cost of ownership	Reduce demand activity, complexity, and variability	Increase business value derived from spend rather than just reducing total cost/spend
Procurement's Role	Buyer-Planner	Negotiator	Supply expert team leader, project manager, supplier manager	Spend/budget consultant ("money manager") and procurement relationship manager	Trusted business advisor and change agent
Key Output Metrics	Perfect order (on-time delivery, defect-free, accurate documentation, etc.)	1. Present Value and/or spend cost savings/ avoidance 2. Performance to market	1. Cost of quality 2. Cost of capital 3. Freight, handling, duties, tariffs, taxes 4. Write-offs and disposal 5. Opportunity cost from lost profits and brand damage	1. Percent of spend/sourcing activity with early demand influence 2. Maverick spend percentage (not channeling demand to best supply) 3. Internal customer satisfaction rating	1. Net income, return on investment, economic value added, net present value, etc. 2. Market cap/ stock price 3. Operation metrics of the spend owners
Practices/ Tools	1. Enterprise Resource Planning 2. Supplier scheduling 3. Long term contacts, dual sourcing, etc.	1. Separation of strategic sourcing and tactical buying 2. Basic "n-step" strategic sourcing methodology 3. Price savings tracking 4. Competitive bidding techniques/ tools	1. Deep cost modeling and management 2. End-to-end functional teams (suppliers, too) 3. Supplier management, collaboration, and development 4. Working capital management 5. Complexity/ waste reduction (lean, Six Sigma, etc.) 6. Supply chain management (e.g., extended network design, multi-tier sourcing) 7. Design for cost 8. Supply risk mitigation (supplier, capacity, market, network, etc.)	1. Customer Account Management (account managers, co-location, stakeholder surveys, contract centers) 2. Demand visibility (e.g., forecasting project portfolio planning, demand planning) 3. Supply planning and demand supply matching 4. Demand shaping (joint planning/ budgeting, promotions, postponement)	1. Business process sourcing (e.g., make vs. buy, shoring) 2. Design for supply 3. Hoshin Planning and Quality Function Deployment (QFD) 4. Customer's customer focus and customer specific methodologies

SUMMARY

In retrospect, this chapter provides a detailed discussion of ten critical challenges that U.S. federal government prime contractors typically encounter in managing their respective supply chains in order to comply with all of the government's laws, regulations, and policies and to achieve high performance results. To help meet those challenges, this chapter offers ten supply chain best practices, which have been successfully implemented by numerous world class companies and/or leading government organizations. Too many organizations in both the public and private sectors over-promise and underdeliver. Remember, the promise of successful outsourcing and contract administration can only be realized through the discipline of effective supply chain management.

In the next chapter, the importance and value of government property management as a vital aspect of contract administration will be discussed.

QUESTIONS TO CONSIDER

1. Which of the prime contractor critical challenges do you think are most important to remedy?

2. Which of the prime contractor proven best practices do you think are most effective?

3. How many of the prime contractor best practices has your organization implemented?

ENDNOTES

1. U.S. Office of Federal Procurement Policy, Federal Procurement Data System, FY08 Procurement Statistics (February 2009).
2. If Key Suppliers are Struggling Financially, What Should Procurement Organizations Do? *Supply Chain Digest*. (New York: January 7, 2009).
3. For Procurement Managers, a Bit of Pay Back Time. *Supply Chain Digest*. scdigest.com (January 27, 2009).
4. Garrett, Gregory A., *Contract Negotiations*. (Chicago: CCH, 2005).
5. Garrett, Gregory A. & McDonald, Peter, Preparing for Change: The Obama Administration Effect on Government Contractors, NCMA, *Contract Management Magazine* (February 2009).
6. Garrett, Gregory A., Commercial Contracting Best Practices, NCMA, *Contract Management Magazine* (January 2008).
7. Ibid.
8. Ibid.

CHAPTER  8

GOVERNMENT PROPERTY MANAGEMENT: CHALLENGES AND BEST PRACTICES

INTRODUCTION

The following situations all have something in common. In August 1990 Iraq suddenly invaded and annexed Kuwait. The United Nations sent coalition forces from 34 nations to expel the Iraqi forces. The U.S. Army's main battle tank, the M1A1, obliterated Iraqi armored forces consisting primarily of Russian designed T-72 tanks. In July 2009 Marines on patrol in a mine resistant ambush protected vehicle near Kabul, Afghanistan, drove over a pressure sensitive improvised explosive device (IED) that was buried in the road. The resulting explosion would have been fatal except that their MRAP did what it was designed to do—deflect the force of the explosion and save lives. On a blustery winter evening in January a school bus with a wheelchair assist mechanism comfortably and safely delivered its precious young passengers to their waiting families in rural Clark County, Ohio. A few days before Thanksgiving grocery stores were experiencing peak demand for the food that would be prepared, served, and enjoyed by friends and family. A regional Midwest supermarket chain had been preparing for this season for months and its distribution centers were delivering the goods as promised. Sharks, orcas, sea lions, penguins, walrus, polar bears, and a variety of other marine animals at a large marine theme park provided entertainment and educational enjoyment to hundreds of thousands of visitors from around the world. The environment in which these animals cohabit, along with their admiring human visitors, is carefully monitored to make sure that everything is safe, secure, and enjoyable.

What do these events have in common? These products or services all depend on the efficient management of property and assets that are there when they are needed. Best practices make it possible for an organization to effectively control, protect, preserve, maintain, and dispose of its property and assets—using a property management system. Embedded within that system are ten key processes that help to lower costs and achieve efficiencies that would not otherwise be possible. In this chapter we will identify these processes and describe their function within the organization. Even though the title of this chapter is "*Government* Property Management: Challenges and Best Practices," the fundamental concepts can be applied to non-governmental entities (organizations) as well. One of the

EIGHT

contractors responsible for an item in the scenario above found that the contractually required government property management system worked so well for the military side of its business that it adopted the system for its commercial business as well– this helped the commercial side of the business to significantly increase efficiency and profitability.

CHALLENGES AND BEST PRACTICES

Any firm needs to be able to use its assets and property in the most efficient and cost- effective way to provide products and services to its customers. In order to do this it needs to focus on the processes that will contribute to the success of the mission. Contractors are strongly advised to read their contracts before they decide what best practices they should or should not use. Information on establishing a contractor's property management system is required to be part of the contract. If it is not or if there are questions regarding your contract, it is advisable to contact the appropriate government representative such as the Contracting Officer or Property Administrator.

Businesses depend upon the establishment of systems, procedures or methods, and best practices to consistently produce the desired results. The method by which the federal government requires contractors to manage its property and assets is found in the Federal Acquisition Regulation (FAR), which provides "uniform policies and procedures for acquisitions by executive agencies" of the federal government.[1] A contractor is required to

> "have a system to manage (control, use, preserve, pro-
> tect, repair and maintain) Government property in its
> possession. The system shall be adequate to satisfy the
> requirements of this clause. In doing so, the Contrac-
> tor shall initiate and maintain the processes, systems,
> procedures, records, and methodologies necessary for
> effective control of Government property, consistent
> with voluntary consensus standards and/or industry-
> leading practices and standards for Government
> property management except where inconsistent with
> law or regulation. During the period of performance,
> the Contractor shall disclose any significant changes
> to their property management system to the Property
> Administrator prior to implementation."[2]

The challenge is to determine the "voluntary consensus standards and/or industry-leading practices and standards" that are appropriate for the organization and the required task that must be performed.

According to FAR 2.202 "voluntary consensus standards" means common and repeated use of rules, conditions, guidelines, or characteristics for products or related processes and production methods and related management systems. Voluntary consensus standards are developed or adopted by domestic and international voluntary consensus standard–making bodies." The FAR does not provide a definition of "industry leading practices" but the available literature has many descriptions of "best practice." Gulati and Smith state in their book *Maintenance and Reliability Best Practices* that best practices "is an idea that asserts that there is a technique, method, or practice that is more effective at delivering a desired outcome than any other technique, method, or process."[3] A best practice is superior to other methods or processes. They provide an example of a person who went on to develop a superior method that was widely copied by others and became a best practice– Olympian Dick Fosbury.

> *The 1968 Mexico City Olympics marked the international debut of Dick Fosbury and his celebrated "Fosbury flop," which would soon revolutionize high-jumping. At the time, jumpers took off from their inside foot and swung their outside foot up and over the bar. Fosbury's technique began by racing up to the bar at great speed and taking off from his right (or outside) foot. Then he twisted his body so that he went over the bar head first with his back to the bar. While the coaches of the world shook their heads in disbelief, the Mexico City audience was absolutely captivated by Fosbury and shouted, "Olé" as he cleared the bar. Fosbury cleared every height through 2.22 metres without a miss and then achieved a personal record of 2.24 metres to win the gold medal.[4]*

By 1980 approximately three of every four Olympic high jumpers were using this new technique as a best practice.

Henry Martin Leland was a precision machinist who moved from Vermont to Detroit. He helped found Cadillac in 1902 and was instrumental in helping the company to design and build the

Model K to unbelievable standards in 1905. Leland sent three Model Ks to London to compete for the Dewar Trophy, one of the most prestigious automotive awards at that time. The Cadillacs were driven on city streets and on a track and then they were totally disassembled. After the parts were mixed up they were randomly selected so that three cars could be fully assembled and tested. One crank of the starter was enough to start two of the cars while the third required two cranks. Before the invention of the electric starter, a crank was used to start the engine in a car, and such quality and precision was unprecedented at that time. Cadillac won the Dewar Trophy and became known as the "Standard of the World." A new best practice was born in the fledgling automotive world.

Best practices are being established every day by individuals interested in achieving the best that can be obtained in almost any field of endeavor with the technology and knowledge available to them. For example, Jimi Hendrix used the feedback and distortion on his Fender Stratocaster to set new standards for the electric guitar. Daily news releases are constantly illustrating the latest trends in best practices. Technology is driving the need for new standards and best practices. As we learn more about the processes that affect the way in which we live, we will be able to develop ones that yield better results. The best practices of today eventually will be overtaken by the best practices of tomorrow.

Ten Process or Outcomes Essential for Property Management

The Federal Acquisition Regulation provides ten primary processes that are necessary to facilitate the effective management of government or commercial property and assets. Subsumed under these primary processes are several additional ones, which are described in the Government Property Clause at FAR 52.245-1 under section (f), Contractor plans and systems. They include acquisition; receipt; records; physical inventory; subcontractor control; reports; relief of stewardship responsibility; utilization; maintenance; and property closeout. The effective management of government property and assets depends on these processes when they are provided to a contractor under a contract. There are many industry leading practices and voluntary consensus standards that are applicable to the processes identified in this clause. The government allows a contractor to select which one is best for its particular operation. A contractor's size, along with the type of products and services it is involved with, help to determine the best practice for its business. These processes are outlined below.

Establishing Contractor Plans and Systems

The Government Property Clause at FAR 52.245-1 states that "Contractors shall establish and implement property management plans, systems, and procedures at the contract, program, site or entity level to enable the following outcomes." The order in which the processes are presented is often referred to as the "life cycle" of government property because it follows an orderly progression of events that mimic the birth, life, and conclusion of a project or program. These ten outcomes or processes are discussed below.

1. Acquisition of Property

Under the Federal Acquisition Regulation, the process related to the acquisition of property requires a contractor to "document that all property was acquired consistent with its engineering, production planning, and material control operations."[5]

Acquisition is typically the first process associated with the life cycle of managing property and assets and occurs. when items are acquired from a vendor or subcontractor. This process may also include the fabrication of items in-house; issuing items from contractor-owned stores or stock or stockrooms; transfers; and reutilization. [6]

When a contract is awarded, the products and/or services are carefully assessed to determine what items are needed and when they will be needed. The person responsible for purchasing will contact suppliers and place orders using subcontracts, purchase orders, etc., to ascertain that the items will be available when needed. When making purchases that will be used to support a contract, the purchasing agent needs to know if they will be purchased with company or government funds and who will have title to the acquired items.

Even though the government prefers a contractor to use its own property, there are times where it is in the government's best interest to furnish it. Property may be provided if government requirements cannot otherwise be met. There are additional exceptions where it may be more advantageous for the government to provide property, including when it is economically beneficial to the government, and for security, standardization, expedited production, scarcity of assets, to maintain the industrial base, and to support small business. A contractor's inability or unwillingness to use its own property is not a reason for the government to furnish its property. In order for acquisitions to be legitimate they must be consistent with the policy on providing property, including what is in the best interest of the government.

In government contracting there are times when a contract stipulates that the government will directly furnish property to the contractor as government- furnished property (GFP). By definition government-furnished property "means property in the possession of, or directly acquired by, the Government and subsequently furnished to the contractor for performance of a contract."[7] Title to government-furnished property always vests in the government.

Contractors should be mindful that the government does not arbitrarily provide government-furnished property to contractors. FAR 45.102 provides that "Contractors are ordinarily required to furnish all property necessary to perform Government contracts." Contracting Officers need to know if furnishing government property to a contractor can provide the contractor with a significant competitive advantage over other contractors, because doing so is prohibited in FAR 45.103: agencies must "eliminate to the maximum practical extent any competitive advantage a prospective contractor may have by using Government property." Because the government must treat all contractors equally, the Contracting Officer must obtain consideration or a cost adjustment in situations where one contractor is provided government property and another is not. This can be done using an equitable adjustment to the contract or by obtaining a rental equivalent in accordance with the Use and Charges Clause at FAR 52.245-9. Rental charges are more applicable after the award of a contract and the contractor must compensate the government for using its property in a manner that was not expressed in the contract.

The Federal Acquisition Regulation is quite clear when it comes to title. The government retains title to all government-furnished property. If the contractor has a cost-reimbursable contract, then the contractor is authorized to acquire items for contract performance so long as the acquisitions are reasonable, allowable, and allocable. The term that describes this situation is contractor acquired property (CAP). This includes "property acquired, fabricated, or otherwise provided by the contractor for performing a contract and to which the Government has title."[8] Any item purchased for the government must be consistent with contractual authorizations. If the contractor has a cost-reimbursement type contract, then any acquisition must be reasonable, allowable, and allocable, as these terms are described in FAR 31.201.

Reasonable costs are those that would be expected of a wise and thoughtful person in conducting a competitive business. Reasonableness can be determined by the terms and conditions of the contract if items to be acquired are specifically mentioned and by reviewing blueprints, drawings, bills of material, or other documents that show the item and the quantity needed.

Costs are allowable only when specified by the FAR, which requires reasonableness, allocability, comportment with standards promulgated by the Cost and Accounting Standards Board, if applicable or otherwise with generally accepted accounting principles and practices appropriate to the circumstances, and compliance with the terms of the contract or any limitations set forth in the FAR.[9] Consistent with the requirements of Public Law 100-679 some contractors and subcontractors must comply with Cost Accounting Standards, which will affect the way in which a contractor can charge general purpose equipment to a contract. In other words, the government does not want a contractor to be charged one way while other commercial contractors are charged another.

A large aerospace defense contractor directly charged the government for an item listed as a "data transfer unit." When the auditors asked the contractor what a data transfer unit item was, the response was somewhat elusive. After the auditors insisted that they take a look at it, the contractor acknowledged that it was a Lincoln Town Car. When asked what qualified it as a data transfer unit, the contractor replied that it was used to transfer the data its executives had from the airport to the nearby corporate headquarters. Since the purchase of this item was not allowed in the contract, the government disallowed the cost, and the contractor had to reimburse the government for this acquisition. Items must not be acquired without the required authority, and   property management systems should describe the acceptable methods or processes for acquiring property and assets.

2. Receipt and Identification of Government Property

This process associated with the receipt of government property requires a contractor to

> receive Government property (document the receipt), record the information necessary to meet the record requirements of paragraph (f)(1)(iii)(A)(1) through (5) of this clause, identify as Government owned in a manner appropriate to the type of property (*e.g.*, stamp, tag, mark, or other identification), and manage any discrepancies incident to shipment. [10]

(Identification of government will be discussed toward the end of this section since it is subsumed under receipt.)

The Federal Acquisition Regulation requires a contractor to describe its standard operating procedure for receiving property in its property management system, including the two methods by which government property is provided in a contract: government-furnished and contractor-acquired. Here is what the Government Property clause requires:

> (A) *Government-furnished property.* The Contractor shall furnish a written statement to the Property Administrator containing all relevant facts, such as cause or condition and a recommended course(s) of action, if overages, shortages, or damages and/or other discrepancies are discovered upon receipt of Government furnished property.

> (B) *Contractor-acquired property.* The Contractor shall take all actions necessary to adjust for overages, shortages, damage and/or other discrepancies discovered upon receipt, in shipment of Contractor-acquired property from a vendor or supplier, so as to ensure the proper allocability and allowability of associated costs. [1]

It is an industry leading practice for contractors to establish a process to receive property from internal and external supply sources such as vendors, suppliers, individuals, internal warehouses, etc. When these items are delivered they must be identified and recorded as being received. Any discrepancies incident to shipment is noted and corrections are made. It is at the point of receipt that the contractor becomes accountable and responsible for the property and stewardship is established. According to the Merriam-Webster dictionary stewardship is "the careful and responsible management of something entrusted to one's care."

There are a number of controls associated with the process of receiving. Contractors must include this process in their property management system and then make sure that their employees follow the specified procedure. This includes notifying the receiving department of assets that are due-in. Receiving documents and due-in data are provided for comparison with items physically received, as well as for proper posting to the accounting record. A physical delivery may be followed by an inspection of the property to make sure that it is what was ordered and to ascertain that there is no obvious or visible damage and the quantity of items agrees with the transportation document. Identification and resolution of discrepancies may occur at any time in this process. These actions may be accomplished either manually or through electronic methods such as bar code or RFID. The assets received are reconciled against due-in records. If a government supply source discrepancy is noted, then a "Supply Discrepancy Report" (SDR), SF 364, will be prepared by the appropriate government representative, unless contractor preparation of the form is contractually specified. Before acceptance of a shipment, the carrier's signature should be obtained to acknowledge any discrepancies. A "Transportation Discrepancy Report" (TDR), SF361, will be prepared by the appropriate government representative, unless contractor preparation of the form is contractually specified, to report discrepant conditions disclosed as a result of the inspection, when appropriate. Receiving documents, such as receiving reports, are prepared. They must clearly indicate the quantity and condition of the property at the time of receipt and any discrepancy must be noted, including overages, shortages, incorrect item(s), misdirected shipments, and/or damage disclosed during the receiving operation. The items are eventually released from the receiving area. After the receiving department prepares and processes appropriate documentation, the assets are generally released for quality or technical acceptance inspection, storage, or use as required. Upon completion of any required quality inspection, acceptance testing, and/or physical identification, the items are delivered to the appropriate storage area or stockroom, or they are released for use as authorized. Concurrent with the distribution of assets, the associated receiving notification is distributed, either manually or electronically. The distribution generally includes a copy that is retained in the Receiving Department files, one or more copies that go to purchasing, a copy that goes to the department to which the asset is delivered, and a copy to the Accounting Department to use as a voucher for invoices.

Subsidiary receiving areas in outlying locations are usually responsible for performing the same processes as the main receiving areas and should be required to submit necessary documentation to the main receiving activity. The contractor's written procedures need to ensure discussion of this action, i.e., the use of alternate or subsidiary receiving areas.

Some contractors maintain separate receiving areas that specialize in the receipt, inspection, identification, and release of government property for certain classes of property such as sensitive, classified, etc. Normally special tooling, special test equipment, or other items fabricated in-house do not go through the receiving process. Care should be taken to ensure that these items are recorded on the stewardship records upon completion of the fabrication in accordance with the contractor's established procedures.

Identification

Identification is the act of providing or ascribing a unique characteristic to an item for the purpose of distinguishing it from other items. It may be accomplished by placing a mark on the item, labels, stickers, atomic or chemical tracers, stamping, etching, engraving, bar codes, unique identifiers (UID), radio frequency identification (RFID), bio-metrics, and nano-technology. The choice will depend on a number of factors, including the type of property, type of surface, whether or not the identification is permanent or temporary, convenience, and cost. There are many excellent identification methods or best practices available. Contractors are encouraged to check the voluntary consensus standards and/or industry-leading practices and standards applicable to the type of property or asset requiring identification.

3. Records of Government Property

Establishing and keeping records is perhaps the most important requirement for effectively managing assets and property. Al Capone was a notorious gangster from Chicago during the depression who was eventually sent to the federal prison at Alcatraz, but not for murder, extortion, bootlegging, etc. He served time because he lied to the government on official records...his tax forms!

A record is permanent evidence of an event such as a financial transaction, proof of ownership, or the quantity of specific items in a warehouse. It preserves knowledge and can be used as evidence to settle accounts such as property disputes in a court of law. Contractors may use either paper or electronic records or a combination of both. The Government Property Clause requires a contractor to "create and maintain records of all government property accountable to the contract, including Government-furnished and Contractor-acquired property." Furthermore, it requires that a contractor "enable a complete, current, auditable record of all transactions." [12] The following information is required:

(1) The name, part number and description, manufacturer, model number, and National Stock Number (if needed for additional item identification tracking and/or disposition).

(2) Quantity received (or fabricated), issued, and balance-on-hand. (For example, shipping, receiving, transfer, inspection, issue documents, reports, etc.)

(3) Unit acquisition cost. [For example, the cost each, per ounce, or per gallon]

(4) Unique-item identifier or equivalent (if available and necessary for individual item tracking).

(5) Unit of measure. [For example: inch, foot, yard, centimeter, meter, ounce, pound, ton, gram, kilogram, etc.]

(6) Accountable contract number or equivalent code designation. [Note: an equivalent code may be used in lieu of the contract number but it must be auditable back to the contract.)

(7) Location. [Note: This is important because if an item cannot be located, then it cannot be used for the intended purposes and will have a detrimental effect upon the products and services being provided.][13]

(8) Disposition (current status of the property or asset);

(9) Posting reference and date of transaction;

(10) Date placed in service.

The government acknowledges that there may be situations when the standard method of establishing records is not adequate for the task. An allowance is made for a variation to the standard records requirement by the use of a Receipt and Issue System for Government Material but it must be approved by the Government Property Administrator. The Government Property Clause states that "the Contractor may maintain, in lieu of formal property records, a file of appropriately cross-referenced documents evidencing receipt, issue, and use of material that is issued for immediate consumption."[14] This permission to deviate from the standard procedure would be very useful in a situation where the contractor exhausts its supply of a critical item required for production or it is necessary to maintain the service being provided. For example, if a contractor fabricating armor plates for the Army's MRAP vehicle runs out of welding wire that is essential for production, the fabrication work would cease until the welding wire could be supplied. If the contractor had a Receipt and Issue System, the purchasing agent could contact a supplier of the welding wire and request an emergency shipment of that critical item, and the supplier would rush the material directly to the fabrication department where it is needed. Upon receipt the welding wire would be used for "immediate consumption." Although this action would circumvent the contractor's standard method for establishing records, the property management system would allow it because the shipping documents from the supplier would contain the information necessary to satisfy the record-keeping requirements for this emergency, including the name, part number, description, quantity received, unit of measure, etc.

Records must account for other contractor transactions, including physical inventories, reports, acquisitions, receipts, subcontract controls, relief of stewardship responsibility, utilization, consumption, maintenance, liability actions, property disposal, and closeout. The contractor also is required to keep records of its internal self-audits.

Section 4.703 of the Federal Acquisition Regulations requires that contractors make records available to the government "to satisfy contract negotiation, administration, and audit requirements of the Contracting Agencies and Comptroller General." The length of record retention varies depending on the event. It includes the following:

- After final payment is received: three years
- Accounts receivable invoices: four years
- Material, work order, or service order files, including purchase orders for material or services: four years
- Accounts payable records to support disbursement of funds for materials: four years
- Store requisitions for materials: two years
- Work orders for maintenance: four years
- Equipment records: four years
- Expendable property: four years
- Receiving and inspection report records: four years
- Purchase Order files for supplies, equipment, and material: four years.

Contractors should check their contract for specific requirements on establishing, maintaining, and retaining records. There are many voluntary consensus standards and/or industry-leading practices and standards available, including commercially available software that will facilitate this process.

4. Physical Inventory

A physical inventory is the process of going to a location and, using an orderly methodology and process, locating the physical property, verifying the count (i.e., how many are there), recording that information, comparing that information with the record, reconciling any discrepancies, and reporting the results. This process is described in the Government Property Clause as follows:

> Contractor shall periodically perform, record, and disclose physical inventory results. A final physical inventory shall be performed upon contract completion or termination. The Property Administrator may waive this final inventory requirement, depending on the circumstances (*e.g.*, overall reliability of the Contractor's system or the property is to be transferred to a follow-on contract).[15]

It is the contractor's responsibility to establish the process (i.e., the methods and methodologies) to accomplish this outcome in accordance with and using industry leading practices and voluntary consensus standards. Barron's describes this as the "actual count of items in inventory, as contrasted with accepting the values shown on accounting records."[16] The National Property Management Association states that it is "The determination of inventory quantity by actual count."[17] ASTM calls it "the verification of the existence, location and quantity of property items."[18]

Some of the methodologies that are available for performing physical inventories are sighting, tagging, or marking using a manual methodology. This may include the use of stickers, labels, tags, paint, marker, etching, etc., to identify and count items. Contractors may also use electronic readers for recording and reporting inventory, such as bar codes and scanners. Radio frequency identification (RFID) may use an active or passive method to collect the required information.

There are many types of physical inventories. The traditional wall-to-wall type is performed by many companies on an annual basis where everything within a defined space is counted "wall to wall." Closed stores are another type of physical inventory where the defined space is closed and restricted to the personnel who are counting. Retail and department stores typically perform an annual physical inventory after the Christmas-New Year's Holiday, which is a wall-to-wall inventory with the doors closed to the public. Open store inventory is not as restrictive and can be undertaken during normal business hours. Supermarket chains often employ people with hand held recording devices to check inventory while the store is open for business. One of the most widely used types is the cyclic inventory in which a segment is completed within a set period of time. For example, ten percent of the inventory could be completed monthly, twenty-five percent quarterly, or fifty percent semiannually. Sampling involves taking a representative sample of the population, and if statistically valid, then it is possible to predict the count of the inventory with extremely high levels of accuracy. When sampling is used on inventories consisting of high-, medium-, and low-value items, the statistical probability of including low-value items is very high. High-value items have a lower statistical probability of being selected. To compensate for this stratified or ABC sampling, where representative samples are selected from populations according to value or other criteria, can be included. Using this method a representative sample can be selected consisting of separate populations of low-, medium-, and high-value items, for example, from $0 to $100; over $100 to $1,000; and above $1,000. This will assure that low-, medium-, and high-value items are accurately counted. The setting of values is arbitrary and will depend upon the value of assets and property examined.

The contractor is responsible for establishing the type and frequency of physical inventory, which based on the following criteria: the established practices of the contractor; the type of government property; the use of government property; dollar value; whether or not the property is critical or sensitive; and the reliability of the contractor's property management system. The contractor must provide the written procedures describing the process and the outcomes.

ASTM E-2132 describes the key points of physical inventory planning. They include

- management and accountability;
- key results required;
- population (determination and selection);
- independence;
- data requirements;
- validation techniques;
- result validation (third-party independent validation);
- period (for performance);
- resources;
- information management;
- training and communication; and
- project plan..

Contractual and regulatory requirements stipulate that the results of physical inventories be reported to the Government Property Administrator. The minimum reporting requirements include prompt reporting as well as the identification of all discrepancies. This not only includes shortages but also the inventory that is above the recorded amounts (overages). These need to be posted to the record after reconciliation by the contractor. The Government Property Administrator does

EIGHT

not need to review or approve these adjustments before the contractor's posting to the record for two reasons: (1) It does not affect the actual count and (2) the issue of liability must still be addressed and resolved.

The profit margin on grocery store items is reported to be approximately one percent. That means that for every $100 of inventory sold, the store makes $1. At a very large grocery distribution and warehousing center in the Midwest the management reported the results of their physical inventory to be consistently above 99%, which is surprising because the inventory results are for low-dollar grocery items. In contrast, many Department of Defense contractors do not want to control so-called low-value government property. This low-value property was initially valued at $1,500 in 1995 but was raised to $5,000 in 1999. The reason for not wanting to control this property is that it is time consuming and expensive to manage. Another reason is that the government would be responsible for any loss, damage, destruction, or theft to this property. When the manager of the grocery distribution/ warehouse center was asked what was driving it to maintain such high inventory accuracy levels, his response was that maintaining high inventory accuracy levels gave it a competitive edge.

The Government Property Clause states that "A final physical inventory shall be performed upon contract completion or termination." However, the Government Property Administrator may "waive this final inventory requirement, depending upon the circumstances (e.g., the overall reliability of the contractor's system or the property to be transferred to a follow-on contract." If the contractor transfers property to a follow-on contract, the Property Administrator should check to make sure that authorization exists to transfer property and that record balances have been transferred and accountability moved to a follow-on contract.

In general, the personnel who perform the physical inventory should not be the ones who maintain the records or who have custody of the property, which should help to make the results less subjective and more accurate.

5. Subcontractor Control

Prime contractors are allowed to provide government property to subcontractors as long as doing so directly supports the effort on the prime contract. The subcontract must include language that is similar to the prime contract for controlling, protecting, preserving, maintaining, and disposing of the government property. This is often referred to as the "flow down" of contract terms and conditions. The subcontract should include the provisions for limitations for use, liability, title, sensitive property, disposal, etc. The Government Property Clause specifies that "The Contractor shall award subcontracts that clearly identify assets to be provided and shall ensure appropriate flow down of contract terms and conditions (*e.g.*, extent of liability for loss, damage, destruction or theft of Government property)"[19]

The prime contractor is responsible for monitoring the subcontractor's property management system for compliance with contract/subcontract requirements. The prime contractor may choose to audit the subcontractor or may ask the government to do so. The subcontractor control section of FAR 52.245-1 states "(B) The Contractor shall assure its subcontracts are properly administered and reviews are periodically performed to determine the adequacy of the subcontractor's property management system." If the government performs an audit of the subcontractor at the prime contractor's request, then the government may be entitled to an equitable adjustment.

It must be remembered that the government cannot audit a subcontractor without the written approval of the prime contractor because of privity of contract. (Privity of contract is the contractual relationship that exists between the parties to a contract that makes the contract legal.) The prime contractor normally has privity of contract with its subcontractors but the government does not. Unless the subcontract authorizes the government to conduct an audit, perform surveillance, or do other tasks, the government must ask the prime contractor for permission to do so. Failure to ask for permission may create legal problems for the government.

Alternate contractor locations are not considered subcontractor controlled. Since an alternate location is just another physical extension of the prime contractor, the government does not need the contractor's permission for an audit.

6. Reports

A report is a written record or summary providing a detailed account of an event. A contractual requirement mandates that contractors have a process for managing the generation/creation of reports. The Government Property Clause requires contractors to "have a process to create and provide reports of discrepancies; loss, damage, destruction, or theft; physical inventory results; audits and self-assessments; corrective actions; and other property related reports as directed by the Contracting Officer.[20] Under the receiving process, a contractor is required to manage any discrepancies incident to shipment and submit a report for government-furnished property. The contractor submits a Supply Discrepancy Report (SDR), formerly known as a "report of discrepancy" (ROD), using a Standard Form 364. To report a transportation discrepancy, a contractor should use a Standard Form 361.

The Government Property Clause requires a relatively detailed report for property that is lost, damaged, destroyed, or the result of theft. The clause requires the contractor to "investigate and promptly furnish a written narrative of all incidents of loss, damage, destruction, or theft to the property administrator as soon as the facts become known or when requested by the Government."[21] The report shall contain the following information:

(1)   Date of incident (if known).
(2)   The name, commercial description, manufacturer, model number, and National Stock Number (if applicable).
(3)   Quantity.
(4)   Unique Item Identifier (if available).
(5)   Accountable Contract number.
(6)   A statement indicating current or future need.
(7)   Acquisition cost, or if applicable, estimated scrap proceeds, estimated repair or replacement costs.
(8)   All known interests in commingled property of which the Government property is a part.
(9)   Cause and corrective action taken or to be taken to prevent recurrence.
(10) A statement that the Government will receive any reimbursement covering the loss, damage, destruction, or theft, in the event the Contractor was or will be reimbursed or compensated.
(11) Copies of all supporting documentation.
(12) Last known location.

(13) A statement that the property did or did not contain sensitive or hazardous material, and if so, that the appropriate agencies were notified.[22]

These data elements should be addressed in the contractor's property management system and procedures. The procedures must also address the party responsible as well as the specific time frame for reporting. A contractor should report the loss of small quantities of material or the destruction of low-value items that are not sensitive or critical and are not needed for replacement due to a bulk purchase on a quarterly or biannual basis. The exception would be for sensitive or classified property.

The contractor is also required to report government property in excess of the needs of the contract through the use of scrap lists or inventory schedules or electronically via the Plant Clearance Automated Reutilization Screening System (PCARSS). Along with the reports mentioned above, the Contracting Officer may direct the contractor to furnish other reports to satisfy contractual requirements.

The contractor's property management system shall ensure that reports of audits and self-assessments provide a process to ensure that the reporting of these findings has materiality or is significant. Timely reporting needs to be defined in the contractor's property management system.

7. Relief of Stewardship Responsibility

In general, contractors are not held liable for loss, damage, destruction, or theft of government property under cost reimbursement, time and material, labor hour, and negotiated fixed-price contracts for which price is not based upon an exception at FAR 15.403-1. However, contractors are liable under fixed-price contracts for which there is an exception at FAR 15.403-1. The two forms of liability are (1) the limited risk of loss and (2) the full risk of loss.

If the contractor has a fixed-price contract with FAR 52.245-1 alternate I then "the contractor assumes the risk of and shall be responsible for any loss, damage, destruction, or theft of Government Property upon its delivery to the contractor as Government-furnished property.[23]" The exception to the full risk of loss provision is "fair wear and tear" or when the property has served its useful life and has simply worn out. Contractor liability was decided in *Dynalectron Corp. v. U. S.*, ASBCA No. 29,831; 85-3 BCA ¶ 18,320 (July 31, 1985). According to an opinion by Administrative Judge Freeman, Dynalectron destroyed three segments of exposed government motion picture film while it was being developed under an audio-visual production and services contract. The destruction of two segments was attributed to operator negligence, and faulty equipment destroyed the third. Since Dynalectron's contract contained the full risk of loss provision, the court ruled that it was liable. The court also decided that the government was owed the intrinsic value of the property or the value of the film to the owner. Since the destroyed film was taken at an airbase in Korea, the contractor was required to pay the costs associated with retaking the destroyed segments in Korea.[24] This court case is important because it helped to determine the value of the property to the owner. Records of government property normally list the acquisition cost of an asset, which might lead one to believe that the acquisition cost is owed the government when property is lost, damaged, destroyed, or the result of theft, but that is not the case. Intrinsic value could result in the contractor's being assessed the replacement value where the government has current or future needs, or the contractor could be responsible for any repairs to damaged property. Intrinsic value could also mean the salvage or scrap value for damaged property if the government has no need for it.

The limited risk of loss provision is applied to contractors with cost-reimbursement, time and material, labor hour, or non-competitive fixed-price contracts. FAR Section 45.107, Contract clauses, requires a contracting officer to insert the appropriate government property clause (limited risk or full risk) in accordance with the provisions of this section. Carefully read your contract before deciding which risk is applicable to the property in question.

When the limited risk of loss provision is included in a contract, the contractor is liable when the risk is covered by insurance. Since the government is a self-insurer, the cost of insurance is normally not an allowable expense, although sometimes it is., In other situations insurance may cover the loss, damage, destruction, or theft of government property. This may happen, for example, when the owner of an insured vehicle (car, truck, motorcycle) runs into and damages or destroys government property. The contractor is liable when the loss, damage, destruction, or theft is due to willful misconduct or lack of good faith on the part of the contractor's managerial personnel. If the contractor's property management system is not in compliance with contract terms and conditions and the contractor's managerial personnel fail to adequately correct the problems, then the government may withdraw the its assumption of risk. If the loss were to occur after the withdrawal of the assumption of risk, then the contractor would be liable.

The Fairchild Hiller Corporation had an inspect and repair as necessary (IRAN) contract for the stripping, washing, and cleaning of C-130 aircraft. The contract stipulated that the contractor could only use a prescribed soapy water solution to clean the aircraft. One of the contractor's employees had difficulty cleaning one of the aircraft's wheel wells and decided to add methylethyl-ketone (MEK) to the soapy water and try again. MEK is a highly flammable cleaning fluid with a flash point of 140° F. After spraying the solution on the wheel well he took a break, and when he returned he brought a quartz-iodine floor light to inspect his work. A short circuit in the quartz light ignited the volatile mixture, destroying the aircraft. The contractor requested relief from liability for damaging the aircraft, but the contracting officer denied this request because the contractor did not comply with the terms and conditions of the contract related to washing and cleaning the aircraft. Cited was the contractor's inappropriate use of MEK and a faulty portable light not authorized for use in a volatile environment.

The case went to court as the *Fairchild Hiller Corp. v. U. S.*, ASBCA No. 14387 (1971). The contractor argued that it had been relieved of liability for other accidents in the past and that it should also be relieved in this instance. The contracting officer found that the contractor's managerial personnel had shown a lack of good faith and willful misconduct in regard to the program for aircraft maintenance and administration. Furthermore, the contracting officer said that a warning was given to the contractor after a similar accident. The contractor's management personnel had failed to maintain proper training and supervision of employees and also failed to comply with the instructions of authorized government representatives regarding the proper procedures for controlling, using, and storing hazardous solvents. The board decided that the government could not prove that the contractor was liable for willful misconduct and lack of good faith on the part of managerial personnel. The board said that "there is no evidence that they subordinated their responsibility for safety to other goals to such an extent that one could find willful misconduct or lack of good faith in regard to safety concerns...willful misconduct or lack of good faith of top management are not proven."[25] This case serves as the benchmark for solving liability claims involving the limited risk of loss provision of a contract when government property is involved.

There are other situations where contractors may be relieved of stewardship responsibility. The Government Property Clause mentions that contractors may be relieved when government property is

> Consumed or expended, reasonably and properly, or otherwise accounted for, in the performance of the contract, including reasonable inventory adjustments of material as determined by the Property Administrator; or a Property Administrator granted relief of responsibility for loss, damage, destruction or theft of Government property; (Note: read the section on consumption) (B) Delivered or shipped from the Contractor's plant, under Government instructions, except when shipment is to a subcontractor or other location of the Contractor; or (C) Disposed of in accordance with paragraphs (j) and (k) of this clause.[26]

8. Utilizing Government Property—Consumption, Movement, and Storage

It is an industry leading practice for contractors to establish and maintain procedures and processes to insure that government property be used only for purposes authorized in the contract and that the degree of utilization justifies retention. Equipment, real property, special tooling, and special test equipment is utilized; material is consumed and not utilized (see consumption below). The Government Property clause states that:

> (A) The Contractor shall utilize, consume, move, and store Government Property only as authorized under this contract. The Contractor shall promptly disclose and report Government Property in its possession that is excess to contract performance.[27]

Contractual authorization to use Government Property is normally specified in the contract under which it is accountable. Contractors cannot use this property for any other purpose, including commercial contracts or even other government contracts without the express written approval of the contracting officer. Contractors wishing to use such property for government or commercial purposes must obtain written approval prior to use from the contracting officer having cognizance over the property. In the event the contractor uses government property without authorization, the contractor may be subject to fines, imprisonment, or both under 18 U.S.C. 641.

Government property that has no current usage or activity should be periodically reviewed to initiate disposal action or to justify continued retention. This process must be responsible for contract modifications, completion, and terminations, as well as reduced production rates, reduced demand rates, and engineering changes.

If government property will be used for purposes not originally authorized in the contract, the contractor's property management system must provide a basis for determining and allocating rental charges to comply with the requirements of the Uses and Charges Clause at FAR 52.245-9. The contracting officer is responsible for collecting any rent due from the contractor in accordance with this clause.

The contractor is prohibited from modifying, cannibalizing, or making alterations to any government property unless it is permitted in the contract.

The FAR prohibits contractors from commingling government property with property that is not owned by the government. It states that

> (B) Unless otherwise authorized in this contract or by the Property
>
> Administrator the Contractor shall not commingle Government property with property not owned by the Government.[28]

Commingling is a process where material that is used on multiple projects is stored in a common area and loses its identity. The government wants the contractor to be able to readily distinguish its property from the property of the contractor. Government material that is stored in a common area is co-located (not commingled) as long as it can be immediately identified as government property.

Consumption

Consumption is the process of using, expending, attaching, or incorporating material into an item being produced under a contract. Contractors may be relieved of stewardship responsibility if an item is properly consumed. Consumption consists of four stages

(1) Issuing the material in the proper amount required by the contract;
(2) Using the material for the intended purposes;
(3) Returning any unused material to stock with the appropriate annotation to the record;
(4) Returning parts removed from repair, rework, testing, or cannibalization.

Unreasonable consumption occurs when the amount of material used exceeds what would be considered normal for the work being done. If a contractor overconsumes, then it will need to procure more material to cover the requirements specified in the contract. The government is not responsible for reimbursing the contractor for unreasonable costs incurred during the performance of a contract. FAR 31.201-3 provides information on determining the reasonableness of a cost, and it is the contractor's responsibility to prove that its costs are reasonable. Unreasonable consumption is not to be handled in the same way as government property in accordance with the risk of loss provisions in the contract (lost, damaged, destroyed, or stolen). Contracting Officers may disallow any excess costs associated with overconsumption in accordance with FAR Part 31, Cost Principles. What this means is that the contractor is responsible for all costs that would be required to replenish the overconsumed material.

Movement

Movement is another process that is subsumed under utilization, and is the physical relocation of property. It may consist of local movement, where items are transported from one location to another with the proper authorization and documentation. While property may be moved off-site, there must be an authorization to do so, along with the proper documentation. The user responsibilities and limitations on use must be clearly stated. The maintenance and/or repair responsibility must be assumed by the user; the property records must be annotated; and there must be periodic reviews and re-approval for this process.

The contractor's property management system must provide sufficient procedures for packaging, cradling, and handling of government property during movement. The procedures should include environmental protection against heat, cold, moisture, contaminants, electro-static discharge, infestation, shock, etc. Personnel assigned the responsibility for movement should be qualified to handle the equipment necessary to accomplish the move (forklift trucks, overhead cranes, hoists, tractor-trailers, etc.).

Records must include the local/off-site change of location, change in custodianship, the time frame for such recording, and the documentation of the move. Property movement records may be electronic or paper and may consist of move tickets, travelers, transfer and accountability forms, hand receipts, or electronic or automated property passes. Unless otherwise specified, the responsibility for movement remains with the contractor/shipper of the property until it is safely received at the destination.

Storage

Storage is a process subsumed under the Government Property Clause for utilization. It refers to the act of placing an item into a specific location or space such as a storage yard, warehouse, building, room, closet, shelf, bin, etc. Storage can be temporary such as when an item is placed in a staging area awaiting the next phase of processing or assembly. Or it can also be long term, for example, when crude oil is placed in the strategic petroleum reserve where it will remain until the President of the United States declares a national emergency.

The contractor must include procedures in its property management system for proper storage of government property, including physical security and protection for the property. When required, the items must be properly packaged and preserved. Access to items in storage must be limited to authorized personnel, and if sensitive or classified property is involved, then the contractor must include procedures that address the requirements for additional physical security and protection. Special controls and storage may be necessary for items susceptible to contamination, humidity, corrosion, temperature (heat and cold), vibration, shock, electrostatic discharge, aging, etc.

A contractor must comply with all statutory, regulatory, and contractual requirements, including those that could have an impact on the environment (i.e., the Hazardous Materials Transportation Act, the Resource Conservation and Recovery Act, the Comprehensive Environmental Response Compensation and Liability Act, and the Federal Facility Compliance Act). The contractor must read and understand the contract in order to be compliant these and other requirements.

9. Maintenance

Maintenance is the process of providing the amount of care necessary to obtain the most useful service life from property and equipment. It means taking care of property and assets as well as providing for, repairing, keeping in an existing state, calibrating, or preserving from failure or decline. The Government Property Clause requires a contractor to have a process to maintain all accountable government property:

> The Contractor's maintenance program shall enable the identification, disclosure, and performance of normal and routine preventative maintenance and repair. The Contractor shall disclose and report to the Property Administrator the need for replacement and/or capital rehabilitation.[29]

In order to keep the property in the best possible condition and to maximize its service life, the contractor should follow the manufacturer's recommended maintenance procedures and use established practices and standards that include voluntary consensus standards and industry leading practices and standards. A good example is the maintenance manual that manufacturers include with cars and trucks. Almost anything purchased today has recommended maintenance procedures.

It is important to distinguish between general maintenance and major capital-type rehabilitation. The first type, general or routine maintenance, is the day-to-day maintenance that is required for efficient and economical operation of property and equipment. It includes inspecting, cleaning, adjusting, calibrating, lubricating, changing filters, parts replacement, and performing the manufacturer's recommended maintenance procedures according to a schedule. Preventive maintenance is part of the general maintenance requirement; it is performed on a regularly scheduled basis to prevent the occurrence of defects and to detect and correct minor defects before they result in serious consequences. General and/ or preventive maintenance is to be performed by the contractor as part of its standard operating procedure. The costs associated with this program are already included in the contract. The government is not required to pay any additional costs for this type of maintenance.

The second type of maintenance is major or capital-type rehabilitation. This maintenance exceeds the general and preventative requirements stated in the contract and the contractor's property management system (procedures). Because this type of maintenance exceeds the standard requirements, it becomes the financial responsibility of the government. Prior to performing any major maintenance or capital-type rehabilitation, the contractor is required to obtain the advance written approval of the Contracting Officer. Failure to do so may result in the rejection of any claims for reimbursement or consideration by the government.

10. Property Closeout and Disposal

There are a number of actions that must be completed prior to closing out a contract. Contractors must perform a final physical inventory, make sure that all liability actions have been resolved, and dispose of government property in accordance with contract requirements and/or directions of the plant clearance officer, including demilitarization, if required. Demilitarization is the process of removing the defensive or offensive capabilities of a military item.

Property Disposal

Disposal includes compliance with environmental laws and the proper handling of sensitive and classified property. The basis for disposing of government property is the Federal Property and

Administrative Services Act of 1949, as amended (P.L. 81-152). This law created and established the General Services Administration (GSA) as the government-wide property manager.

The Government Property Clause sets forth the requirements that a contractor is required to follow under are driven by the Federal Property and Administrative Services Act. A contractor must list the property to be disposed of on a standard form SF 1428 electronically using the Plant Clearance Automated Reutilization Screening System (PCARSS). This excerpt from the FAR describes what the government requires for contract property closeout:

> (1)(x) *Property Closeout..* The Contractor shall promptly perform and report to the property administrator contract property closeout, to include reporting, investigating and securing closure of all loss, damage, destruction, or theft cases; physically inventorying all property upon termination or completion of this contract; and disposing of items at the time they are determined to be excess to contractual needs.
>
> (2) The Contractor shall establish and maintain Government accounting source data, as may be required by this contract, particularly in the areas of recognition of acquisitions and dispositions of material and equipment.
>
> (3) The Contractor shall establish and maintain procedures necessary to assess its property management system effectiveness, and shall perform periodic internal reviews and audits. Significant findings and/ or results of such reviews and audits pertaining to Government property shall be made available to the Property Administrator.[30]

SUMMARY

Any firm or organization needs to be able to use its assets and property in the most efficient and cost- effective way to provide products and services to its customers. In order to do this well an organization or entitiy needs to have a property management system with good procedures. This chapter provides a fundamental outline for these essential processes. It is recommended that contractors read and understand their contractual requirements for property and asset management.

The Federal Government requires contractors to have a property management system that includes ten key outcomes or processes. They are:

1. Acquisition;
2. Receipt (Identify);
3. Records;
4. Physical Inventory;
5. Subcontractor Control;
6. Reports;
7. Relief of Stewardship Responsibility;
8. Utilizing Property (Consumption, Movement, and Storage);
9. Maintenance; and
10. Property Closeout (Disposal).

These processes are also found in organizations that do not do business with the federal government. The ten processes are frequently described as the "life cycle" of government property because they follow an orderly progression of events that mimic the birth, life, and conclusion of a project or program.

The government describes the basic components of this system in the Government Property Clause at FAR 52.245-1. In addition, this system must include existing voluntary consensus standards and/or industry leading practices and standards, and there are many that can be used. Together they contribute to the use of best practices by the contractor. This gives contractors greater flexibility in designing a system that will meet their needs based on a contractor's size, product line, and personnel.

In the next chapter, we discuss the use of earned value management systems by government contractors as a project management tool to reduce risks and improve project performance results.

ENDNOTES

1   FAR 1.101.
2   FAR 52.245-1(b).
3   Gulati, Ramesh and Smith, Ricky. *Maintenance and Reliability Best Practices*. New York: Industrial Press, 2009.
4   Official website of the Olympic Movement (www.olympic.org) 2009.
5   FAR 52.245-1(f)(i).

6   FAR 52.245-1(f)(1)(i).

7   FAR 52.245-1.

8   FAR 52.245-1.

9   FAR 31.201-2.

10   FAR 52.245-1(f)(1)(ii).

11   FAR 52.245-1(f)(2)(A), (B).

12   FAR 52.245-1(f)(1)(iii)(A).

13   FAR 52.245-1(f)(1)(iii)(A).

14   FAR 52.245-1(f)(1)(iii)(B).

15   FAR 52.245-1(f)(1)(iv).

16   Friedman, J.P. Barron's Dictionary of Business Terms, 2nd ed. (Barron's, 1995).

17   NPMA Standard Property Book, 1st ed. (1999).

18   ASTM E2132-01, Practice for Physical Inventory of Durable Moveable Property (September 2004).

19   FAR 52.245-1(f)(1) (v)(A).

20   FAR 52.245-1(f)(1)(vi).

21   FAR 52.245-1.

22   FAR 52.245-1(f)(1)(vi)(B).

23   FAR 52.245-1.

24   Wehrle-Einhorn, Robert J. Selected Cases in Government Contract Law. Air Force Institute of Technology School of Systems and Logistics, 1990.

25   Ibid.

26   FAR 52.245-1(f)(1)(i)(A).

27   FAR 52.245-1.

28   FAR 52.245-1(f)(1)(viii).

29   FAR 52.245-1(f)(1)(ix).

30   FAR 52.245-1(f)(1)(x)—(3).

CHAPTER

9

EARNED VALUE MANAGEMENT SYSTEMS (EVMS)

INTRODUCTION

This chapter provides information pertaining to project planning, scheduling, and the earned value management system (EVMS) required by the U.S. Department of Defense's (DOD) Instruction 5000.2 and the Defense Acquisition Guidebook. It should be helpful to project managers, program managers, technical representatives, project control managers, contract managers, subcontract managers, and others involved in project management.

EARNED VALUE MANAGEMENT (EVM)

Earned value management (EVM) is now a hot topic within the U.S. Department of Defense (DOD) and defense industry for a couple of reasons. First, the Office of Management and Budget (OMB) has added the requirement for EVM to the *Federal Acquisition Regulation.* Second, the Department of Defense (DOD) has recently made some relatively significant changes to its policy on this key project management process that has been used in the defense acquisition process for more than 35 years.

EVM is a widely accepted industry best practice for project management used across the DOD, the federal government, and the commercial sector. A common operational definition of EVM is "the use of an integrated management system that coordinates work scope, schedule, and cost goals and objectively measures progress toward these goals." EVM replaces the old term Cost/Schedule Control Systems Criteria (C/SCSC) used since the 1960's.

On March 7, 2005, the defense acquisition executive signed a memorandum approving revisions to the department's EVM policy. The policy has been modified to provide consistency in application across DOD programs and to better manage programs through improvements in DOD and industry practices.

NEW APPLICATION THRESHOLDS FOR EVM

EVM compliance is required on cost or incentive contracts, subcontracts, intra-government work agreements, and other agreements valued at $20 million and above . An EVM system that has been formally validated and accepted by the cognizant contracting officer is required on cost or incentive contracts, subcontracts, intra-government work agreements, and other agreements valued at $50 million and above.

CONTRACT IMPLEMENTATION OF EVM

The changes to DOD's EVM policy are required to be implemented on applicable contracts that are awarded based on solicitations or requests for proposal valued at $20 million and above issued on or after April 6, 2005, using Defense Federal Acquisition Regulation Supplement (DFARS) clauses 252.242-7005 and 252.252-7006. The revised policy has been incorporated into DOD Instruction 5000.2 and the Defense Acquisition Guidebook. And the changes have been incorporated into the EVMIG, the principal reference for detailed implementation guidance, which is available on the Defense Contract Management Agency (DCMA) Web site at http://guidebook.dcma.mil/79/guidebook_process.htm.

UNDERSTANDING THE EARNED VALUE MANAGEMENT SYSTEM (EVMS)

To understand how an earned value management system (EVMS) works you must be familiar with the ten basic project management building blocks of (1) organizing; (2) authorizing; (3) scheduling; (4) budgeting; (5) cost accumulation; (6) performance measurement; (7) variance analysis; (8) changes management; (9) internal audit; (10) performance formulae, analysis, DoD reviews, and reports.

Organizing Work

Organizing the work is the initial task of project management. The operations organization is made up of those individuals responsible for the various tasks required by the contract statement of work (SOW), or performance work statement (PWS).

Work Breakdown Structure (WBS)

The WBS provides the framework for organizing the contract effort. It is an indentured listing of all of the products (e.g., hardware, software, services, and data) to be furnished by the seller. It is used as the basis for all contract planning, scheduling, and budgeting; cost accumulation; and performance reporting throughout the entire period of project performance.

Integrated Project Team (IPT)

The integrated project team structure reflects the organization required to support the project. The project manager is responsible for ensuring the cost, schedule, and technical management of the project. The project manager utilizes the functional groups to accomplish the work by assigning responsibility to appropriate managers.

Responsibility Assignment Matrix (RAM)

The RAM ties the work required by the WBS elements to the organization responsible for accomplishing the assigned tasks. The intersection of the WBS with the integrated project team structure identifies the control account. The RAM identifies the organization and the individual responsible for the work, which is then tracked to a control account.

Authorizing Work

All work within a project should be described and authorized through a contractor's work authorization system. Work authorization ensures that performing organizations are specifically informed regarding their work scope, schedule for performance, budget, and charge number(s) for the work assigned to them.

Work authorization is a formal process that can consist of various levels. Each level of authorization is agreed upon by the parties involved, leaving no question as to what is required.

The document involved in work authorization should be maintained in a current status throughout the life cycle of the contract as revisions take place.

Customer Authorization

Customer authorization is comprised of the basic contract, contract change notices, and engineering change notices.

Internal Authorization

Internal authorization comprises these steps:

- Upon receipt of a contract (or change notice), the contracts management team provides the project manager authorization to perform the contract work in the form of a project authorization notice (PAN) or equivalent document.
- The project manager prepares a document authorizing the assigned functional manager to perform the work. This authorization is a contract between the functional manager and the project manager.

Figure 9-1 shows the typical contractor work authorization flow.

Figure 9-1
Work Authorization Documentation Flow

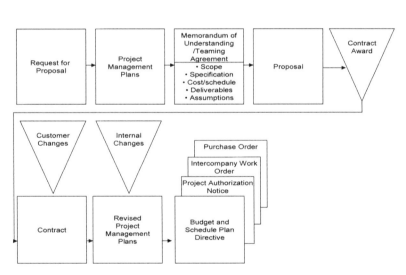

Scheduling Work

Scheduling and budgeting are interrelated and iterative. In order to develop a time-phased budget plan, the schedule must be prepared first. Scheduling is the process of integrating activities and resources into a meaningful arrangement, depicting the timing of the critical activities that will satisfy the customer's requirements.

Project Scheduling

Project scheduling is a logical time-phasing of the activities necessary to accomplish the entire project scope. The most important tool for cost and schedule, it includes the following:

- Planning
- Tracking
- Analysis of variances
- Reporting of project performance

Each activity in the network is characterized by scope, logical relationships, duration, and resources.

Figure 9-2 shows the steps required to build a project schedule.

Figure 9-2
Building Project Schedule

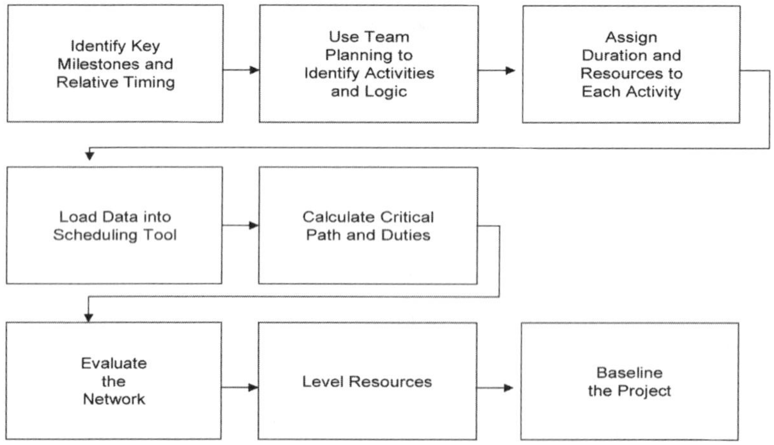

Scheduling Definitions

- **Milestone** An event of particular significance that has no duration.
- **Activity** Something that occurs over time; work that must be accomplished, also referred to as a "task."
- **Sequential** Activities that are performed in sequence or one after another.
- **Concurrent/Parallel** Two or more activities that are performed at the same time or that overlap.

Scheduling Terms

- **Finish-to-Start** The predecessor activity must be completed before the successor activity can begin.

- **Start-to-Start** The predecessor activity must begin before the successor activity can begin.

- **Finish-to-Finish** The predecessor activity must end before the successor activity can end.

- **Lag** Any schedule time delay between two tasks; lags can be positive or negative.
- **Critical Path** Longest continuous sequence of tasks through the network, given the underlying relationships that will affect the project end-date.
- **Float** Difference between the time available (when tasks can start/finish) and the time necessary (when tasks must start/finish).

Schedule Outputs

The three basic scheduling outputs are

- network diagram,
- Gantt chart, and
- resource histogram.

Once the project schedule is complete, the cost/schedule performance baseline is established. Figure 9-3 shows the steps required to establish the baseline and track and analyze performance on the project.

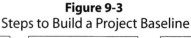

Figure 9-3
Steps to Build a Project Baseline

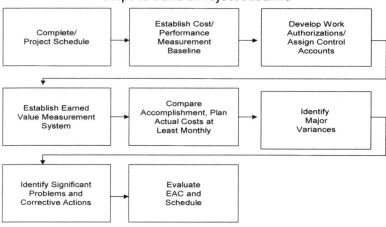

Figure 9-4
– A Typical Performance Measurement System

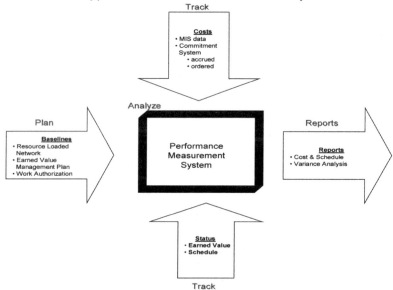

Budgeting Work

Budgeting is the process of distributing budgets to individual work segments. The following top-down illustration (Figure 9-5) provides an overview of the relationships.

Figure 9-5
Typical Budget Relationships

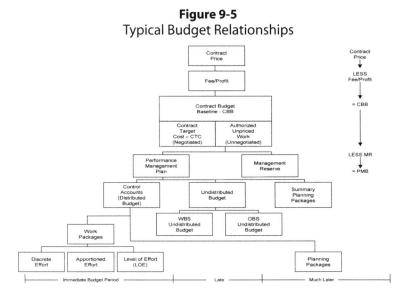

Total Allocated Budget (TAB)

The TAB is the sum of all budgets allocated to the contract. It is the same as the contract budget base (CBB) unless an over target baseline (OTB) has been established. (See *Changes* for an explanation of OTB.)

Contract Budget Base (CBB)

The CBB is the sum of the contract target cost (CTC) plus the estimated cost of any authorized unpriced (not yet negotiated) work. It is made up of the performance measurement baseline and management reserve.

Performance Measurement Baseline (PMB)

The PMB is the time-phased budget plan against which contract performance is measured. It is composed of the budgets assigned to control accounts and undistributed budget. It equals the TAB minus management reserve.

Management Reserve (MR)

The management reserve is a budget amount that is set aside to provide for unforeseen, within-contract scope requirements.

Control Account (CA)

The control account is the focal point for planning, monitoring, and controlling project work as it represents the work within a single WBS element, and is the responsibility of a single organizational unit.

Virtually all aspects of the performance management system come together at the control account level, including budgets, schedules, work assignments, cost collection, progress assessment, problem identification, corrective actions, and estimate at completion (EAC) development. Day-to-day management is performed at the control account level.

The level selected for the establishment of a control account must be carefully considered to ensure that work is properly distributed into manageable units with responsibilities clearly delineated.

Undistributed Budget (UB)

The undistributed budget is the budget that is applicable to a specific contract effort, but that has not yet been distributed to the WBS elements. Undistributed budget is intended to serve only as a temporary holding account until the budget is properly distributed

Summary Planning Packages

Summary planning packages are used to plan time-phased budgets for far-term work that cannot practically be planned in full detail.

Work Packages

A work package is a detailed job that is established by the functional manager for accomplishing work within a control account.

A work package has these characteristics:

- Represents units of work (activities or tasks) at the levels where the work is performed.
- Is clearly distinct from all other work packages, and is the responsibility of a single organizational element.
- Has scheduled start and completion dates (with interim milestones, if applicable) that are representative of physical task accomplishment.

- Has a budget or assigned value expressed in terms of dollars, labor hours, or other measurable units.
- Has a duration that is relatively short, unless it is subdivided by discrete milestones to permit objective measurement of work performed.
- Has a schedule that is integrated with all other activities occurring on the project.
- Has a unique warned value technique, either discrete, apportioned effort, or level of effort (LOE).

Planning Package

If a control account cannot be subdivided into fully detailed work packages, the far-term effort is identified in larger planning packages for budgeting and scheduling purposes. The budget for the planning package is identified according to the work for which it is intended, is time-phased, and should have controls that prevent its use in the performance of other work. Eventually, all work in planning packages will be planned to the appropriate level of detail in work packages.

Cost Accumulation

Cost accumulation is the process of recording and assembling the actual costs for a project. The lowest level of accumulation is the work package, although many large projects accumulate costs at the control account level. These actual costs plus accruals are called actual cost of work performed (ACWP).

Direct Cost Elements

Within the control account or a work package (depending upon the level of cost accumulation), there are direct cost elements. Direct cost elements are

- Direct Labor.– Timekeeping/cost collection for labor costs uses a labor distribution/accumulation system. The MIS reports biweekly expenditure data based on labor charges against control accounts or work packages.
- Other Direct Costs (ODCs).– ODCs include charges for items such as travel and per diem, service centers, and purchased services.
- Materials
  - Subcontracts

Indirect Cost Elements

Indirect cost elements consist of multiple sub-elements:

- *Overhead (OH) and Fringe.*–Overhead and fringe costs, accumulated in pools for biweekly distribution to projects, are allocated to each charge number in each organization based on the individual organization's overhead and fringe rates.
- *General and Administrative (G&A).*–These indirect costs also are accumulated in pools for biweekly distribution to project charge numbers.

Performance Measurement

Performance measurement for functional managers, project control managers, and others consists of evaluating work packages status calculated at the work package level. A comparison of the planned value (budgeted cost for work scheduled (BCWS) to earned value (budgeted cost for work performed (BCWP) is made to obtain the schedule variance. A comparison of the BCWP to the actual costs (ACWP) is made to obtain the cost variance. Performance measurement provides a basis for management decisions by the project manager, the organization's management and, in some cases, the customer.

Performance measurement provides:

- Work progress status
- relationship of planned cost and actual cost to actual accomplishment
- valid, timely, auditable data
- basis for EAC.

Elements required to measure project progress and status are:

- Work package schedule status
- BCWS or the planned expenditure
- BCWP or earned value
- ACWP or MIS costs and accruals.

Control account/work packages:

- Measurable work and related event status form the basis for determining progress for BCWP calculations. BCWP measurements at summary WBS levels result from accumulating BCWP upward through the control account from the work package levels.

- Within each control account, the inclusion of LOE is kept to a minimum to prevent distortion of the total BCWP. Calculation methods used for measuring work package performance are:
  - Short work packages (2 months or less) may use the measured effort or formula method, e.g., 0-100%, where a status can be applied each month.
  - Longer work packages (over 2 months) should have milestones assigned. The milestones are then used monthly for the life cycle of the work package.
  - In manufacturing, work packages may use the earned standards or equivalent units method to measure performance based on the manufacturing work measurement system output.
  - Effort that can be measured in direct proportion to other discrete work may be measured as apportioned effort work packages. Apportioned effort is used primarily in manufacturing.
  - Sustained efforts are planned using the LOE earned value method. The earned value for LOE work packages is equal to the time-phased plan (BCWS).
- The measurement method used depends on an analysis of the work to be performed in the work package. Whichever method is selected for planning, (BCWS) must also be used for determining progress (BCWP).

Estimate to Complete (ETC) Preparation

To develop an ETC, the CAM must consider and analyze:

- Cumulative ACWP/ordered commitments
- schedule status
- BCWP to date
- remaining control account scope of work
- previous ETC
- historical data
- required resources by type
- projected cost and schedule efficiency
- future actions
- approved contract changes.

The functional managers or control account managers (CAM) prepare the ETC as required by the project manager.

EAC Preparation. The ETC is then summarized to all necessary reporting levels, added to the ACWP and commitments, and reported to corporate management and the customer, as appropriate.

A bottom-up EAC should be prepared quarterly for all contracts at an organization.

The EAC is the estimated cost at the end of a project. It is the cost of what has been accomplished and the estimated cost of the remaining work. This graph in Figure 9-6 illustrates the two primary components of the EAC.

Figure 9-6

Primary EAC Components

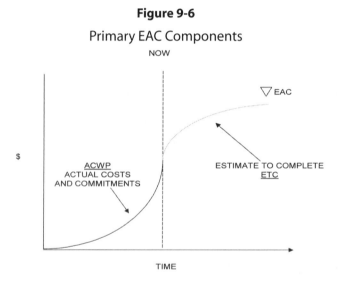

Figure 9-7, below, shows the components of the EAC.

Figure 9-7
Components of EAC

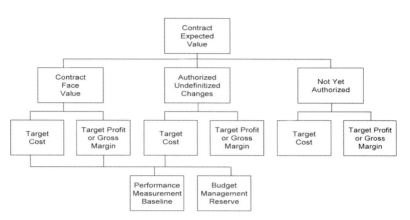

Revenues at Completion

Revenues at completion are the total revenues anticipated on a contract at the completion of the project. Revenues at completion are composed of the EAC and EAC profit.

Estimate at Completion (EAC)

EAC is the cost of work performed to date plus the estimated cost of all remaining work on a project. The EAC is made up of five components: ACWP, accruals, ordered commitments, ETC, and hard reserves.

EAC Profit

EAC profit is the profit expected to be achieved at the completion of a project.

Actual Cost of Work Performed (ACWP)

ACWP is the cost of work performed to date plus accruals.

Accruals

Accruals are costs for goods or services received by an organization, but not yet paid.

Ordered Commitments

Ordered commitments are costs for goods or services on order where the work has not yet been performed.

Estimate to Complete (ETC)

ETC is the estimated cost of the remaining work on the project.

Hard Reserves

Hard reserves are reserves associated with the EAC and cover the potential cost of risks to be mitigated on a project. The hard reserves equal the sum of the mitigation costs plus the sum of the residual risk remaining.

Variance Analysis

If performance measurement produces schedule or cost variances in excess of pre-established thresholds, the cause must be determined. The functional managers or CAM is responsible for the analysis of the control account and recognizing trends that indicate potential future problems.

Variance Calculations

There are three types of variances: schedule variances, cost variances, and variances of completion (VACs). They are calculated as follows:

$$SV = BCWP - BCWS$$
$$CV = BCWP - ACWP$$
$$VAC = BAC - EAC$$

Variance Thresholds

Variance analysis is required when one or more of the variances exceed the threshold established for the project. Variance thresholds are defined by a percentage, a dollar amount, or a combination of the two. The latter method is usually more appropriate since it eliminates very small variances from the analysis requirement. The thresholds are generally established by the Sector, but may be provided by the customer.

Variance Analysis Operation

■ The Variance Analysis Reports (VARs) provide current period, cumulative, and at-completion data. CAMs provide VARs for control accounts that have a schedule variance, cost variance, or VAC that exceeds the established thresholds.

■ The CAM completes the VAR by providing a description of the cause of the variance, its impact on the control account and other elements of the project, the corrective action to be taken, and any follow-up on previous actions taken.

■ The VAR is submitted through the appropriate project channels for approval.

■ The project manager uses the control account VARs to report project status to upper management.

■ The Project Manager has a continuing responsibility for monitoring corrective actions.

■ Periodic, formal project reviews, scheduling meetings, and staff meetings serve as forums for variance trend analysis and corrective action monitoring.

Changes

When an authorized change is received, all affected work authorization, budget planning, and scheduling documents should be updated in a timely manner to reflect the change.

Revision Types

The three types of planning revisions are

■ *Internal Replanning.* This is the replanning that is undertaken within the scope, schedule, and budget constraints of the current contract. It is often associated with the use of management reserve.

■ *External Replanning.* These are contract changes directed and authorized by the customer.

■ *Over Target Replanning.* This type of replanning results in planning a new PMB that is above the CBB. It results in a plan to overrun the contract value.

Replanning Rules

Four replanning rules are:

- Retroactive changes to BCWS, BCWP, or ACWP already incurred are strictly prohibited, except to correct accounting errors.
- Closed work packages or control accounts may not be re-opened.
- Work scope may not be transferred from one control account to another without the associated budget transfer.
- Work packages that are open (in process) may not be re-planned.

Internal Audit/Verification

The functional manager or CAMs are the most significant contributors to the successful operation of the earned value management system and to the successful completion of any subsequent audits or customer reviews, if appropriate. Day-to-day management of a project takes place at the control account level. If each control account is not managed competently, project performance suffers. Because organizations emphasize cost schedule and technical performance, the functional managers must be proficient in all areas of control account management. Audits are performed periodically to ensure that the management system is fully operational.

In addition to auditing the internal system, there is a responsibility to periodically audit subcontractors to ensure that an organization receives reliable schedule and performance measurement data.

Performance Formulae, Analysis, DoD Reviews, and Reports

This legend is applicable to the formulae and charts that follow:

BCWS – Budgeted Cost for Work Scheduled
BCWP – Budgeted Cost for Work Performed
ACWP – Actual Cost of Work Performed
BAC   – Budget at Completion
ETC   – Estimate to Complete
EAC   – Estimate at Completion

Cost Variance

$$CV = BCWP - ACWP$$

Cost Variance Percentage

$$CV\% = \frac{CV}{BCWP} \times 100$$

Cost Performance Index

$$CPI = \frac{BCWP}{ACWP}$$

To Complete Performance Index

$$TCPI = \frac{BAC - BCWPcum}{EAC - ACWPcum}$$

Schedule Variance

$$SV = BCWP - BCWS$$

Schedule Variance Percentage

$$SV\ Percentage = \frac{SV}{BCWS} \times 100$$

Schedule Performance Index

$$SPI = \frac{BCWP}{BCWS}$$

Schedule Variance in Months

$$SV\ months = \frac{SV\ cum}{BCWP\ current\ period}$$

Percent Spent

$$Percent\ Spent = \frac{ACWPcum}{BAC^*} \times 100$$

Percent Complete

$$Percent\ Complete = \frac{BCWPcum}{BAC^*}$$

*EAC, PMB, CBB, or TAB also may be used.

Statistical Examples

Independent EAC

The basic formulae are:

$$EAC1 = ACWPcum + (BAC - BCWP\ cum)$$

$$EAC2 = \frac{BAC}{CPIe}$$

$$EAC3 = [(BAC - BCWP)/(CPI \times SPI)] + ACWP$$

Variance at Completion Percentage

$$VAC\ Percentage = \frac{VAC \times 100}{BAC}$$

Budget/Earned Rate

$$B/E\ Rate = \frac{BCWP\ dollars}{BCWP\ hours}$$

Actual Rate

$$Actual\ Rate = \frac{ACWP\ dollars}{ACWP\ hours}$$

Rate Variance

$$Rate\ Variance = (B/E\ Rate - Actual\ Rate) \times Actual\ Hours$$

To-Go Rate

$$To\text{-}Go\ Rate = \frac{ETC\ dollars}{ETC\ hours}$$

Efficiency Variance

$$Efficiency\ Variance = (BCWP\ hours - ACWP\ hours) \times B/E\ Rate$$

Price Variance

$$PV = (Planned/Earned\ Price - Actual\ Price) \times Actual\ Quantity$$

Usage Variance

$$UV = (Planned/Earned\ Quantity - Actual\ Quantity) \times Earned\ Price$$

Cost and schedule performance data are often displayed graphically to give the analyst and the manager a picture of the trends. The two most common displays are shown here. These graphs (Figure 9-8 and Figure 9-9) can be used for a control account, an organization, a WBS element, or an entire project.

Figure 9-8
Cumulative BCWS, BCWP, and ACWP

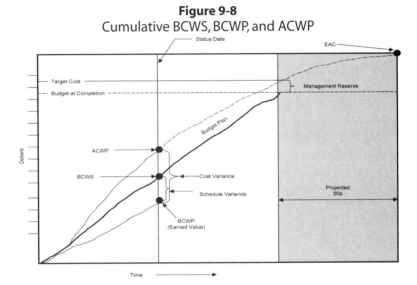

Figure 9-9
CPI and SPI

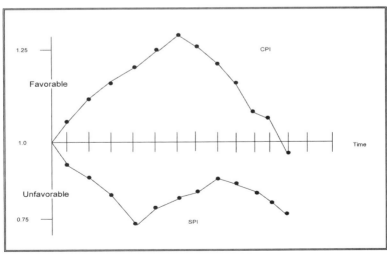

DoD Performance Reviews and Reports

Integrated Baseline Reviews (IBRs)

An IBR is a joint assessment of the performance measurement baseline (PMB) conducted by a government program manager and a contractor. The IBR is not a one-time event but a process, and the plan should be continually evaluated as changes to the baseline occur (modifications, restructuring, etc.). IBRs should be used as necessary throughout the life of a project to facilitate and maintain mutual understanding.

- The scope of the PMB consistent with authorizing documents;
- Management control processes;
- Risks in the PMB associated with cost, schedules, and resources; and
- Corrective actions where necessary.

IBRs should be scheduled as early as practicable and the timing should include consideration of the contract period of performance. The process should be initiated not later than 180 calendar days (six months) after (1) contract award, (2) the exercise of significant contract options, and (3) the incorporation of major modifications.

IBRs also are performed at the discretion of the program manager or within a reasonable time after the occurrence of major events in the life of a project, such as completion of the preliminary or critical design review, a significant shift in the content and/or time phasing of the PMB, or when a major milestone such as the start of the production option of a development contract is reached. Continuous assessment of the PMB will identify when a new IBR should be conducted.

In accordance with USD (AT&L) policy memorandum dated March 7, 2005, program managers are required to conduct IBRs on all cost or incentive contracts that require the implementation of EVM (contracts valued at $20 million or above). However, conducting an IBR is not dependent on formal validation of a contractor's earned value management system's (EVMS) complying with the EVMS guidelines in ANSI/EIA-748. Subcontractors, intragovernment work agreements, and other agreements should also require IBRs, as applicable. The scope of IBRs should be tailored to the nature of the work effort.

Contract Performance Management Reporting

The Contract Performance Report (CPR) and the Integrated Master Schedule (IMS) apply to all contracts that meet the EVM applicability requirements in USD (AT&L) policy memorandum dated March 7, 2005. On contracts valued at $20 million and above but less than $50 million, it is recommended that CPR and IMS reporting be customized. See the DoD Earned Value Management Implementation Guide for additional guidance on customized reporting.

A common work breakdown structure (WBS) that follows the DoD Work Breakdown Structure Handbook (MIL-HDBK-881A) is required for the Contractor Performance Report (CPR), Integrated Master Schedule (IMS), and Contractor Cost Data Report (CCDR). Except for high-cost or high-risk elements, the required level of reporting detail should not normally exceed level three of the contract WBS.

Contract Performance Report (CPR)

The CPR provides contract cost and schedule performance data that is used to identify problems early in the contract and to forecast future contract performance. The CPR should be the primary means of documenting the ongoing communication between a contractor and a program manager to report cost and schedule trends to-date and to permit assessment of their effect on future performance.

The program manager should obtain a CPR (DD Form 2734) on all cost or incentive contracts, subcontracts, intra-government work agreements, and other agreements valued at $20 million and above. The CPR is not typically required for cost or incentive contracts valued at less than $20 million, contracts less than 12 months in duration, or firm-fixed price contracts regardless of dollar value. The DoD Earned Value Management Implementation Guide (EVMIG) discusses some circumstances where the CPR may be appropriate for contracts in these categories.

Data Item Description (DID) DI-MGMT-81466A should be used to obtain the CPR. The contracting officer and contractor should negotiate reporting provisions in the contract, including frequency and selection of formats, level of detail, submission dates, variance thresholds and analysis, and the contract WBS to be used. The program manager should tailor the CPR to the minimum data necessary for effective management control, particularly on contracts valued at less than $50 million. See the DoD EVMIG for additional guidance on customizing CPR reporting.

In exceptional cases, a contractor may determine that the performance measurement budget or existing contract schedule cannot be achieved and no longer represents a reasonable basis for management control. With government approval, the contractor may implement an over target baseline or over target schedule. For cost-reimbursement contracts, the contract budget base excludes changes for cost growth increases, other than for authorized changes to the contract scope.

Integrated Master Schedule (IMS)

The IMS is a time-based schedule containing the networked, detailed tasks necessary to ensure successful program/control execution. The IMS is traceable to the integrated master plan, the contract work breakdown structure, and the statement of work. The IMS is used to verify attainability of contract objectives, to evaluate progress toward meeting program objectives, and to integrate the program schedule activities with all related components.

The program manager should obtain an IMS on all cost or incentive contracts, subcontracts, intra-governmental work agreements, and other agreements valued at or above $20 million. The IMS is applicable to development, major modification, and low-rate initial production efforts; it is not typically applied to full-rate production efforts. Nor is it normally required for contracts valued at less than $20 million, contracts less than 12 months in duration, or firm-fixed price contracts, regardless of dollar value. The DoD Earned Value Management Implementation Guide (EVMIG) discusses some circumstances where the IMS may be appropriate for contracts in these categories.

Contract Funds Status Report (CFSR)

The CFSR supplies funding data about defense contracts to program managers to be used for:

- Updating and forecasting contract funds requirements;
- Planning and decision-making on funding changes in contracts;
- Developing funds requirements and budget estimates in support of approved programs;
- Determining funds in excess of contract needs and available for de-obligation;
- Obtaining rough estimates of termination costs; and
- Determining whether sufficient funds are available by fiscal year to execute a contract.

The program manager should obtain a CFSR (DD Form 1586) on contracts over six months in duration. The CFSR has no specific application thresholds; however, the program manager should carefully evaluate its application to contracts valued at less than $1.5 million (in then-year dollars).

DID DI-MGMT-81468 should be used to obtain the CFSR. The contracting officer and contractor should negotiate reporting provisions in the contract, including level of detail and reporting frequency. The program manager should require only the minimum data necessary for effective management control. The CFSR should not be applied to firm-fixed [rice contracts unless unusual circumstances dictate specific funding visibility.

Contractor Cost Data Reporting (CCDR)

CCDR is the primary means that the Department of Defense uses to collect data on the costs incurred by DoD contractors in performing DoD programs (Acquisition Category ID and IC). DoD Instruction 5000.2 makes CCDR mandatory. This data enables reasonable program cost estimates and satisfies other analytical requirements. The Chair, Cost Analysis Improvement Group (CAIG) ensures consistent and appropriate CCDR application throughout the Department of Defense by defining the format for submission of CCDRs and CCDR system policies and by monitoring implementation.

CCDR coverage extends from Milestone B or equivalent to the completion of production in accordance with procedures described in this section. Unless waived by the Chair, CAIG, CCDR reporting is required on all major contracts and subcontracts that support Acquisition Category ID and IC programs, regardless of contract type, when the contracts are valued at more than $50 million (FY2002 constant dollars). CCDR reporting is not required for contracts below $7 million. The CCDR requirements on high-risk or high-technical-interest contracts between $7 and $50 million is left to the discretion of the cost working-level integrated product team.

Exclusions.– CCDR reporting is not required for procurement of commercial systems or for non-commercial systems bought under competitively awarded, firm fixed-price contracts, so long as competitive conditions continue to exist.

Software Resources Data Report (SRDR)

SRDR is a recent initiative with a primary purpose of improving the ability of the Department of Defense to estimate the costs of software-intensive programs. DoD Instruction 5000.2 requires that data be collected from software development efforts with a projected value greater than $25 million (FY2002 dollars) contained within major automated information systems (Acquisition Category IA) and major defense acquisition programs (Acquisition Category IC and Acquisition Category ID).

Data collected from applicable projects describe the type and size of software development and the schedule and labor resources needed for the development. There are three specific data items to be provided.

The Initial Government Report (DD Form 2630-1),records the government program manager's estimate-at-completion for the project. This report is due 180 days prior to contract award and is part of the cost analysis requirements description.

- The Initial Developer Report (DD Form 2630-2) records the initial estimates by the developer (i.e., contractor or government central design activity). This report is due 60 days after contract award.
- The Final Developer Report (DD Form 2630-3) is used to report actual experience. This item is due within 60 days after final deliver.

For particularly small or large software developments, the program manager may choose to shorten or lengthen the submission deadlines, accordingly. Also, for projects with multiple releases, the program manager may elect to combine the SRDR reporting of incremental releases within a single contract and provide SRDR data items for the overall project.

Further information is available in an on-line SRDR Manual. The manual provides additional background and technical details about the data collection. In particular, the manual contains information about the process by which each project defines, collects, and submits the data. The manual also contains sample data items and provides suggested language to include in a request for a proposal for this reporting requirement.

SUMMARY

This chapter provides a wealth of information explaining the ten building blocks of earned value management systems (EVMS). Specifically, this chapter is a guide to understanding how government contractors should develop EVMS and prepare for EVMS compliance reviews conducted by the Defense Contract Management Agency (DCMA). Increasingly, U.S. federal government agencies are following the U.S. Department of Defense's lead requiring government contractors to implement effective EVMS on their critical government contracts and projects.

Chapter 10 discusses contract terminations and contract closeouts, and Chapter 11 provides an understanding of the actions government contractors should take to reduce the risk and expense of litigation.

QUESTIONS TO CONSIDER

1. Does your organization have an effective EVMS?

2. Have you received education and training on EVMS?

3. Has you organization's EVMS been reviewed and validated by DCMA? If so, when?

CHAPTER **10**

HOW IT ALL ENDS: CONTRACT TERMINATIONS AND CLOSEOUT

INTRODUCTION

Every contract ends. Sometimes contracts end in an unexpected manner or at an unexpected time, but regardless of the timing, manner, or method, every contract ends.

This chapter reviews three aspects of the last days of a contract, beginning with a discussion of the various ways that a contract can be discharged and the rights, duties, obligations, and responsibilities of all parties at cessation of a contract. After it is over, we will look more specifically at the affirmative discharge of contracts via termination for convenience or termination for default, discussing when these actions may be appropriate, and the specific procedural process that must be followed. Finally, we examine the closeout process, a step that is too often ignored or not completed properly. Unfortunately, it is an exception when contracts are closed out timely. Best practices dictate that the closeout process be followed to ensure that lingering issues do not grow into major problems.

DISCHARGE

The concept of contract discharge is common to all contracts whether or not the government is a party. Contract discharge methods arise from the common law of contracts and occasionally via statute (also called civil law). One of the seemingly simple, but amazingly difficult questions to answer concerning a contract is, When is it done? Why is this question so difficult to answer? It might be due to sloppy drafting at its inception. It might be due to unexpected events arising during performance. It might be due to a failure in the inspection and acceptance process. The reasons are countless. Yet it is important for good contract administration to understand when *exactly* a contract ends.

Lawyers like to collect the various rules of law in a concise format. One of those is the *Restatement of the Law of Contracts* published by the American Law Institute.[1] According to this publication there are no less than 23 different ways to discharge a contract. The most common method is when all parties have fulfilled their obligations, goods or services have been delivered at the right quantity and quality, and the price has been paid. But this is just one way to discharge a contract. The termination of a contract for default or convenience is discussed below, but first let's look at other methods by which a contract can be discharged. Suppose you agree to buy your neighbor's car and the day before you have agreed to go to the bank and complete the transaction the car is stolen. Since the contract was executory (meaning that the agreement had been reached but full performance had not yet occurred), this contract would be discharged due to the inability of the seller to perform through no fault of his/her own. The same would be true if the car caught on fire and was destroyed. Destruction of the subject matter discharges a contract.

When we refer to the "terms and conditions" of a contract we don't usually think of these as two separate things, but they are. Terms address a particular aspect of a contract, such as the delivery date. Conditions, on the other hand, set up options for unknown events that might impact performance. For example, you might enter into a contract conditioned on approval by a regulatory body. If the approval is not granted within the time allotted in the contract, the deal ends and the contract is discharged. This is called a condition precedent; an event must occur before the other party's obligations arise. Consider also the situation called a condition subsequent, where a full agreement exists, but a future event could negate the obligation. Suppose you agree to buy gasoline at a specific price so long as the price of a barrel of oil stays above a certain level. If the price of oil falls below that level, the deal is over. The condition subsequent has occurred and discharges the contract. So the failure of a condition precedent or the occurrence of a condition subsequent can both serve to discharge a contract.

Another way that a contract can be discharged is through legal impossibility. If Congress were to decide to prohibit credit card interest rates above a certain level, imposition of a contractually agreed-to rate would now be illegal. While the contract might survive due to a standard term that permits such continuation, it is also possible that absent such a clause the contract would end.

Can the parties to a contract simply agree to end it earlier than originally planned? Absolutely. A contract can be discharged by agreement of the parties. They might decide to rescind the contract, offer and accept some alternative performance (often referred to as an "accord and satisfaction"), or the contract might permit novation of the contract (substitution of one contract for another) to other parties, thereby discharging the party initiating the novation.

Discharge by operation of law is another common method of discharge. The two most common of these are through bankruptcy or by the passage of time that exceeds the statue of limitations.

Consequently, a contract can end in an unexpected manner or at an unexpected time. The key point is that once a contract is discharged, it is over in the eyes of the law—work stops; obligations cease; duties are no longer required to be performed. The contract is considered "physically complete" whether or not the parties got what they wanted or expected.

TERMINATIONS

Another effective way to discharge a contract is by way of termination. There are two basic types of terminations—those done for the convenience of one of the parties and those caused by the default of one of the parties. In the commercial would a default is often referred to as a "breach" of the contract. Contrary to what some believe, the existence of a breach, or a condition of default, does not automatically discharge a contract. Even when there is a reason to terminate the contract, some affirmative act must occur to cause it to end.

In the government contracting environment, the right to terminate for convenience is reserved through the inclusion of a clause by that name. The government reserves this right so that the public is not required to continue with a contract that will no longer be in the government's interest, which would be considered a waste of taxpayer dollars. Commercial parties can also agree to terminate for convenience and if they do that clause has to be specifically drafted and included in the contract. The government, however, has an added benefit. Due to the case of *GL Christian & Associates v. United States*, 312 F.2d 418, aff'd on reh'g, 320 F.2d 345 (1963), a case that specifically considered the government's termination-for-convenience clause, the Court of Claims (as that court was then known) determined that certain clauses were so important to the effective administration of government contracts that even if they were omitted, they would be read into the contract by operation of law. In other words, every government contract contains the termination-for-convenience clause whether or not it is physically inserted or incorporated by reference within the words of the agreement. It is there regardless.

The right is not unlimited. There is another principle of the common law of contracts that states that a contract has to be supported by the mutuality of obligation between the parties. In other words, a completely one-sided deal would not withstand legal scrutiny. No contract would be found to exist. This poses the question, then, if one party to a contract can simply walk away from its obligation, doesn't that make the deal so one-sided that it is not a legally recognizable contract? The short answer is no. Aside from the public policy issues mentioned above, what the government's termination-for-convenience clause does is provide a limited remedy for the contractor in the event of the government's breach. The government cannot in fact just walk away, but must reimburse the contractor for all work actually performed, and also must pay certain other costs, or "damages," that the contractor incurs in winding up the contract. What is limited is the contractor's right to recover other legally recognized "damages" that it would normally be entitled to.

For example, in a commercial setting an innocent contractor would be entitled to be placed in the same position as if the contract had been fully performed. If the contractor would have made $100,000 in performing the contract but the contract ended prematurely, the innocent contractor would normally be able to recover $100,000 in lost anticipated profits (along with other lawful damages). In a contract with the government, however, the innocent contractor whose contract is terminated for the convenience of the government cannot recover those lost anticipatory profits. Rather than being put in the position it would have been in if the contract were completely performed, the contractor is put in no worse a position than it were when the contract ended. What the contractor has earned up to that point, it can keep. And whatever costs are occasioned by the winding up of the contract, the contractor will receive as well. What the contractor will not be able to recover is any fee or profit on those costs, and whatever intangibles the contract might have brought, such as technical improvements, a fully engaged labor force, or the recovery of continuing indirect costs of its operations. The contractor simply must go find other work to perform.

The government's right to terminate a contract for convenience is the preferred method of terminating a contract if the goods or services are no longer required. This is true even if the contractor is in default on its contract obligations. The FAR provides that even when a contractor could be terminated for default, if the government no longer needs the goods or services, a convenience termination should be issued. Within some agencies there are warranted contracting officers whose sole responsibility is to settle terminated contracts. The important aspect of such an action, however, is that, once issued, a termination for convenience serves to discharge the contract. It is over and must move to closeout.

An astute reader, however, might note that there is a FAR provision that permits the reinstatement of terminated contracts. And this is correct. That provision also clearly states that "with the consent of the contractor" the contracting officer may take such an action. This is because, in the eyes of the law, the original contract is complete, it is done The "reinstatement" constitutes the creation of a new contract on the same terms and conditions as the terminated contract. If the contractor does not agree, however, the original contract is still over, and no new contract comes into existence

Default Terminations

A default termination is a very serious matter. A contractor that has been terminated for default has a negative past performance rating and must certify to the government to the existence of a default in its background. Given the seriousness of the action, FAR provides very detailed guidance on the procedures, alternatives, and other considerations that a contracting officer must address before issuing a default termination.

The default clause provides three reasons that a contract can be terminated for default. The first and most common cause for default is simple failure to deliver. If the contract is clear as to delivery and the contractor fails to deliver, absent some excuse that is permitted under the clause, the contract can be terminated for default immediately. In the other two situations, immediate termination for default is not permitted. If a contractor has failed to make progress so as to endanger performance, or has failed to perform any other term or condition of the contract, the contract is still subject to termination, but the contracting officer is required to give the contractor notice of the deficiency and at least 10 days to provide any excuse, justification, or correction for its lack of progress or performance.

Two concepts are important here. The first is the concept of forbearance. This means that one of the parties has a right they can exercise, but chooses to delay the exercise of that right for some short period of time. The second concept is waiver, which means that any right you might have had has now expired. Waiver occurs with the passage of time, by actions that indicate waiver (even if waiver was not intended), or by affirmative action that clearly waives a right. A period of forbearance can lead to a waiver. A right that is waived is forever lost. When are these concepts used?

Assume that a contractor is required to deliver 32 mugwumps (because widgets have become boring) by June 10. On June 11 the contracting officer is contacted by his technical representative and informed that the mugwumps were not delivered and the rep wants to know what the contracting officer is going to do about it. The contracting officer could, by the terms of the contract, terminate for default immediately since failure to deliver gives rise to an immediate right to terminate. But is that the most judicious course of action?

To answer, let's look at FAR and see what guidance it offers. The text of FAR 49.402-3(f) states:

> The contracting officer shall consider the following factors in determining whether to terminate a contract for default:
> (1) The terms of the contract and applicable laws and regulations.
> (2) The specific failure of the contractor and the excuses for the failure.
> (3) The availability of the supplies or services from other sources.
> (4) The urgency of the need for the supplies or services and the period of time required to obtain them from other sources, as compared with the time delivery could be obtained from the delinquent contractor.
> (5) The degree of essentiality of the contractor in the Government acquisition program and the effect of a termination for default upon the contractor's capability as a supplier under other contracts.
> (6) The effect of a termination for default on the ability of the contractor to liquidate guaranteed loans, progress payments, or advance payments.
> (7) Any other pertinent facts and circumstances.

Note first that this regulation provides that the contracting officer "shall" consider these factors. In the FAR, "shall" is mandatory, meaning that the contracting officer must consider these items before making the decision to terminate for default. Second, note that subsection (f)(2) poses the possibility of the contractor's having an excuse. How do you find out? Some government personnel might be aware of an excuse, but that is not a certainty. The simplest method is—just ask! This is where a "show cause" notice serves a useful purpose. This language is provided in FAR 49.607(b) and essentially informs the contractor that to the best of the contracting officer's knowledge, the contractor is in default and could be terminated immediately. It requests any facts or other information that would provide an excuse. Examples of excuses that would in fact excuse performance include unusually severe weather, government interference or delay, war or insurrection, and the government's failure to perform a proper inspection, among several other possibilities. If the contractor provides a legitimate excuse, then a new delivery date must be set. Some of the excuses might provide a day-for-day extension while others might require an entirely new date be established.

FAR 49.607(b) *Show Cause*, states:

> Since you have failed to _____ [*insert* "perform Contract No. ___ within the time required by its terms," *or* "cure the conditions endangering performance under Contract No _____ as described to you in the Government's letter of _____ (date)"], the Government is considering terminating the contract under the provisions for default of this contract. Pending a final decision in this matter, it will be necessary to determine whether your failure to perform arose from causes beyond your control and without fault or negligence on your part. Accordingly, you are given the opportunity to present, in writing, any facts bearing on the question to _____ [*insert the name and complete address of the contracting officer*], within 10 days after receipt of this notice. Your failure to present any excuses within this time may be considered as an admission that none exist. Your attention is invited to the respective rights of the Contractor and the Government and the

liabilities that may be invoked if a decision is made to terminate for default.

Subsections (3) and (4) of the FAR citation concerning things the contracting officer should consider suggest that whether or not the government can get a substitute contractor should figure into the decision to terminate. Likewise, how long it will take to obtain another source should be considered. Therefore, even though the contractor has defaulted on its responsibilities, the guidance states that it is often preferable to work with the contractor to encourage performance.

What about the contractor's importance in government acquisition or the impact on its reputation if it defaulted? To some this might seem to be an odd consideration, but in fact FAR is quite clear that default terminations are a very severe action and should only be taken when no other option is appropriate. This does not mean that the contractor gets off the hook completely. A contract modification that resets the delivery date needs to obtain some consideration from the contractor, but that is far short of the consequences of a default termination.

Another consideration is the effect a termination would have on other aspects of government operations. If the government has guaranteed a loan and default will interfere with the recovery of the funds loaned, the contracting officer must consider that impact. And lastly FAR suggests that there are "other pertinent facts and circumstances" that should be considered. Thus, the contracting officer has very broad discretion in determining whether a default termination, even if warranted, is going to ultimately be in the government's best interest. FAR suggests very strongly that default terminations should be a solution of last resort.

So let's return to our scenario:

> What action should the contracting officer take upon receiving the call from his technical rep that the contractor failed to deliver the much-needed mugwumps?

Let's review the options. The contractor could terminate immediately for failure to deliver. He could draft a formal show cause letter in conformance with FAR 49.607 and demand an explanation from the contractor. He could pick up the phone and call the contractor to find out what is causing the delay. He could ignore the whole thing and wait a few more days to see if the mugwumps show up on the dock. He could get the technical rep in a room and demand to know what he did to cause the contractor to fail to deliver.

What would you do?

While all of the options are possible, the most immediately productive would be to pick up the phone and call the contractor. If the delay is minor, perhaps nothing more should happen. If the contractor has no excuse and no plan of recovery, an immediate termination might be appropriate. If there was in fact some government interference or other excuse, it is best to know that sooner rather than later. After considering all of the factors listed in FAR 49.402-3(f), it is appropriate to permit a period of forbearance before taking the precipitous action of a termination for default. If a contracting officer waits too long, however, or if the technical rep did indeed take some action to encourage continued performance past the original due date, the right to a termination for default will be deemed to have been waived. the contracting officer cannot now issue a termination for default and must bilaterally (if possible) reset the delivery date. If the contractor is recalcitrant, the contracting officer can reset the date unilaterally but might be called upon to defend the date as reasonable if challenged. If the contracting officer chooses to make the phone call, file documentation can become critical in defending a termination for default and the contracting officer should be prepared to immediately issue a show cause letter in order to put the contractor on formal notice, provide the contractor a reasonable period in which to respond, and provide file documentation that the FAR guidance has been followed in attempting to ascertain the facts before issuing a termination for default.

Before issuing a termination for default, a contracting officer is required to place a memo in the contract file explaining his or her actions. There may also be other actions a contracting officer can take that is short of a full termination for default, again emphasizing FAR's preference for almost anything other than a termination for default. Examine FAR 49.402-4, Procedure in lieu of termination for default, which states:

The following courses of action, among others, are available to the contracting officer in lieu of termination for default when in the Government's interest:

(a) Permit the contractor, the surety, or the guarantor, to continue performance of the contract under a revised delivery schedule.

(b) Permit the contractor to continue performance of the contract by means of a subcontract or other business arrangement with an acceptable third party, provided the rights of the Government are adequately preserved.

(c) If the requirement for the supplies and services in the contract no longer exists, and the contractor is not liable to the Government for damages as provided in 49.402-7, execute a no-cost termination settlement agreement using the formats in 49.603-6 and 49.603-7 as a guide.

What if in the exercise above the contracting officer selected the option to terminate for default immediately, and later discovered that there was in fact an excusable delay? One of two options is available. If the termination was recent, the government still needs the goods or services, and the contractor agrees, the contract can be reinstated. If too much time has passed before the government discovers its error, or the matter is litigated before a Board or court and the government loses, the default termination is considered a breach of the contract by the government. This has the effect of converting the termination for default into a termination for convenience, and thereby gives the contractor all the rights to recover its costs up to the point of termination. Keep in mind, however, that any termination is a discharge of the contract. The only issue is what the contractor can recover, if anything.

Recall that the ability to terminate for default immediately after a failure to deliver is just one of three potential situations that permit a termination for default. The second instance is when the contractor fails to make progress toward contract completion that threatens success. In most cases this is a matter of judgment. How is progress measured? Are there activities going on behind the scenes that might not be obvious? In order to justify a termination on this basis a contracting officer must provide a notice to the contractor of his or her belief of the failure to make progress and provide 10 days (or more) for the contractor to respond. If the contractor does not respond or provides an inadequate response within the 10-day window, the contract can then be terminated for default. The text of FAR 49.607(a), Cure Notice, reads:

> You are notified that the Government considers your
> _____ [*specify the contractor's failure or failures*] a condi-
> tion that is endangering performance of the contract.
> Therefore, unless this condition is cured within
> 10 days after receipt of this notice [*or insert any longer
> time that the Contracting Officer may consider reasonably
> necessary*], the Government may terminate for default
> under the terms and conditions of the _____ [*insert
> clause title*] clause of this contract.

What should happen if the contractor contacts the contracting officer and manifests some intent not to perform the contract? In the commercial world this is called "anticipatory repudiation." Generally, a party does not have to wait until an actual failure to perform occurs, which is a hindrance to commerce and typically not in the best interest of the government. As a result both the FAR and the Uniform Commercial Code (UCC), which applies to commercial transactions, provide a solution. Under the FAR, the procedures described above would apply. Whether the denial of performance is a failure to make progress or considered a breach of another term or condition of the contract, the result is the same. The contracting officer can request that the contractor "cure" the perceived deficiency. Language for such a demand is contained at FAR 49.607(a), above. In the commercial world, UCC Section 2-609 provides that either party that becomes concerned about the future performance of the other has an absolute right to request "adequate assurances" that a party will perform. This might be due to an act of perceived anticipatory repudiation or even perhaps some other hindrance. If you heard that there was a big fire at the plant where your products are being made, that could be sufficient to cause concern and prompt a request for adequate assurance.

Thus, both the government, whose purchases are governed by the federal common law and the Federal Acquisition Regulation, and commercial parties, whose transactions are governed by their respective state version of the UCC, have a mechanism to prompt a party to assure the other party that they will indeed perform in accordance with the terms of a contract. Failure to respond, or failure to respond adequately, gives rise to a right to terminate for default (or a breach in the commercial world) and permits the innocent party the freedom to find another way to meet its needs.

Let's return to our example. The government was trying to buy 32 mugwumps and on the delivery date the contractor failed to deliver. The contracting officer decided to call the contractor and ask what was going on. Assume now that the government has placed a moratorium on importing any more mugwumps. The contractor has 23 of them, but cannot get the other 9. Is it possible to partially terminate the contract? The answer is yes, and the termination clauses anticipate that a default or a convenience termination can be partial or complete. Whether the contracting officer determines that the inability to import the mugwumps is "beyond the control and without the fault or negligence of the contractor" or not, he or she can terminate that portion of the contract for the nine unavailable mugwumps. If the contractor is at fault, it can be a termination for default; otherwise (or if it is in the best interest of the government, even though a cause for default exists) a partial termination for convenience can be issued, and the other 23 mugwumps can be accepted.

Does it make a difference if the contract is awarded on a fixed-price or cost-reimbursement basis? The effect on the contractor directly reflects the risk that the contractor accepts with each contract type. In fact, in cost-reimbursement contracts, there is not a separate convenience or default termination clause as there is, for example, in fixed price supply contracts. The clause is entitled "terminations" and whether the contractor is at fault or not for the failure to perform, the contractor recovers its costs expended and fee earned up to the point of termination. The only practical impact is that the contractor is not reimbursed for the settlement proposal preparation as it would be if the termination were not it's the contractor's fault. Because the government assumes the risk of performance under a cost-type contract, it also assumes the risk of non-performance.

In a fixed-price contract, however, the results are quite different. The full risk of performance rests on the contractor, and its failure to perform can lead to the government's recovering its entire investment in the contract. If no deliveries have been accepted, the government can recover any progress or advance payments made to the contractor. The government is not required to accept or pay for any items under a contract after it is terminated. Remember that the contract is discharged when it is terminated. It is like the Monty Python parrot—it has ceased to exist. But, as the late Billy Mays would remind us, there is more!

One additional remedy that the government has is to repurchase the needed supplies from another source and charge the defaulted contractor for the difference in cost. The government has to act promptly and reasonably, but if the same products are repurchased, the defaulting contractor must pay the government the difference between the contract price on the defaulted contract and the contract price on the repurchase contract. The government is also entitled to levy an administrative charge on the defaulted contractor for its efforts in placing and administering the new contract. These repurchase rights can result in significant expense to a defaulted contractor and can be used as an effective negotiating tool. There is a benefit to the government in these situations in that the government need not follow all of the formal competition requirements, must only act reasonably in the acquisition process, and the money from the defaulted contract remains available for re-obligation under applicable fiscal law rules even if it is from a prior year.

The government is also entitled to "other damages" in addition to the repurchase costs. If the contract provided for liquidated damages, the government is entitled to recover them, as well as any other damages that are legally allowed. In very serious cases of misconduct, the government can also pursue suspension, debarment, or prosecution of a contractor under federal criminal statutes.

Termination Timelines

When a termination is issued, the clock begin running on a variety of events that follow. The following chart reviews the key events.

Table 10-1

Event	FAR Reference	Time After Effective Date of Termination
Funding requirements identified	FAR 49.105-2	30 days
Inventory schedules	FAR 49.206-3, 49.303-2	120 days
Vouchering period for cost-type contracts	FAR 49.302	Not later than the first month end after six months have passed.
Submission of final termination settlement proposal	FAR 49.206-1, 49.303-1	One year (unless extended for good cause by TCO)
Partial payments	FAR 49.112-1	After submission of interim or final termination settlement proposal
Final settlement	None	Depends on the size and complexity of the contract, settlement issues with subcontractors, continuing litigation, audit schedules, and thoroughness of the settlement proposal. This can often be from one to five years.

This chart contains a few items of interest. The property disposition is a high priority. The sooner property can be dispositioned, the sooner it can either be put to productive use or simply removed from circulation and scrapped. Disposition of property reduces maintenance, storage, and tracking costs more quickly. Thus, property inventories are required within 120 days of a termination notice.

Under cost-type contracts, a contractor can continue to voucher costs, but doing so is limited to six months. After that, some alternative funding process needs to be agreed-to with the contracting officer. The final settlement proposal is typically required within one year. While the termination contracting officer can grant an extension, it is in everyone's best interest to get the matter settled as quickly as possible. Many things can delay the submission, including failure to reach agreement with subcontractors, resolving cost issues, and litigation.

Terminations, whether for convenience or default, are just one of the ways that a contract can end–or to use the legal term, be discharged. In government contracting, it is a process that is automatically reserved to the government as a matter of public policy, permitting the cessation of effort and the associated cost to the government. Terminations are a drastic action and contracting officers are encouraged by the controlling regulations to avoid using the default termination option unless absolutely necessary. If the default option is selected, the government can recover its excess reprocurement costs, administrative costs, and any other damages to which it is legally entitled. And while the regulation permits the "reinstatement" of defaulted contracts, such an action may only be taken with the consent of the contractor. When a contract is terminated for convenience, the contractor has one year to submit its settlement claim, but when possible, best business practices suggest that the matter be settled as promptly as possible. Subcontractors receive their entitlement, property is dispositioned for reuse where possible, and both the government and the contractor can move on to more productive work.

CLOSEOUT

Once a contract has been performed it is tempting to think that everything is finished. However, except in the instance of a simplified acquisition, a series of additional events must occur to close out the contract. The actual performance and verification of adequate performance is one step in that process, but it is only ONE part of the process. When a contract has been performed, it is "physically complete." As defined in FAR, physically complete means the contract has been completely terminated for convenience or default OR the contractor has completed the required deliveries and the government has inspected and accepted the supplies, the contractor has performed all services and the government has accepted these services, and all option provisions, if any, have expired. In other words, everyone has completed what they were expected to do and there is no "performance" remaining by any of the parties.

Contract closeout is a team effort and preferably should include people who worked on the program. Memories fade quickly and people are often reassigned to new projects. It is therefore imperative that contract administrators use forms, checklists, and reliable databases to complete the process. Good closeout preparation—from the moment the contract is awarded—is one of the most important techniques for contract closeout success. To borrow from Steven Covey, use a habit highly successful people use and begin with the end in mind.

Closeout is not merely getting the files ready for storage. The closeout process is the means by which contractors get any withholding released and the government de-obligates funds remaining on the contract. There is a time value of money for both parties, especially for the government if the contract can be closed out while the funds are still available for obligation. If you wait too long, most funding has a time limit after which the funds "expire." In those cases the agency loses 100% of the remaining funds .

While this means more to contractors than to the government, there is also a cost for keeping the books open longer than necessary. If there is any withholding, the contractor has probably not recovered its fee or profit on the work. These funds provide working capital so that the contractor can perform the next job without a loan. Because a contractor's interest is not an allowable expense , whenever funds can be released and the contract closed out, the contractor generally benefits.

FAR 42.708 provides a Quick Closeout procedure that permits physically complete contracts to be closed even though every detail has not been verified. This process recognizes that it can be more time-consuming and costly to try to nail down every detail than to just get reasonably close and negotiate a settlement of any outstanding issues.

Administrative Closeout

Administrative closeout is the process of settling all outstanding issues to ensure that each party has met its obligations and the contract file has been documented accordingly. It includes the ultimate archiving of files in a manner consistent with the contract terms and applicable law, and provides for the possibility of future retrieval if necessary. The key objectives of administrative closeout are to identify and resolve any uncompleted obligations or pending liabilities on the part of either the government or the contractor. It also ensures that any issues related to the contract, including outstanding claims or litigation, have been properly documented.

How do you know that a contract is physically complete and ready for closeout? There are many mechanisms or documentation trails that verify the completion of performance. The DCMA or the contracting officer might sign off on a DD250 or there might be a Notice of Completion. There might be an observation that the contract period of performance has passed or that all of the level of effort allocated to the contract has been expended. Other forms also may document receipt and acceptance, such as an approved and paid final invoice from the contractor. Even with this evidence, it must be determined whether or not there are other outstanding issues related to the contract. Are there any requests for equitable adjustment still pending? Were all change orders closed? Is there a warranty period that has not yet expired or are there outstanding issues related to contract data? Do the final reports carry the correct proprietary legends? Have all patents been disclosed? Is all property dispositioned? Closeout is designed to answer these and other questions.

Although contracts should be closed out in a timely manner, that is often the exception. FAR provides the following time lines for closeout.

Table 10-2
FAR Closeout Time Lines

Type of Contract Action	Usual Time Frame	FAR Reference
Simplified Acquisition	When CO receives evidence of receipt of property and final payment (unless agency regulations provide otherwise)	4.804-1(a)(1)
Firm Fixed Price	6 months from date CO receives evidence of physical completion	4.804-1(a)(2)
Contracts that require settlement of indirect cost rates	36 months from the month the CO receives evidence of physical completion	4.804-1(a)(3)
All others	20 months from the month the CO receives evidence of physical completion	4.804-1(a)(4)

A few things stand out in Table 10-2. Indirect cost audits may slow down the process considerably. This is driven in large measure by the need for an incurred-cost audit. Larger contracts, and contractors with more sophisticated accounting systems, naturally take the longest. Sometimes the audit agency simply cannot get the audit completed within the required time frame and contracts remain physically complete but still open for more than five years. Litigation also prevents a contract from being closed out, and that can extend the process many years—and sometimes decades!

Table 10-3 is an audit closeout checklist used by Certified Contracting Solutions, LLC, . While some contracts may require slightly different tasks, this checklist provides an excellent starting point for determining when a contract is physically complete and the closeout process may begin. Once these steps are taken, the parties can construct a final release to serve as the closing modification. Ideally, both sides will release the other of any further obligation under the contract. The release reflects any money owed.. Any outstanding claims also are dispositioned. Any withholding due the contractor is paid (and vice versa if money is owed the government), and the agency deobligates the remaining funds on the contract.

The resolution of financial issues is one of the keys to proper contract closeout. Depending on the contract, many questions should be asked and answered to assure both parties that the numbers have been calculated properly. The government occasionally makes double payments, might not timely release withholding, often changes payment offices, and periodically introduces new automated systems with sometimes irregular results. If the government is found liable for amounts due beyond the prompt payment windows it pay interest on such amounts, but to many businesses the interest is a minor point. The principal amount of the invoice is a business's cash flow and the importance of cash flow to any business should never be underestimated.

Generally, closeout is designed to close and archive the entire contract. In some situations when that is not possible, portions of the contract can be closed. Perhaps all subcontractor claims can be settled and paid. The government and the prime contractor might decide to enter into a settlement agreement that recognizes the subcontract closures. Partial closeout modifications are appropriate and sometimes necessary. To the degree that the parties can agree to close out aspects of the contract, they should pursue that option. Later, when the rest of the contract is ready for closeout, such as at the conclusion of litigation or the expiration of a warranty, the remaining issues can be closed out with a subsequent settlement modification.

Many questions may be considered during closeout. For example:

- Was an audit conducted and have its recommendations and findings been resolved?
- Are the indirect rates subject to final settlement?
- Has the contractor timely submitted the final invoice based on those rates?
- If funds are due the government, have they been remitted?
- Were all ODCs captured (material, travel, etc.)?

- Are there special financial provisions that must be considered, such as indirect cost ceilings, travel limitations, or the limitation-of-funds clause?
- Are the cumulative billings proper and within contract dollar limits?
- Have the financial issues been documented in the contract file and, where appropriate included in a final release modification?

Although contract closeouts should proceed expeditiously, as Table 10-2 shows, many of them are not closed out even routinely for two to three years. Cost contracts can be vouchered for six months past their termination, but sometimes there are expenses for which the government is responsible that extend past that period. As a result, some payment mechanism should be put in place, and the contracting officer should have some method to track what is going on. Often a continuing reporting process is instituted, which is most commonly structured as monthly report. Like any contract tracking tool, the report should be meaningful and should track those items that are most important to the parties. In the shutdown and closeout of a significant DOE facility, for example, one of the primary teammates brought its activity to an end and entered the closeout phase. The monthly report included personnel layoffs, closed subcontracts, expended costs (in this case in accordance with an earned value management system), property disposed of, and special issues that arose that might delay final closeout. The estimate was tracked at completion and the entire process proceeded ahead of schedule and below cost.

Another useful tool is a series of form letters or communication formats. For example, there might be a quick closeout procedure request or letters specific to cost-type or fixed-price contracts that will facilitate the closeout process by initiating communications. Generally, the closeout documentation is similar on many programs, so the letter could be pre-drafted to request, for example:

- The final technical report
- Project officer certification
- A patent and copyright infringement report
- A patent rights report for inventions
- A royalty statement
- Request for closeout of any value engineering proposals

- Documentation related to any outstanding data requirements
- Final property inventory
- A request to status the closeout of significant subcontractors
- Completion invoice including:
  - A statement that all subcontracts have been settled
  - A statement that the final invoice has been submitted for payment (fixed-price contracts)
  - The final invoice number and date, the total amounts paid, and the total amount due on the contract.
  - Contractor's release for all contracts
  - Contractor's assignment of refunds, rebates, and credits
  - A letter documenting final price revision calculations, such as may relate to an incentive contract or a fixed-price redeterminable contract.

Other useful letters include those most commonly needed during closeout, such as a letter questioning costs, past performance reports/requests, and correspondence related to the disposition of classified or other sensitive information. If the contract was terminated, there should also be a termination docket assuring that the termination procedures were followed, and the file will reflect that the proper actions were taken, including the implementation of any board or court decision related to the contract. Having these letters in a template format before they are needed will greatly facilitate closeout. Experienced contracting professionals keep a file of such documents. Once you have been through the process of developing them from scratch, you quickly learn the benefit of using the best practice of cataloging such sample correspondence.

FAR provides the following as the complete statement on how to close out a contract:

> **4.804-5 Procedures for closing out contract files.**
> (a) The contract administration office is responsible for initiating (automated or manual) administrative closeout of the contract after receiving evidence of its physical completion. At the outset of this process, the contract administration office must review the contract funds status and notify the contracting office of any excess funds the contract administration office might deobligate. When complete, the administrative closeout procedures must ensure that–

(1) Disposition of classified material is completed;
(2) Final patent report is cleared;
(3) Final royalty report is cleared;
(4) There is no outstanding value engineering change proposal;
(5) Plant clearance report is received;
(6) Property clearance is received;
(7) All interim or disallowed costs are settled;
(8) Price revision is completed;
(9) Subcontracts are settled by the prime contractor;
(10) Prior year indirect cost rates are settled;
(11) Termination docket is completed;
(12) Contract audit is completed;
(13) Contractor's closing statement is completed;
(14) Contractor's final invoice has been submitted; and
(15) Contract funds review is completed and excess funds deobligated.

(b) When the actions in paragraph (a) of this subsection have been verified, the contracting officer administering the contract must ensure that a contract completion statement, containing the following information, is prepared:

(1) Contract administration office name and address (if different from the contracting office).
(2) Contracting office name and address.
(3) Contract number.
(4) Last modification number.
(5) Last call or order number.
(6) Contractor name and address.
(7) Dollar amount of excess funds, if any.
(8) Voucher number and date, if final payment has been made.
(9) Invoice number and date, if the final approved invoice has been forwarded to a disbursing office of another agency or activity and the status of the payment is unknown.
(10) A statement that all required contract administration actions have been fully and satisfactorily accomplished.
(11) Name and signature of the contracting officer.
(12) Date.

(c) When the statement is completed, the contracting officer must ensure that–

(1) The signed original is placed in the contracting office contract file (or forwarded to the contracting office for placement in the files if the contract administration office is different from the contracting office); and
(2) A signed copy is placed in the appropriate contract administration file if administration is performed by a contract administration office.

Note that the government has the added requirement of a closeout statement be placed in the file. Closeout, like most other contract actions, can be enhanced with complete documentation. Of all the possible failures of a contracting professional, the most egregious is the lack of documentation. Have you ever handled a file and commented that it contained too much documentation? Of course not. The common complaint is that the file is too thin and the details of what actually transpired are simply missing.

This leads us to the final part of closeout–record retention. Most companies and the government have detailed document retention policies and procedures. The requirements for record retention vary, often conflict, and sometimes depend on the nature of the records, e.g., hard copy versus electronic only. Problems have arisen from retaining records only in electronic formats, as ultimately that format becomes obsolete and the records become useless. Even printed paper has been known to fade or darken or simply deteriorate. Natural disasters such as floods, broken pipes, or fires have also had their impact on record retention efforts.

One critical issue to keep in mind is that the FAR rules on contract file retention relate ONLY to those issues unique to contract files. There are also rules that relate to file retention covering a great multitude of situations. Drug experiment records, tax records, injury statistics related to consumer product safety, and many, many other rules cover record retention. It is best to check with legal to make sure that the rules and regulations covering the longest applicable period for retaining records are followed. This is a complicated area that is regularly challenged with new technologies. For example, can messages sent via Twitter be considered "records"? Are instant messages between two government officials "records" of an "official meeting" ? Clearly we are evolving faster with technology than are the methods used to manage the data being generated.

The government has its own rules, which are found at FAR 4.805, Storage, handling, and disposal of contract files.

4.805 Storage, handling, and disposal of contract files.

(a) Agencies must prescribe procedures for the handling, storing, and disposing of contract files. These procedures must take into account documents held in all types of media, including microfilm and various electronic media. Agencies may change the original medium to facilitate storage as long as the requirements of Part 4, law, and other regulations are satisfied. The process used to create and store records must record and reproduce the original document, including signatures and other written and graphic images completely, accurately, and clearly. Data transfer, storage, and retrieval procedures must protect the original data from alteration. Unless law or other regulations require signed originals to be kept, they may be destroyed after the responsible agency official verifies that record copies on alternate media and copies reproduced from the record copy are accurate, complete, and clear representations of the originals. Agency procedures for contract file disposal must include provisions that the documents specified in paragraph (b) of this section may not be destroyed before the times indicated, and may be retained longer if the responsible agency official determines that the files have future value to the Government. When original documents have been converted to alternate media for storage, the requirements in paragraph (b) of this section also apply to the record copies in the alternate media.

(b) If administrative records are mixed with program records and cannot be economically segregated, the entire file should be kept for the period of time approved for the program records. Similarly, if documents described in the following table are part of a subject or case file that documents activities that are not described in the table, they should be treated in the same manner as the files of which they are a part. The retention periods for acquisitions at or below the simplified acquisition threshold also apply to acquisitions conducted prior to July 3, 1995, that used small purchase procedures. The retention periods for acquisitions above the simplified acquisition threshold also apply to acquisitions conducted prior to July 3, 1995, that used other than small purchase procedures.

Document	Retention Period
(1) Records pertaining to Contract Disputes Act actions.	6 years and 3 months after final action or decision for files created prior to October 1, 1979. 1 year after final action or decision for files created on or after October 1, 1979.
(2) Contracts (and related records or documents, including successful proposals) exceeding the simplified acquisition threshold for other than construction.	6 years and 3 months after final payment.
(3) Contracts (and related records or documents, including successful proposals) at or below the simplified acquisition threshold for other than construction.	3 years after final payment.
(4) Construction contracts:	
(i) Above $2,000.	6 years and 3 months after final payment.
(ii) $2,000 or less.	3 years after final payment.
(iii) Related records or documents, including successful proposals, except for contractor's payrolls (see (b)(4)(iv)).	Same as contract file.
(iv) Contractor's payrolls submitted in accordance with Department of Labor regulations, with related certifications, anti-kickback affidavits, and other related papers.	3 years after contract completion unless contract performance is the subject of an enforcement action on that date.
(5) Solicited and unsolicited unsuccessful offers, quotations, bids, and proposals:	.
(i) Relating to contracts above the simplified acquisition threshold.	If filed separately from contract file, until contract is completed. Otherwise, the same as related contract file.
(ii) Relating to contracts at or below the simplified acquisition threshold.	1 year after date of award or until final payment, whichever is later.
(6) Files for canceled solicitations.	5 years after cancellation.
(7) Other copies of procurement file records used by component elements of a contracting office for administrative purposes.	Upon termination or completion.
(8) Documents pertaining generally to the contractor as described at 4.801(c)(3).	Until superseded or obsolete.

(9) Data submitted to the Federal Procurement Data System (FPDS). Electronic data file maintained by fiscal year, containing unclassified records of all procurements other than simplified acquisitions, and information required under 4.603.	5 years after submittal to FPDS.
(10) Investigations, cases pending or in litigation (including protests), or similar matters.	Until final clearance or settlement, or, if related to a document identified in (b)(1) - (9), for the retention period specified for the related document, whichever is later.

Again, these rules solely address contract files. Be sure to check with legal for the variety of rules that might affect the retention of specific files. An interesting aspect about these retention periods is the odd "3 months" that is tacked on to some of the retention periods. The primary reason for this is that the statute of limitations for most contract claims is six years after final payment. As lawyers are known for filing claims on the last possible day of eligibility, the extra "three months" additional retention gives the government time to receive service on a claim and prepare to preserve the records for litigation.

SUMMARY

The methods by which a contract can be discharged are many, and not all are as anticipated or planned. It is nonetheless important to know when the contract is "done." While the vast majority of contracts end through performance and payment, there are other events and situations that can result in a contract's coming to an early end.

One of these methods is a termination for convenience or default. While default, or breach, under a contract does not automatically discharge it, a default event gives the other party the right to declare the contract over. For either party to exercise a termination for convenience, that right must be reserved in the contract as it is not normally part of a commercial contract. A different rule applies to government contracts where the standard FAR Termination for Convenience clause is read-into all government contracts as a matter of public policy.

After a contract is performed, or as it is often called "physically complete," there remains the administrative process of closing the contract, verifying that all administrative actions have been completed, necessary audits and reports have been completed, and

TEN

the parties released from any further obligations. The complete contract files are then cataloged and archived in accordance with applicable laws, rules, and regulations.

In the next chapter, we discuss the need to take appropriate action to mitigate the risk of litigation on U.S. government contracts.

This chapter has prepared you to answer the following review questions:

1. T F When a contractor has failed to meet a delivery schedule, it should be sent a "cure notice" and given ten days to correct the failed delivery.

2. T F If a contract is terminated for convenience and later the government discovers that the contractor was in default, the contracting officer should convert the termination to a default.

3. When a contractor has performed the work described in the statement of work, we say that the contract is _____. [physically complete]

4. T F When considering record retention periods, there are applicable retention rules for the records beyond those required of contract records.

5. Name three events that can cause a contract to be discharged even though discharge was not the original intent of the parties.

ENDNOTES

1   *Restatement of the Law, Second, Contracts.* Philadelphia, PA: American Law Institute, 1981.

CHAPTER

MITIGATING THE RISK OF LITIGATION

INTRODUCTION

Importance of Managing Litigation Risk Throughout the Procurement Life-Cycle

Litigation is expensive and time-consuming. It is a distraction from a company's core business activities. But litigation is also a risk that each government contractor faces in relationships throughout the supply chain (from subcontractors and vendors to the government), which requires planning and preparation. Too often, government contractors that believe a case will never go to litigation end up struggling to gather their resources for just that eventuality. Had they identified and managed their litigation risk better, beginning as early as contract formation, the company would have been in a dramatically better position to either recover monies owed it or defend against government claims.

Litigation is extremely expensive compared to other business activities and, except in limited circumstances, a contractor that prevails will not be able to recover its litigation costs.[2] Under the applicable Federal Acquisition Regulation (FAR) cost principles, costs incurred in the defense of government claims or the prosecution of claims against the government are unallowable.[3] Similarly, costs incurred in the protest of a government solicitation or contract award are unallowable unless the costs of defending against a protest are incurred pursuant to a written request from the contracting officer.[4]

Litigation is also extremely disruptive to a company's day-to-day business activities. Over the course of a single case, parties will have to collect and produce thousands, if not millions, of pages of documents. In light of the proliferation of the types and amounts of electronic media used by companies, document production can be a very expensive endeavor. Moreover, courts will usually require a company to incur the time and expense associated with the production of relevant electronic media (e.g., e-mails, electronic versions of documents, spreadsheets, databases, program management files).

In addition to physically producing their documents, parties will be obliged to provide written responses to requests for production of documents, interrogatories, and requests for admissions. Further, companies must make individuals available for depositions.

These depositions may involve individuals who were involved in the day-to-day management of the contract under dispute; the financial people responsible for tracking the programs costs; or even a company's chief executive officer (CEO). Alternatively, an opposing party may request that your company designate an individual to speak on behalf of the corporation on a host of topics. Finally, to resolve a suit successfully, a company must undertake a substantial amount of factual development and analysis. This fact-gathering and analysis focuses on past problems rather than present or future business operations. Litigation is very rarely a profit center.

Consequently, before entering into a business relationship with the government or another contractor, companies must assess the risk associated with the relationship. Typically, there are at least three types of risk that must be assessed in considering the possibility of litigation that may arise in the course of government procurements (both before and after award): (1) performance risk; (2) contractual risk; and (3) financial risk.

> **Performance risk** is the risk that contract award or performance will be adversely affected if a contractor fails to anticipate potential litigation. For example, failing to document discussions with the government concerning a contractor's understanding of a statement of work (and to preserve the documentation) may undercut the contractor's ability to provide supplies or services in the manner in which it intended if the government subsequently disagrees and claims an understanding that is different from the contractor's.

> **Contractual risk** is the risk that a contractor's rights and duties under the terms of its contract or sub-contract will be adversely affected. A contractor's failure to confirm or correct its understanding of a solicitation or a contract's scope of work and terms will usually result in any doubts being resolved in favor of the government, as the contractor usually bears the risk of confirming these matters prior to award or, at a minimum, prior to problems arising, as a matter of law.

Financial risk is the risk that a contractor will not optimize its profit or that the contractor will suffer unanticipated losses. Failing to anticipate potential pre- and post-award litigation may result in a contractor's losing its ability to protest or defend a contact award or to successfully prosecute a claim that arises in the course of performance. All of these possibilities may result in lost revenue and profit.

Not assessing litigation risk and having the right policies and practices in place will compromise chances of success if a contractor is forced to pursue or defend a bid protest or claim. Thus, these risks must be addressed at the outset of every contractual relationship.

MANAGING RISK DURING THE FORMATION OF A GOVERNMENT CONTRACT

It makes the most sense to identify risk and take affirmative steps to manage the identified risks prior to contract award, when a contractor's ability to shape or clarify a contract's terms and conditions is greatest. However, to fully and accurately identify the risks in a solicitation, a contractor must have a thorough understanding of the type of procurement as well as the scope of the project.

Determining and Mitigating Risk in Contractual Terms

To limit risk at the contract's outset, contractors must have a thorough understanding of the contract type.[5] The two types of contracts predominantly used by the government are either fixed-price or cost-reimbursement contracts. Within each of these categories, there are a number of variations that may impact the ultimate risk borne by the contractor. Pursuant to a fixed-price contract, the contractor bears the risk of performing the contract at the fixed price the government has agreed to pay. In contrast, the government bears the risk of performance under a cost-reimbursement contract.

Irrespective of the procurement vehicle, contractors must read the solicitations and ensure that they understand the project's scope of work. Frequently, many performance problems arise because the contractor failed to fully analyze the scope of the contract. Prior to submitting a proposal or signing a contract, contractors should ask themselves:

- What does the contract require us to do?
- Who will judge whether we successfully meet the terms of the contract?
- Does the individual that will evaluate our performance have a stake in the outcome of the contract?[6]
- What standards will the individual use to determine whether our performance was successful?
- What are the terms of the contract?
- What contract terms have been incorporated by reference?
- To the extent a dispute arises, what law will apply to the resolution of the dispute and what forum will handle the resolution of the dispute, *i.e.*, a court or an arbitrator?
- What notice must the company give the other party if a dispute arises under the contract?
- If a dispute arises, does the contractor have an obligation to continue performance?
- Does the contract obligate the contractor to indemnify my company for the violation of a patent? Does my company have to indemnify the government or the other contractor if the company violates a patent?
- What type of warranty will the company receive or be required to provide under the contract?
- Are there clauses that must be flowed-down to our subcontractors?
- Are there contract terms that may apply by "operation of law" even if the government failed to include them in the written contract?

Prime contractors can make a number of mistakes at the outset of a contract that potentially increase the risk of performance or that may increase costs or have adverse contractual consequences. For example, government contracts often contain a boilerplate clause such as "this contract is subject to all applicable rules and regulations." In other instances, the contract incorporates an entire host of regulations and standards by reference. Before signing the contract, a company should expend the effort to determine the regulatory framework under which it will perform the contract. Contractors can mitigate this risk by commenting on or submitting questions.

Subcontractors also make a number of mistakes at the outset of a contract. A common mistake occurs when subcontractors fail to analyze all the terms and conditions that are "flowed down" by the government prime contractor. Today, many large government prime contractors incorporate a very large numbers of FAR, DFARS, and other clauses into virtually all of their subcontracts through incorporating, by reference, a website that lists the standard terms and conditions. Unfortunately, these often detailed terms and conditions are not provided with every subcontract or purchase order and, in their haste to close a deal, the subcontractor simply does not review the clauses even though they are readily available on the Internet. Moreover, these "standard" terms and conditions may include a number of certifications and representations that can result in civil or even criminal liability if they are violated. An example that has led to many problems for subcontractors supplying material and components for major weapons systems involves compliance with the Berry Amendment's requirement that only domestic specialty metals be used in these systems. The failure to confirm and analyze these requirements, which are largely "incorporated by reference" into subcontracts and purchase orders, can lead to prosecutions or government claims against a number of commercial suppliers/subcontractors of items such as metal fasteners and parts.

Whether your company is a government prime or subcontractor, there are a number of steps you can take at the outset to reduce the litigation risk inherent in your contract.

- First, the contractor should determine whether any contract terms can be interpreted in more than one way. If they can, the contractor has an obligation to seek clarification of the ambiguous terms.[7]
- Second, contractors must identify the standards and regulations incorporated into the contract.
- Third, the contractor must identify the areas where it lacks relevant experience and determine whether it will need to acquire that experience through a teaming agreement or subcontract arrangement.

Determining and Mitigating Performance and Financial Risk

Another common source of risk that can be determined and addressed at the outset of a program relates to the financial and performance assumptions. Overly-optimistic financial and performance assumptions, in particular, are areas that can doom a contract to a poor outcome if not carefully considered prior to contract or subcontract award.

For example, if a company historically has had an overhead rate of forty-eight (48) percent, senior management should aggressively challenge an assumption in a bid or proposal that performance efficiencies will somehow reduce the overhead rate to thirty-two (32) percent and therefore support a potentially unrealistic price. Likewise, if a proposal relies on a cutting-edge technology, management should ensure that the assumptions relating to the maintenance and operation of the project are not overstated.

Other bid or proposal terms and assumptions, which should trip alarms and increase scrutiny, include the following items:

- **Schedule** – A contractor must ensure that it has the resources, financial and otherwise, for the contract's required delivery or completion schedule. Be very wary of assumptions that rely on dramatic improvement in the company's or in you're the subcontractor's "efficiency" to meet schedule requirements. When a critical-path or similar schedule methodology is available, look carefully for performance paths that have no "lag time" or that rely on a number of tasks being completed before a critical activity can be started.
- **Cost** – Where a company's bid relies upon a number of vendors or subcontractors, determine whether the vendors' prices are confirmed and will remain binding for a reasonable time after contract award; failure to do so can be disastrous if you win a bid, only to find that your actual costs will be substantially higher than planned. Where a bid calls for pricing for a number of years, or for a base period and optional periods, carefully examine annual escalation rates and projected cost increases for reasonableness.
- **Assumption of Performance Risk** – Carefully review the solicitation's specifications or statement of work to determine which party (i.e., the government or the contractor) bears the risk of not being able to satisfy the contract's performance requirements. For example, unless a contract is truly a "build to print" project where the government provides detailed design specifications, the contractor typically assumes the risk that it will be able to achieve the specification's performance require-

ments (and assumes risk of nonpayment and liability to the government for default and excess reprocurement costs).

Some of the techniques that a contractor can use to reduce this risk include rejecting unrealistic assumptions and revising its bid based on a more realistic assessment of the performance, contractual, and financial risks under a contract. Any assumptions upon which a proposal is based must be grounded on a complete and careful evaluation of the solicitation's terms, conditions, and specifications. It may be possible to include contingencies in a proposal or to take exception to terms and conditions that a contractor determines are unrealistic, but this can be difficult under government contracts because many terms and conditions are required by law or require that the solicitation be amended (which many government contracting agencies may be reluctant to do). To identify these issues, companies should involve a company's legal counsel in key decisions and proposal submissions to better identify the pre-award risks under a solicitation.

MANAGING RISK DURING PERFORMANCE OF A GOVERNMENT CONTRACT

Once a company has been awarded a government contract, it must continually monitor the performance, contractual, and financial risks that arise in the course of contract performance. To do this, a contractor must have controls in place that accurately track every aspect of its performance. Of particular importance are tools that track cost and schedule.

Risks in Taking Direction from Unauthorized Government Representatives

One of the most important principles for a government contractor to understand in order to protect itself from all of the risks attendant to performing a government contract is to ensure that the government representative with whom it is dealing has the *actual* authority to bind the government. It is an axiom of government contract law that only actual authority binds the government. "Where a party contracts with the government, apparent authority of the government's agent to modify the contract is not sufficient; an agent must have actual [express or implied] authority to bind the government."[8]

In *Winter v. Cath-dr/Balti Joint Venture*, the underlying contract explicitly set forth the limit of the authority of the government representative. Specifically, the government representative did not have the authority to obligate the government.[9] Although the court in *Winter* acknowledged that the "government [was] not without blame," it held that no implied authority could exist where the contract language and incorporated references were clear.[10] Thus, there was no express or implied authority and apparent authority was held insufficient to bind the government.

The issue of authority frequently arises with government program managers, inspectors, and contracting officer representatives. To protect your company, if you are unsure whether a government official has the authority to issue contractual direction, you should not follow the instructions until you have verified them with the contracting officer. If the contracting officer approves of the direction orally, you should send a confirmation letter or e-mail that documents the instructions. Failure to follow this process often results in the loss of a contractor's ability to recover any increased costs it incurs in complying with the unauthorized direction (and sometimes *demands*) of a government official who lacks contractual authority to bind the government.[11]

Managing Risks of Contract Changes

Even when dealing with authorized government representatives, a contractor must implement procedures to identify and manage changes to the contract in order to mitigate risks. Most importantly, the contractor must ensure it can recover increased costs or show that it is entitled to a revision of the contract schedule or other terms. In contrast to most commercial contracts, the government has the ability to order changes to a contract unilaterally.[12] While the formal changes clauses vary with the type of contract, a changes clause generally requires the contractor to continue with performance of the contract and to submit a request for an equitable adjustment seeking relief for any increased costs in performance as well as any required changes to the contract's performance schedule.

To recover for changes to the contract, a contractor first must have a thorough understanding of what the contract requires. Then, the contractor must give prompt notice of the change so that the contracting officer has an opportunity to determine whether the directed course of action constitutes a change. If the government decides to require the contractor to continue performance with the government's interpretation of the contract, the contractor generally has 30 days to submit its claim for equitable adjustment. To recapture the costs, the contractor should establish a separate charge number for the changed work. Failure to segregate and provide an accurate accounting of the direct costs of a change will compromise a contractor's ability to recover any increased costs at a later date.

Contractors should also implement policies to identify changes and to ensure that they meet any contractual notice requirements. All government contracts require contractors to provide notice of a change to the contract. Although there is no particular format that this notice must follow, it must include, at a minimum:

- The date, nature, and circumstances of the conduct or government direction that the contractor regards as a change;
- The name, position, and office of the government officials who are involved in, or know of, the change;
- An identification and description of any documents and oral communications relating to the change;
- If the change is in the form of an acceleration of the delivery or performance schedule, the circumstances under which the acceleration arose; and
- A description of the particular elements of the contract for which the contractor believes it is entitled to an adjustment (e.g., line items, labor or material required to complete the change; description of any delays or disruptions caused by the change; adjustments to delivery schedule, price, or other contract terms that must be made to accommodate the change).[13]

Failure to timely notify of a change may severely undercut or even defeat a contractor's ability to pursue a claim successfully, especially where the government argues it lost the opportunity to direct the contractor not to perform the change.

Managing the Risk of Potential Litigation

All contractors should ensure that their existing company policies, procedures, and internal controls do not undermine their ability to prosecute a claim (or defend against a government claim). These policies include record retention, telecommunications usage (including e-mail), ethics and compliance, and former employee responsibilities. Contractors must not only have these policies in place and ensure that they are consistent with law and the terms and conditions of their government contracts–*they must actually follow them!*

In too many companies, these items frequently exist in name only and are not followed in practice. Many employees believe that these programs distract from their focus on day-to-day business without providing any benefit to the bottom line. While the benefits of these programs may not be readily apparent on a daily basis, any company that has implemented and followed these policies will see substantial benefits should litigation arise under their contracts.

Some of the issues that document retention policies should focus on include:

- How long documents will be retained;
- Whether or not documents can be removed from the premises by an employee; and
- How to handle documents when employees leave the company.

Of all the documents created by companies, e-mails by far present the most risk. In addition to the expense associated with collecting and analyzing e-mail, people, for whatever reason, write e-mails as if they will never be seen by anyone outside the company. Employers must instruct and remind their employees that business e-mail accounts should be used for business purposes. In addition, employees should keep their work-related e-mails factually accurate. Clarity of e-mail is extremely important, as e-mails can be easily misconstrued and taken out of their original context when reviewed years later by individuals uninvolved in the original communication. Employees should also not attack their colleagues or their counterparts in the government or with other companies. Likewise, employees should not write e-mails that say things like "we are really screwing this project up. I hope we can get well on change orders."

Another common mistake of contractors is seeking to know why there was a problem with the performance of a specific program. While all contractors should seek to reinforce their successful practices and improve in those areas where their performance falls short of the mark, "red team," "tiger team," or "gold team" reviews generate a wealth of information regarding the problems on a program that frequently provide the opposition with ample fodder for discovery. Some of the issues that "red teams" identify as problems include a lack of program direction; poor program management; absence of cost controls; lack of a detailed work breakdown structure; failure to identify critical path activities; lack of skilled personnel; and overly optimistic schedule or cost assumptions.

It is obvious that a catalogue of these types of problems can undercut even the best legal argument. Attorneys love cases where they can state that their client does not have to say a word. If the court wishes to know why the contract failed, it can simply listen to the words of the contractor's [pick your color] team. The people on these teams must be sensitive to potential litigation and avoid the use of phrases that will render any claim or future litigation dead on arrival.

Contractors and their employees must also be sensitive to protecting their attorney-client and other privileged communications. Many documents (including e-mails and electronic documents) are privileged and do not have to be provided to adverse parties, including the government, if they are prepared by or for an attorney to assist in investigating a matter, formulating legal advice, or other purposes. In order retain this privilege, the documents and information they contain must be kept confidential, and the privilege will be lost if the documents or information is disclosed to third parties outside the company. Accordingly, contractors must ensure that any potentially privileged documents are clearly marked as "Attorney-Client Privileged" and are safeguarded so that they are not disclosed, even inadvertently, to anyone outside the company.

With regard to privileged documents, attorneys with the Department of Justice (DOJ) and other government agencies have long treated a company's decision not to turn over attorney-client privileged protected documents as a failure to fully cooperate in an investigation. In response to concerns by Congress and industry, the DOJ has issued updated guidelines regarding waiver of the attorney-client and work-product privileges.

In the Filip Letter, the DOJ provides prosecutors with five guidelines to be followed in evaluating whether a company has cooperated in an investigation:

- Cooperation will be measured by the relevant facts and evidence disclosed by the corporation and not by the waiver of the attorney-client or work product privileges.
- Federal prosecutors will not demand the disclosure of confidential attorney-client communications or an attorney's mental impressions as a condition for credit.
- Federal prosecutors will not consider whether the corporation has advanced attorneys' fees to its employees.
- Federal prosecutors will not consider whether the corporation has entered into a joint defense agreement.
- Federal prosecutors will not consider whether the corporation has retained or sanctioned employees.[14]

Despite the new guidance contained in the Filip Letter, federal prosecutors may continue to seek waivers of the attorney-client and attorney work-product privileges. Accordingly, contractors should consider the following:

- When conducting internal investigations, business organizations should consider that the government may ask for copies of any investigation reports, witness statements, and related documents.
- If the organization wishes to cooperate fully with the government's investigation, but also wants to avoid disclosing internal legal advice and other attorney work product, take reasonable steps, such as those outlined below, to ensure that documents such as investigation reports and witness statements do not include any privileged material. Preparing documents in this fashion may enable the company to provide the government the facts it needs to complete its investigation.
  - Include only information that is "factual" in nature in such documents and consider not reducing initial observations and information to writing until after key facts can be confirmed.
  - Avoid including attorney impressions, conclusions, or legal advice in such documents.

- The government is unlikely to waive prosecution or adverse administrative action in exchange for privileged information where the facts appear to establish a violation. This factor favors not waiving the attorney-client and work-product privileges so that the company's legal advice and strategies remain confidential throughout the course of any investigation as well as any ensuing judicial or administrative proceedings.

Managing Risk When Litigation Appears Possible

The first step that a contractor must take when litigation appears imminent is to ensure that any evidence relating to the dispute is preserved. Failure to preserve evidence at the contract's outset may result in allegations that a contractor has destroyed evidence. This so-called "spoliation of evidence" is taken very seriously by the courts and can result in a host of sanctions against the party responsible for destroying the evidence. These sanctions can include an order preventing the contractor from presenting favorable evidence in the areas relating to the destroyed evidence. In extreme cases, for example when evidence has been intentionally destroyed, a claim may be dismissed by the court or board of contract appeals.

"Spoliation is the destruction or significant alteration of evidence, or failure to preserve property for another's use as evidence in pending or *reasonably foreseeable* litigation."[15] The guiding principle behind the sanctions regime is to ensure that spoliators do not benefit from their conduct. Courts have the inherent authority to sanction spoliation of evidence and may choose from a range of options, from making an adverse inference to declaring a default judgment and imposing costs and attorney fees. Once the spoliation has occurred, the courts give greater leniency where there is disclosure of the spoliation, no future spoliation, and the impact of spoliation can be mitigated through other evidence.

The primary step most companies take to avoid spoliation of evidence is for the Chief Counsel or another senior official within the company to instruct the employees working on a project to take steps to preserve documents relating to the dispute. As part of this notice procedure, companies must notify their information technology (IT) support group not to overwrite back-up tapes that may contain documentation relevant to the dispute. This notice should include a brief description of the kinds of documents (including e-mails and electronic documents) that should be retained and identify an official in the company who should be provided with a description and the location of all such documents.

Early on and as part of the document collection process, contractors must take steps to create a list of individuals who have worked on the project or contract over the years. People frequently move between jobs or provide matrix support for a particular aspect of the project, and these individuals often create their own personal files of documents relating to the case that contain harmful information.

In addition to collecting documentation, contractors need to establish an internal structure with responsibility and authority to manage potential litigation, be it a claim, protest, etc. As part of this process, the company's counsel should prepare a memorandum for potential witnesses that outlines their role in the factual investigation. In addition, it should state unequivocally that legal counsel seeks their assistance so that it may provide legal advice to the corporation. The memorandum should also make it clear that, to the extent outside counsel is conducting the fact-finding, counsel represents the corporation and not the individual. Failure to properly describe the scope of representation may disqualify counsel from defending or prosecuting the case.

The best way to manage risk during litigation is to focus on the litigation. Too many companies view litigation as a minor inconvenience that will go away if ignored. While a company certainly can decide not to pursue litigation as a plaintiff, once a party becomes a defendant, the issue will not simply go away. Rather, the impact on the company will be driven, in large part, from how aggressively the other side decides to pursue the litigation or how vigorously the company chooses to defend the litigation.

Even when litigation is managed well, it can be very expensive. When managed poorly, litigation will drain a corporation's bottom line. To avoid this risk, contractors should designate an in-house representative as the day-to-day manager of the litigation.

Irrespective of whether a company is a plaintiff or a defendant, it should, as a general rule, push to get the matter resolved at the outset of the litigation. Bad facts do not get better with time, and witnesses' memories do not improve the further removed they are from an event. In the government contracts arena, however, what will likely determine the ultimate success or failure of a party's case is its documents. Consequently, the first thing a contractor needs to do when litigation appears imminent is to identify and collect its relevant documents.

After this initial step, contractors should establish realistic expectations, as well as the final desired outcome of the litigation. Discussions regarding these goals should involve both legal and business personnel within the company. In addition, the company should revisit these goals at a minimum of every three (3) to six (6) months to make any adjustments necessary. Objectives may include a monetary settlement, some sort of business capture relationship, or enjoining a competitor from using data to pursue additional contracts.

As part of the process, the company should also require its outside counsel to provide a budget for the litigation. This budget should cover every aspect of the litigation, including document production; written discovery; depositions; pre-trial motions; settlement discussions; and trial. As part of the budget process, contractors should ask for the names of the members of the litigation team as well as their hourly rates. Further, at the outset of the litigation, contractors should attempt to negotiate an agreement with the lawyers to obtain a discount on the attorney's rates or an agreement to freeze the rates for the duration of the litigation. The budget should be updated every three (3) to six (6) months, and counsel should provide a periodic comparison of its fees to the budget.

Because litigation costs are generally unallowable, contractors must take steps to segregate and separately account for these costs.[16] Furthermore, the contracting officer will generally withhold payment of the costs.[17] Consequently, contractors should consider approaching the contracting officer regarding conditional payment of these costs. To obtain conditional payment of litigation costs, a contractor will have to establish that payment is in the best interest of the government and provide adequate assurance, as well as an agreement by the contractor, that all costs will be repaid, plus interest, if the government ultimately deems them unallowable.[18]

In the government contracts arena, litigation may last several years before a case is resolved. For this type of litigation, companies should consider regular meetings or conference calls with their lawyers to discuss progress and key developments likely to affect outcome. At least once every six (6) months, companies should meet with their outside counsel to review the key evidence to date and assess how this data impacts the likelihood of prevailing in the dispute.

Given the cost of formal litigation, it is always prudent to consider whether less formal alternative processes are available to expedite a favorable outcome. These alternatives include various forms of "Alternate Dispute Resolution," or "ADR," that can be customized to the requirements and circumstances of a particular case. For example, it may be desirable to employ an independent legal or technical expert to receive a summary of each party's case and render a neutral evaluation of the likely outcome, from which the parties can fashion a settlement. Use of such a "third-party neutral" may be successful where the contractor and the government have very different views and are unable to agree on key facts or legal issues. Another alternative involves structured mediation, in which a respected third party serves to facilitate communication between the contractor and the government in order to assist the parties in assessing the strengths and weaknesses of their case to arrive at an acceptable settlement. Mediation can be particularly effective where the parties have a relatively good working relationship, but are having difficulty agreeing on the financial aspects of a case. There are many other forms of ADR that a contractor should discuss with counsel with a view towards reducing the financial and opportunity costs of formal litigation.

Once some companies become embroiled in litigation, they simply stop communicating with the opposing side. This is a mistake. If anything, it becomes even more important for the contractor to maintain an open line of communication with the government program and contract personnel involved in a claim. As noted, the contractor is generally required to continue to perform the contract while a dispute is being resolved, and failing to maintain open communication can impair contract performance and lead to even more acrimony. Moreover, a contractor's communication should reassure the government that it is simply looking for a principled, business resolution of the dispute and that it wants to maintain a business relationship with a valued customer. In addition, maintaining communications may serve to remove some of the emotion from the dispute and lead to a more meaningful dialogue between the parties. Prior to these communications, the contractor should consider discussing its conversations with counsel so that it does not inadvertently make a statement that the other side will attempt to portray as an admission. Contractors generally should also never use phrases during these communications that begin with the statement "my attorney told me," as this may result in a loss of attorney-client privilege with respect to the information (and, in any event, is unlikely to impress the government official with whom the contractor is speaking).

Finally, never forget that the government contracts arena is a very small community. Today's enemy is very frequently tomorrow's (if not today's) team member. As a result, throughout this process, contractors and their counsel must take the long view of business relationships. Counsel should be firm, but fair. Counsel should rarely engage in "scorched earth" tactics that damage business relationships, and contractors should be wary and raise any concerns with counsel if this seems to be occurring. Tactics such as deposing the CEO or the Secretary of the Army or contacting the Secretary of Defense or other senior officials that may have minimal or no involvement in a dispute regarding the litigation should only be pursued after very careful consideration. While pursuing such a strategy in a case might assist in short-term gains, it may result in the overall destruction of the business relationship.

Settlement Considerations

No matter what course a dispute with the government or its subcontractor may take, a contractor must always keep the subsequent administrative rights of the government in mind. If litigation is due to a statutory or regulatory allegation, it is likely that the government will also have an administrative cause of action. One such cause of action, the exclusionary action, can have a far more onerous impact on a contractor than a fine, or even a criminal conviction.

There are generally two types of exclusionary actions available to the federal government: (1) discretionary actions, which include both suspension, a temporary form of exclusion, and debarment, an exclusionary action for a fixed period of time, and (2) disqualification pursuant to a statute or executive order (hereinafter "statutory disqualification"). Typically, suspension and debarment actions exclude companies from entering into new contracts or new participation in federal loans, grants, or other federal financial assistance programs. These actions normally do not affect existing contracts or current loan or grant participation. Suspension is normally used where there is adequate evidence, such as an indictment, to believe that a cause for debarment exists but the criminal proceeding is not final. Suspension lasts during the pendency of a proceeding, but generally does not exceed 12 months. Debarments are often based on final adjudications, such as convictions, plea agreements, or settlements, and are for a fixed period of time, typically three years.

Both suspension and debarment involve a complex procedural process and a number of nuances understood by experienced counsel. Further, because these administrative actions frequently run on parallel tracks to the government's criminal and civil actions, it is imperative that a global strategy be developed among counsel to deal with the issues arising in each area in a coordinated matter, as findings and admissions in one action may adversely impact a contractor's position in one or more other parallel actions. Contractors must be mindful of the fact that the resolution or settlement of a fraud claim with the Department of Justice (which handles criminal and civil matters) does not control the resolution of the government's administrative actions, which are handled by other executive agencies that are not typically parties to plea and settlement agreements.

As one can imagine, the ramifications of suspension or debarment may be significant in that they effectively preclude the contractor from new federal work. The extent of a suspension or debarment may also have repercussions outside the federal marketplace as many states and private entities often inquire into a contractor's suspension/debarment status and may withhold offers from contractors that have been suspended or debarred by the federal government, especially for violations implicating the contractor's integrity, such as fraud. Thus, special attention should be given to all suspended or debarred public contracts, because further issues could arise if a contractor were to improperly certify to a suspension/debarment inquiry, such as criminal prosecution under 18 U.S.C. § 1001.

Indeed, a contractor could successfully resolve an alleged fraud claim with the Department of Justice only to find itself suspended or debarred from future government work. Moreover, under recent case law, it is possible for a contractor to successfully resolve a potential debarment with one government agency only to face a potential debarment or adverse responsibility determination by another agency based on the same conduct. Thus, the implications of suspension or debarment can far outweigh the costs associated with a one time civil penalty.

SUMMARY

Litigation is a risk that all government contractors face and involves many nuances and challenges that are not encountered in a purely commercial setting. While litigation cannot always be avoided, the costs and disruption associated with litigation can be mitigated and managed. Considering litigation risk in the course of day-to-day operations and contract performance, in the form of the policies and other measures discussed above, can greatly enhance a contractor's chances of success at a manageable cost. Of course, the foregoing is intended to assist contractors in identifying and managing risks and is not intended as legal advice, which should only be provided by a trusted lawyer after a discussion of all the facts and circumstances.

Chapter 12 provides a simple yet proven highly effective tool that can be used by government contractors to evaluate opportunities and risks prior to making a bid/no-bid decision on a U.S. government contract and/or by government agencies prior to contract award.

QUESTIONS TO CONSIDER

1. In the past three (3) years, has your organization been involved in any litigation, either with government agencies or your organization's subcontractors?

2. Does your organization actively promote and use alternative dispute resolution techniques?

3. How effectively does your organization manage risk in contract changes?

ENDNOTES

1. Partners in the Government Contracts practice group at Venable LLP, 575 7th Street NW, Washington, D.C., 20004 (www.venable.com). The authors gratefully acknowledge the assistance of Dismas Locaria and James Chiow, Associates at Venable LLP, in the preparation of this chapter.

2. For example, a small business may be able to recover some of its costs in successfully litigating claims against the federal government at the Board of Contract Appeals or the U.S. Court of Federal Claims under the Equal Access to Justice Act (5 U.S.C. § 504; 28 U.S.C. § 2812). Similarly, a contractor that successfully protests a solicitation or award to the Government Accountability Office may be able to recover its fees and costs under the Competition in Contracting Act (31 U.S.C. § 3554(c)). Recovery of litigation costs even in these settings, however, may be subject to caps on hourly rates and other limitations and, in practice, contractors rarely recover all of their costs associated with litigation.

3. FAR 31.205-47 (f) (1).

4. FAR 31.205-47 (f) (8).

5. Contractors must be very careful about agreeing to one type of contract and then entering into a different type of contract with its subcontractors that may impact its overall ability to manage the contract. For example, a company that enters into a firm-fixed price contract with the government and then, in turn, enters into cost-reimbursement or time-and-materials contract with its subcontractors may find that it will be unable to control subcontractor costs to the extent necessary to maintain profitability on the prime contract.

6. This issue can be very problematic in contracts where there are multiple stakeholders that have different policy goals and objectives. For example, under environmental remediation contracts, a contractor's performance may have to be approved by the U.S. Department of Energy, the U.S. Environmental Protection Agency, and a state department of health as well as a Management and Operations contractor. As we have seen over the years, each of these entities has a different interpretation of the myriad of regulations that may apply to a project. Likewise, there is no guarantee that these entities have a uniform understanding of the contract.

7. Under no circumstances should a contractor plan to use its more favorable interpretation of the ambiguous term during its performance of the contract. This type of "gamesmanship" with the hope of building in a change order during performance almost always fails.

8. Winter v. Cath-dr/Balti Joint Venture, 2006-1359 p. 7 (Fed. Cir. 2007).

9. Id. at 8-10.

10. Id. at 11.

11. Moreover, most government contracts require the contractor to expressly waive any rights to invoke the jurisdiction of local courts where the contracts are performed and contractors agree to accept the exclusive jurisdiction of a contract appeals board and the United States Court of Federal Claims. The underlying contracts may also contain unambiguous clauses providing (1) that the contract will be construed and interpreted in accordance with U.S. law and (2) that the contracting officer is the only person with authority to bind the government. Government representatives' appointment letters also contain clear prohibitions against obligating government funds and otherwise restrict those employees' authority. With such clear provisions, neither the Federal Circuit nor any other court is likely to find that the government is bound by a government employee's actions, absent government ratification. Ratification occurs when the government knows that an employee exceeded his or her authority, but a person with proper authority subsequently authorizes the action.

12. See FAR 52.243-5 (Changes and Changed Conditions).

13. See FAR 52.243-7 (Notification of Changes).

14. See Letter, July 9, 2008, Deputy Attorney General ("DAG") Mark Filip to U.S. Congress.

15. United States Medical Supply Co., Inc, v. United States, 77 Fed.Cl. 257, 263 (2007) (citing West v. Goodyear Tire & Rubber Co., 167 F.3d 776, 779 (2d Cir. 1999)) (emphasis added).

16. FAR 31.205-47 (g).

17. Ibid.

18. Ibid.

CHAPTER  12

CONTRACT INTERPRETATION, U.S. GOVERNMENT CONTRACTS, POLICIES, REVIEWS, AND AUDITS

INTRODUCTION

Simply stated, contract interpretation is the process of determining what the parties agreed to in their bargain. This process typically involves determining the intent of the parties who actually negotiated and formed the contract, which often requires determining the meaning of words, supplying missing words, and resolving ambiguities and/or contradictions that may appear in the contract. In U.S. federal government contracting, numerous contract performance problems and controversies stem from misunderstandings or disagreements about contract requirements. Thus, it is important for U.S. government agencies, government prime contractors, and subcontractors to understand the guidelines used in contract interpretation and the numerous U.S. federal government's contracting policies, review, and audits.

CONTRACT INTERPRETATION GUIDELINES

The cardinal rule of contract interpretation is to ascertain a single interpretation of the contract that reflects the parties' intent. U.S. courts and boards of contract appeals usually seek to determine the correct interpretation, based upon the intent of the parties, by examining two sources of information: (1) the language in the contract and (2) extrinsic evidence pertaining to facts and circumstances surrounding contract formation and post-award performance.[1]

Clearly, it can prove very difficult to discern what was in the minds of the parties—buyer and seller—unless their intent was well stated in the contract, in post-contract negotiation memoranda, or by their subsequent actions. U.S. courts and boards of contract appeals usually strive to determine the intent of contract parties when a contract dispute/claim arises by using the "objective test."[2]

The objective test is the understanding that U.S. courts and boards of contract appeals interpret a contract in a way that would be consistent with a reasonably intelligent person familiar with all of the facts and circumstances surrounding contract formation.[3]

Figure 12-1, illustrates the seven most common contract interpretation guidelines which are often used by U.S. government contracting officers, U.S. courts, and U.S. Boards of Contract Appeals, when resolving a contract dispute or claim which arises due to a contract interpretation issue.

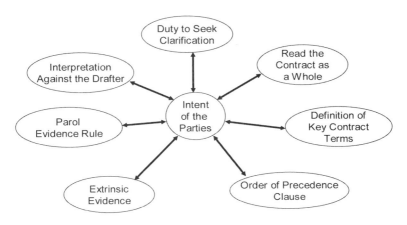

Figure 12-1
Contract Interpretation Guidelines

Read the Contract as a Whole

When a contract is formed, it is the entire document that embodies the agreement of the parties, buyer and seller, not just the scope of work, individual sections, or certain contract clauses. The meaning of the selected language in a contract is often derived from the context in which it appears. Thus, an attempt to interpret a word, term, phrase, or clause independent of the context of the remaining contract document may distort its intended meaning. In numerous U.S. court cases where the contract interpretation guideline "read the contract as a whole" has been used, the courts chiefly rely upon two key principles: (1) parts of a contract must be read together and harmonized if at all possible, and (2) preference is given to an interpretation that gives effect to all terms and leaves no clause meaningless.[4]

Definition of Key Contract Terms

Contracts are composed of words, numbers, and symbols that result in key terms and conditions between the parties, which in turn give rise to specific obligations for the buyer and the seller. In U.S. federal government contracting, generally U.S. courts and boards of contract appeals use three sources to define key contract terms. First, the courts and boards apply any definitions that the parties have incorporated into the contract document. Second, if a key contract term is not defined within the contract, then the courts and boards will use dictionaries or common usage to provide an appropriate definition. Third, if a key contract term is not defined in the contract and circumstances indicate that the intent of the parties was a technical term, not a common usage terms, then an appropriate technical definition is selected.

These latter two definitions are described by *Restatement (Second) of, Contracts,* section 202(3), which states:

> Unless a different intention is manifested, (a) where language has a general meaning it is interpreted in accordance with that meaning; (b) technical terms and words of art are given their technical meaning when used in a transaction within their technical field

It is important to remember that contracts often contain definitions of key terms in numerous places, including: the statement of work (SOW), performance work statement (PWS), performance standards and/or specifications, specific contract clauses, general contract clauses, incorporated by reference, and other contract sections.

Order of Precedence Clause

Given the length and complexity of most U.S. federal government contract documents, it is quite possible conflicting statements and/ or vague requirements may be drafted independently of each other. Thus, it may be quite difficult to arrive at an interpretation that gives a reasonable effect to all sections of a contract. When such contradictions, conflicts, and or ambiguities exist, they may be resolved by use of contract interpretation guidelines via an order of precedence clause contained within the contract. In order for an order of precedence clause to be applied, there must be a conflict between the terms and conditions in question.[5]

The basic order of precedence clause used in sealed bid and negotiated procurements, in FAR 52.214-29 and FAR 52.215-33, respectively, provides:

"Any inconsistency in this solicitation shall be resolved by giving precedence in the following order: (a) the Schedule; (b) representations and other instructions; (c) contract clauses; (d) other documents, exhibits, and attachments: and (e) the specification.

These FAR clauses may also be supplemented by agency clauses. The order of precedence clause guideline to contract interpretation provides an objective and relatively quick resolution of a contractual conflict. However, there is no real assurance that the decision reached will reflect the true intent of the parties.[6]

Extrinsic Evidence

There are three types of extrinsic evidence of surrounding circumstances frequently used to assist in the resolution of contract interpretation conflicts: (1) discussions and concurrent actions, (2) prior course of dealing between the parties, and (3) custom and trade usage.[7]

Evidence of discussions, meetings, teleconferences, emails, or conduct prior to the submission of bids, quotes, or proposals may serve as proof of the intent of the parties when conflicts arise pertaining to terms in a contract. Further, the conduct of the parties after contract award but before the controversy may provide valuable insight into the interpretation of the contract terms in question .

Evidence of prior course of dealings between the parties is an important type of extrinsic evidence to help resolve the meaning of ambiguous language or conflicts. Prior course of dealings can establish precedence based upon past actions, thus it can be used to establish the intent of the parties.

Evidence of related documents, such as a request for quotation, request for proposal, bids, quotes, proposals, or post negotiation memoranda may provide meaning via the custom and trade usage of the language in question.

Parol Evidence Rule

According to the *Restatement, Second, Contracts*, Section 213, the parol evidence rule "renders inoperative prior written or oral agreements that contradict an integrated agreement." If there is no fraud, duress, or mutual mistake, the parol evidence rule prohibits a party from presenting prior agreements to prove the meaning or intent of the words in dispute.

Interpretation Against the Drafter

In accordance with *Restatement, Second, Contracts*, Section 206: "In choosing among the reasonable meanings of a promise or agreement or a term thereof, that meaning is generally preferred which operates against the party who supplies the words or from whom a writing otherwise proceeds."

The Latin phrase for interpretation against the drafter is *contra proferentem.*

Duty to Seek Clarification

Contra proferentem does not apply if the non-drafting party fails before bidding to seek clarification of an ambiguity of which it was or should have been aware.8   If a contractor fails to inquire about an ambiguous term or conflicting requirements prior to the contract, it forfeits the opportunity to rely on its interpretation and thus bears the risk of misinterpretation.

The seven guidelines of contract interpretation explained above can help U.S. government agencies, prime contractors, and/or subcontractors to resolve potential vague, ambiguous, or contradictory contract requirements.

U.S. GOVERNMENT CONTRACTING: POLICIES, REVIEWS, & AUDITS

In an effort to support the Obama administration, the Government Accountability Office (GAO) has created a web site, www. gao.gov/transition 2009, which includes a list of 13 urgent government contracting issues facing the Obama administration and Congress. The GAO Web site lists numerous opportunities to cut government contracting costs, such as improving the Department of Defense (DoD) major weapon systems acquisition process, applying best practices to strategic sourcing, promoting competition for contracts, improving the use of contract award fees and incentives, improving the Department of Homeland Security's acquisition management, improving oversight of oil and gas royalties, reducing improper federal contract payments, and owning instead of leasing property.

■   The Obama administration policy reform, which is widely affecting government contracting, is a movement toward "greater transparency." In brief, this policy means more government oversight of contractors, both on an individual and organizational basis, via the increased focus on the potential for personal conflicts of interest (PCI) and organizational conflicts of interest (OCI). In addition, greater transparency means more reviews and audits conducted by government agencies of government contractors including: contractor purchasing systems reviews (CPSRs); earned value management systems (EVMS); integrated baseline reviews (IBRs); cost estimating and accounting system reviews; government property (GP) management systems reviews; defense contract audit agency (DCAA) audits; inspector general (IG) inspections; and so on. Moreover, effective December 21, 2008, there were new requirements for government contractors pursuant to the Federal Acquisition Regulation (FAR). The new regulations require government contractors to provide timely disclosure to the government of certain violations of criminal law, False Claims Act violations, and any significant overpayment by the government;

- Have a written code of business ethics and conduct and provide education and training to employees; and
- Establish specific internal controls to prevent and detect improper conduct in connection with government contracts.

For this reason, compliance programs will become even more important for government contractors.9

Apart from the heightened scrutiny for all government contractors, there is an intense focus on major Department of Defense and Homeland Security contractors. Clearly, Defense and Homeland Security spending is likely to experience significant programmatic changes as the Obama administration addresses domestic concerns, as well as the global financial crisis. Accordingly, Defense and Homeland Security programs are being forced to adjust to budget realignments, which forces structure trade-offs (some programs are being cancelled outright).

Moreover, the Departments of Defense and Homeland Security will not be the only agencies to undergo internal competition for diminished budget resources. In short, there will probably be an increase in terminations for convenience, especially in the Departments of Defense, Homeland Security, Energy, and NASA, where the majority of funding is spent acquiring products, services, and integrated solutions from government contractors.

In addition, the Obama administration is focused on rebuilding the federal government's workforce, thus, reducing the practice of competitive sourcing, which is currently implemented pursuant to Office of Management and Budget (OMB) Circular A-76. Further, the Obama administration has already requested the Office of Management and Budget's, Office of Federal Procurement Policy (OFPP) to evaluate the definition of the term "inherently governmental function" to possibly include key acquisition workforce functions such as acquisition planning, strategic sourcing, source selection, contract administration, project planning, system engineering, cost/price/analysis, contract auditing, and program management. Currently, tens of thousands of government contractors are filling these key acquisition roles, because the government does not have the expertise required to get the needed work accomplished. Therefore, the Obama administration intends to significantly increase hiring, training, and retaining federal government employees across the civilian service system, with special emphasis on key acquisition positions, which perform inherently governmental functions.10

Where Is the Money Being Spent?

Pursuant to the 2009 American Recovery and Reinvestment Act (ARRA), the Obama administration and the U.S. Congress have already authorized $787 billion in tax relief and increased spending, resulting in huge increases in funding for numerous U.S. government departments and agencies, including:

- U.S. Department of Education
- U.S. Department of Labor
- U.S. Department of Health & Human Services
- U.S. Department of Housing & Urban Development
- U.S. Department of Energy
- Environmental Protection Agency
- U.S. Department of Transportation
- U.S. Department of State
- Many others11

Preparing for Government Contracting Policy Changes

As the saying goes, "It is best to live in interesting times." Clearly, the next several years will be very interesting times for government contractors, and especially so for major defense contractors. Accordingly, we suggest government contractors focus on the following five actions to prepare for the pending changes:

1. Improve performance results on government contracts and programs, especially on-time delivery within budget, and meet or exceed government requirements.
2. Be well prepared for increased government oversight on all business systems, policies, and practices.
3. Increase the use of competition in internal purchasing system and practices.
4. Enhance ethics and compliance programs, especially PCI and OCI aspects.
5. Improve the education and training of accounting, contract management, pricing, supply chain management, and project/program management personnel to address the requirements and elevated scrutiny of government agencies and Congress.12

A Key U.S. Government–Conducted Review of Government Contractors: The Contractor Purchasing System Review (CPSR)

Contractor purchasing system reviews (CPSRs) are governed by the Federal Acquisition Regulation (FAR) Part 44.3. It provides that the contracting officer or administrative contracting officer (ACO) "shall" determine whether a CPSR is needed for a particular prime contractor based on, but not limited to:

- The past performance of the contractor and
- The volume, complexity, and dollar value of its subcontracts.

If a contractor's sales to the government (excluding competitively awarded firm-fixed-price and competitively awarded fixed-price with economic price adjustment contracts and sales of commercial items pursuant to FAR Part 12) are expected to exceed $25 million during the next 12 months, then the ACO must perform a review to determine whether a CPSR is necessary. The term *sales* includes receipts from prime contractors, subcontracts under government prime contracts, and modifications. Generally, a

CPSR is not performed for a single specific contract. The head of the agency responsible for contract administration may raise or lower the $25 million review level if it is in the government's best interest to do so.

In deciding whether to conduct a CPSR, the ACO assesses the risk posed by the contractor's system. In doing so, the ACO considers a number of factors:

- The contractor's CPSR history
- How previous CPSR recommendations were addressed (or not)
- Dates of previous CPSRs
- The mix of contracts performed by the contractor
- Direct material and material overhead as a percentage of total sales
- The percentage of total sales represented by government sales
- Previous DCAA audit reports
- Information obtained from contracting officers and other officials
- Education, training, and experience of the contractor's procurement personnel
- The contractor's efforts to conduct internal audits and other types of self-assessments
- The contractor's position in the industry
- Reorganizations, mergers, and divestitures
- Significant increases or decreases in sales

Once the initial determination to conduct a review has been made, the ACO must make a similar determination at least every three years.

Extent of the CPSR

A CPSR reviews a prime contractor's purchasing system, but it does not include subcontracts that the contractor awards in support of government prime contracts that were competitively awarded firm-fixed price, competitively awarded fixed-price with economic price adjustment, or awarded for commercial items pursuant to FAR Part 12. Special attention is given to:

- The degree of price competition obtained by the prime contractor;
- Pricing policies and techniques, including methods of obtaining accurate, complete, and current cost or pricing data and certifications, as required;

- Methods of evaluating a prospective subcontractor's responsibility under FAR Part 9, including methods intended to avoid awarding subcontracts to suspended or debarred entities;
- Treatment of affiliates and other concerns that work closely with the prime contractor;
- Policies and procedures relating to small business subcontracting;
- Planning, award, and post-award management of major subcontracting programs;
- Compliance with CAS in awarding subcontracts;
- Appropriateness of the types of contracts used;
- Management and control systems, including internal audit procedures, used to administer progress payments to subcontractors.

The government will also look for:

- Noncompliance with public laws;
- Noncompliance with regulations;
- Noncompliance with prime contract requirements;
- Failure to establish sound policies and procedures in subcontracting; and
- Failure to implement sound business practices

Effect of an Approved Purchasing System

ACO approval of a prime contractor's purchasing system lists the plant or plants covered by the approval. Upon approval, the prime is no longer required to provide advance notice to the government in awarding subcontracts under fixed-price contracts, but still is required to provide advance notice under cost-reimbursement prime contracts. Nor is the prime contractor required to obtain the government's consent for subcontracts in fixed-price contracts or specified subcontracts in cost-reimbursement contracts. This exemption does not apply to any subcontracts that are under an ACO's "surveillance" pursuant to FAR 44.304.

Effect of Disapproval of a Government Contractor's Purchasing System

Disapproval means that there are major weaknesses in a contractor's purchasing system. Even if a contractor has an approved system, approval can be withdrawn any time the ACO determines that the contractor's system has deteriorated or that withdrawal is necessary to protect the government's interest pursuant to FAR

44.305-3. The regulation stipulates that approval can be withheld or withdrawn when there is recurring noncompliance with requirements, including, but not limited to:

■ Cost or pricing data;
■ implementation of CAS;
■ advance notification; or
■ small business subcontracting.

A contractor normally has 15 days in which to develop a plan to address the reasons for disapproval.

Without an approved subcontracting system, a firm is unable to award a subcontract without obtaining prior approval from the government. In addition to time (and expense) to a company's business processes, there are a variety of other problems that can flow from disapproval, such as:

■ Losing out on competitive proposals;
■ poor past performance reports;
■ disallowance of certain costs paid to subcontractors;
■ loss of revenue;
■ increased Government oversight;
■ increased overhead; and
■ delayed billings and collections.

How to Approach a CPSR

It is best to view a CPSR as an opportunity, not as a problem, and to keep the following in mind:

■ Don't be reactive—instead, conduct your own risk assessment to determine how well your company is doing;
■ Develop new processes, policies, and procedures where necessary;
■ Train your procurement staff and your end-users;
■ Brief upper management on what is at stake and what you are doing;
   – Make sure your people understand all of the positive things that can come out of a CPSR, especially how it can maintain or improve your relationship with the government.

U.S. Government Audits and Other Reviews

One of the distinctive features of federal contracts is the clause that gives the contracting officer and the Comptroller General the right to review certain prime contractor books and records. FAR Subsection 52.215-2, in part, states the following:

a. *Examination of costs.* If this is a cost-reimbursement, incentive, time-and-material, labor-hour, or price redeterminable contract, or any combination of these, the prime contractor shall maintain and the contracting officer, or an authorized representative of the contracting officer, shall have the right to examine and audit all records and other evidence sufficient to reflect properly all costs claimed to have been incurred or anticipated to be incurred directly or indirectly in performance of this contract. This right of examination shall include inspection at all reasonable times of the contractor's plants, or parts of them, engaged in performance of the contract

b. *Cost or pricing data.* If the prime contractor has been required to submit cost or pricing data in connection with any pricing action relating to this contract, the contracting officer, or an authorized representative of the contracting officer, in order to evaluate the accuracy, completeness, and currency of the cost or pricing data, shall have the right to examine and audit all of the prime contractor's records, including computations and projections, related to (1) the proposal for the contract, subcontract, or modification; (2) the discussions conducted on the proposal(s), including those related to negotiating; (3) pricing of the contract, subcontract, or modification; or (4) performance of the contract, subcontract or modification.

c. *Comptroller General.* The Comptroller General of the United States, or an authorized representative, shall have access to and the right to examine any of the contractor's directly pertinent records involving transactions related to this contract or a subcontract hereunder.13

The federal government contract audit agencies, the largest of which is the Defense Contract Audit Agency (DCAA), are responsible for providing financial and accounting advice to federal government procurement officials. Procurement officials may also call upon agency inspectors general (IGs) or CPA firms under contract to perform this service. The contracting officer may request field pricing support, which includes a government evaluation of any offeror's proposal prior to negotiation of a contract or modification (FAR Subsection 15.404-2). The contract auditor also serves as the contracting officer's representative in the review of prime contractor accounting records and provides advisory comments and recommendations to the contracting officer. While the contract audit opinions are advisory, internal government follow-up procedures have been established to assure that appropriate consideration and action is taken on audit recommendations.

To provide the contracting officer with financial and accounting advice, the contract auditor performs various reviews, such as the following:

- *Pre-award survey.*–Financial capability and accounting system surveys are performed to assess a prospective prime contractor's financial soundness, as well as the adequacy of the accounting system, to accumulate the type of cost information required by the contract.
- *Forward pricing proposals evaluation.*–The contract auditor evaluates cost estimates in the prime contractor's contract-pricing proposal for allocability, reasonableness, and allowability. These government audits may be directed at specific procurement actions or may involve prospective cost rates that may be used to estimate costs on future procurement actions.
- *Postaward review of cost or pricing data.*–This is the government's terminology for reviews intended to test compliance with P.L. 87-653, commonly known as The Truth in Negotiations Act. This legislation states that the prime contractor must provide the government with accurate, current, and complete cost or pricing data when negotiating contracts subject to P.L. 87-653. To the extent that the prime contractor does not comply with the provisions, thereby increasing the contract price, the government is entitled to a corresponding price reduction for the so-called "defective pricing."
- *Incurred cost audit.*–This government audit focuses on the allowability of direct and indirect costs billed to the government on contracts providing for cost reimbursement or settlement of final prices based on costs incurred.
- *Cost accounting standards compliance and adequacy reviews.*–The purpose of the compliance review is to determine whether the prime contractor's accounting practices conform to the standards promulgated by the Cost Accounting Standards Board

(CASB). The adequacy reviews are designed to determine whether the description of the cost-accounting practices contained in the company's CAS Disclosure Statement is accurate, current, and complete.

- *System reviews.*–These audits cover systems related to federal contract pricing, costing, and billing, such as estimating systems, labor reporting systems, and billing systems.
- *Terminated contract audits.* When a contract or subcontract is partially or completely terminated, the termination contracting officer must submit all contractor settlement proposals over $100,000 to the appropriate audit agency for examination and recommendations concerning the allocability, allowability, and reasonableness of costs. (FAR Subpart 49.107).
- *Claim audits.*–These audits include evaluations of requests for equitable adjustments and claims to be resolved under the Contract Disputes Act of 1978, as amended (41 U.S.C. 601-603).
- *Operations audits and other financial reviews.*–Generally, these audits activities involve evaluating those management and operational decisions made by the prime contractor that affect the nature and level of costs being proposed and incurred on government contracts. These reviews usually result in the government auditor's providing the company with recommendations on how to improve controls and the economy and efficiency of prime contractor operations.

In summary, the fundamental purpose of a government contract audit is to determine the allowability (including reasonableness and allocability) of costs contained either in a proposed price or in a statement of costs incurred during contract performance. FAR Part 31 provides the authoritative criteria for making this determination. Furthermore, contracts provide broad access rights, and statutory inspectors general and DCAA have authority to subpoena certain contractor books, records, and other supporting documentation.14

The concept of allowability of costs is derived primarily from the procurement regulations. For most federal agencies, FAR Part 31 contains the criteria for determining allowability, and many agencies supplement these basic criteria with FAR supplements that specify more precise rules for the respective agencies. A cost is considered allowable if it is reasonable and allocable and not prohibited by the provisions of FAR or contractual terms and conditions.

For many prime contractors, the standards promulgated by the Cost Accounting Standards Board provide the guidance for determining the allocability of costs to government contracts. FAR Part 31 also contains some basic guidance relating to allocability. Once the cost is determined to be allocable, the contract cost principles (FAR Part 31) provide the guidance for identifying which of these costs are eligible for reimbursement. Generally accepted accounting principles (GAAP) apply where FAR or CAS fails to address a specific element of cost.

A significant portion of the contract pricing under negotiated procurements is cost-based. Furthermore, the accounting method used in pricing negotiated contracts is full-absorption costing. Therefore, all allowable and allocable costs ordinarily should be identified in conformity with applicable procedures so that reimbursement may be obtained.

The government does not require prime contractors to restructure their accounting systems to accommodate the full absorption concept. Therefore, memorandum records may be used to make the allocations. For example, some companies do not include general and administrative (G&A) expenses in work-in-process inventory. Prime contractors are permitted to use memorandum records to make the allocation because those costs are allocable and allowable. However, the memorandum records are subject to audit and, therefore, should be reconcilable to the formal accounting records.15

Subcontracts Audits

Companies serving as subcontractors, at all tiers, are generally subject to the same terms and conditions that apply to the federal prime contractors. The prime contractor, or higher-tier subcontractor, is responsible for administering the respective subcontracts. This includes performing audits of subcontract prices and compliance with contractual requirements, such as CAS, cost and pricing data, and progress payment provisions.

Understandably, subcontractors are often reluctant to allow prime contractors to review their books and records. The government, in recognizing this sensitivity, may perform these reviews in lieu of the prime contractor. However, the prime contractor still remains contractually liable for its subcontractors' compliance with applicable procurement rules and regulations. The government has the right to reduce the prime contract price for subcontractor violations. The prime contractor is then faced with obtaining indemnification from the subcontractor for losses sustained as a result of the subcontractor's failure to comply with any procurement regulation.

Unique to government contracts is that prime contracts meeting certain dollar thresholds must contain a positive plan for awarding subcontracts to small business concerns (FAR Subpart 19.7). Additionally, the Small Business Act of 1953, as amended, established direct procurement responsibilities for each procuring agency with socially and economically disadvantaged firms under Section 8(a) of the SBA. The program is more commonly known as the 8(a) program. Actually, the procuring agency enters a tripartite agreement with the Small Business Administration and the socially and economically disadvantaged firm. These 8(a) procurements are, by definition, negotiated (FAR Subpart 19.8).16

There are two more important audit functions related to federal government contracting: the Government Accountability Office (GAO) and the Office of the Inspector General (OIGs). The GAO is an agent of Congress and conducts reviews necessary to evaluate all the activities in the executive departments, including procurement. GAO's focus is to ascertain whether the executive agencies are properly implementing the laws passed by Congress. Its examination authority is granted through the audit and records–negotiation clause (FAR Subsection 52.215-2 paragraph [d]). The OIG's examination authority is derived from the Inspector General Act of 1978, as amended. The OIG operates as an oversight function within the agency for which it was established. In connection with its review of the procurement process, OIG has been granted administrative subpoena authority to assure access to the books and records of government contractors. Note that, for some government agencies, the OIG has contract audit responsibility.17

SUMMARY

This chapter has reviewed the seven common contract interpretation guidelines used in U.S. federal government contracts, numerous government contracting policies, government reviews, and audits performed by government auditors on government prime contractors and subcontractors. To achieve success as a government prime contractor and/or subcontractor, it is important to know the rules of the game, be fully compliant with the U.S. government's laws and regulations, and know how to maximize a contract opportunity while mitigating the risk of doing business with the government.

Chapter 13 looks at the future of contract administration and the importance of creating and managing a governance structure.

QUESTIONS TO CONSIDER

1. Which contract interpretation guidelines does your organization typically use to resolve contract disputes?

2. How efficient and effective is your organization's purchasing system?

3. Which U.S. government audits have you participated in, either giving and/or receiving?

ENDNOTES

1   Cibinc, John, & Nash, Ralph C. *Administration of Government Contracts*, 4th ed. Chicago: CCH, 2004).
2   Ibid.
3   Ibid.
4   Ibid.
5   Ibid.
6   Ibid.
7   Garrett, Gregory A., & McDonald, Peter. Preparing for Change: The Obama Administration Effect on Government Contractors. NCMA, *Contract Management Magazine*, February 2009.
8   Ibid.
9   Ibid.
10   Ibid.
11   Federal Procurement Data System, OFPP, Report. Washington, D.C., March 2009.
12   Ibid., note 7.
13   American Institute of Certified Public Accountants, Inc. *Audit & Accounting Guide for Federal Government Contractors*. New York, 2008.
14   Ibid., note 3.
15   Ibid., note 3.
16   Ibid., note 3.
17   Ibid., note 3.

THE FUTURE OF CONTRACT ADMINISTRATION: PURPOSE DRIVEN GOVERNANCE™

INTRODUCTION

What will contract management look like in the future? Will businesses and governments enter into and manage their contracts the same way that they do today? Contract management isn't generally thought of as a dynamic or innovative business activity. But contract management isn't any less subject to change than any other critical business or governmental process. What were considered leading advertising techniques on Madison Avenue in the 1960's (e.g., the HBO series "Mad Men") wouldn't work very well for online advertising in our Internet age.

Similarly, contracts based on an industrial age model *ipso facto* cannot continue to optimally serve the interests of contracting parties. Business culture, politics, growing litigation costs, globalization, technology advances, ethics scandals, lack of trust in business relationships and in government, contraction of credit markets, skilled workforce shortages—all of these forces work to shape how transactions between buyers and sellers are conducted.

The way business and government customers and service providers manage long-term, complex services contracts has undoubtedly undergone a paradigm shift in recent years. Rather than entering into a transaction defined by legally binding terms, parties now purposely enter into a loosely defined cooperative relationship intended to produce business outcomes more like the cost-efficient operations or increased competitive advantage in the marketplace.

Nowhere is this shift more evident than in outsourcing. The size and complexity of outsourcing deals, often reaching into the billions of dollars; the long and captive nature of outsourcing relationships lasting five years or more; and the unpredictability of changes in business conditions, technology, and market forces have increasingly lead away from reliance on contracts to manage and control outsourcing, and towards the joint and dynamic "governance" of outsourcing relationships independent of definitive contractual terms.[1]

The End of Contract Management?

Prominent outsourcing experts Sara Cullen and Leslie Willcocks maintain that aligning and maintaining "values" is more important to outsourcing than written contracts or arms-length dealing.[2] Management consulting firm Vantage Partners, a spinoff of the

Harvard Negotiation Project, brazenly states that written contracts are detrimental to the management of outsourcing:

> Looking to the contract to determine how to manage the chaos of [outsourcing] transition is fruitless; while outsourcing contracts serve many useful purposes, they fall short on informing the customer and service provider exactly how they will work together to manage all of the changes outsourcing requires. Contracts are written in legal language and focus on what the parties will do, but little on how they will operate together.[3]

Within government contracting, the Procurement Round Table (PRT) has addressed the problems faced by the government and contractors when outsourcing or contracting for long, complex services under current acquisition regulations:

> The PRT thinks it is unrealistic to ask agencies to specify services at the time of contract award in clear, specific, objective, and measurable terms when future needs are not fully known or understood, requirements and priorities are expected to change during performance, and the circumstances and conditions of performance are not reliably foreseeable. Yet those are the difficulties faced by agencies and their contractors when they negotiate long-term and complex service contracts.
>
> In real life, parties to long-term and complex service contracts do not specify all requirements at the time of contract award in clear, specific, objective, and measurable terms; instead, they engage in ad hoc decision making in response to emerging and changing requirements, shifting priorities, and unexpected circumstances."[4]

Scholars in the fields of management and information systems sciences have also argued that contracts and the negotiation process undermine outsourcing governance for several reasons. Contract negotiations and reliance on terms creates distrust between customer and provider, whereas governance is based on the existence of trust. Specification of service terms induces the moral hazard of not doing what is not written in the contract, while governance promotes it. The negotiation process required by contracts creates substantial up-front transaction costs not present with governance. Creating detailed, complex contracts inhibits the free exchange between customer and provider that is at the heart of governance. The net effect of relying on both contracts and governance to manage outsourcing is a negative one.[5]

Governance Models

The Carnegie Mellon eSourcing Capability Model for Client Organizations (eSCM-CL) is the most comprehensive and detailed model available of outsourcing and services governance.[6] The mission of the eSCM is "to continuously evolve, improve, and innovate [customer organizations'] capabilities to develop stronger, enduring, and more trusting relationships with their service providers, and to meet the dynamic demands of their business while effectively managing service delivery by their service providers."[7] The goals of eSCM are fewer failures in customer-provider relationships, better provider performance, more efficient management of providers, and increased value derived from those relationships.[8]

The eSCM breaks out governance into a set of management functions called ongoing capabilities areas: sourcing strategy; governance (establishing a governance organization and processes); relationship (dealing with stakeholders and with the other party); performance (meeting customer requirements); value (aligning services strategy and performance); organizational change; people; knowledge; technology; and threat (managing risk).[9] Practice mgt04, Agreement Management, and the other Practices in the Sourced Services Management Capability Area (located in the Delivery Phase of the model's Sourcing Life-cycle) are the eSCM's brand of contracts management.[10] The scope of eSCM's concept of governance overlaps with what most in the government and corporate sectors would define as the practices that make up traditional contracts management. But the subject areas for management in the eSCM go well beyond traditional contract management's parameters.[11] More profoundly, contracts are not the final authority in the eSCM model that they are in contracts management.

Figure 13-1 gives an overview of how established contracts management practices sit within a governance model such as eSCM.

Figure 13-1

Overview of Contract Management Function Within Representative Governance Model

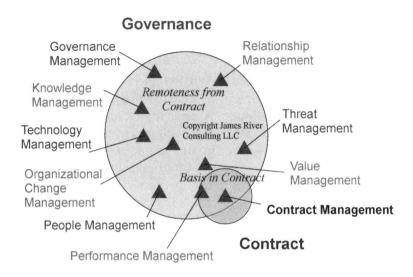

Governance

Governance Management

Relationship Management

Knowledge Management

Remoteness from Contract

Technology Management

Copyright James River Consulting LLC

Threat Management

Organizational Change Management

Basis in Contract

Value Management

People Management

Contract Management

Performance Management

Contract

Philosophy of Governance

The eSCM's Value Management Ongoing Capability Area illustrates the philosophical differences between contracts management and governance.

Value management is "fostering and managing the culture of continuous improvement so that the client derives value from the sourcing engagement, and ensuring ongoing alignment of the sourcing strategy and the organization's sourcing performance with the organization's objectives."[12] Following the individual practices that make up value management, a sourcing organization (the people within the customer organization responsible for managing services delivery) measures, in addition to service provider performance, the performance of the sourcing organization itself using selected performance measures. Sourcing capabilities are then benchmarked (i.e., industry performance data, industry best practices, sourcing models), and the sourcing organization may take corrective actions by both renegotiating service delivery terms with the service provider and improving its own sourcing processes and resources to address recurring problems and increase stakeholder value.[13]

Value management turns contracts management on its head. The purpose of contracts management is to enforce defined and legally binding service delivery terms. Success or failure of contracts management is determined by whether contract terms have been performed. But in value management, an assessment of the management of the services delivery may lead to changing the terms of the service delivery so that they are better manageable.

In another example, Practice mgt08, Review Service Performance (Sourced Services Management Capability Area) addresses contract non-performance as follows: "A procedure to reconcile service provider performance against expectations as a trend over time will lead to fact-based decisions for fine-tuning client requirements and expectations, the services delivered and their performance, and, eventually, for future sourcing decisions..."[14] Any actions to be taken in response to identified gaps between services and documented service terms must be done "jointly" between client and service provider under mgt08.[15] In contract law, non-performance of terms is a breach that entitles one of the parties to seek cure or assurances from the other party. Review Service Performance does not recognize non-performance as an event that creates legal rights and remedies upon its occurrence, but as a subject for continuous and joint management.

In Practice mgt05, Problem & Incident Monitoring, a process for resolution of service problems must be mutually agreed to by the customer and provider; the process may be documented in the contract but may also be documented in other ways outside the actual contract, such as in the governance charter. There is a general assumption in mgt05 that service providers are responsible for correcting service problems; however, the customer is expected to collaborate with the provider in responding to the problem.[16] The service resolution process in mgt05 is intended only to modify the delivery of services. It is not an adjudication of rights under the contract, equivalent to the dispute resolution clause in most contracts. Disputes over service delivery in the eSCM are separately addressed in Practice rel04, Issue Management, which directs the parties to resolve issues using a collaborative method instead of taking a positional approach[17]

Figure 13-2 describes the key discriminating features between contracts management and governance.

Figure 13-2

Key Discriminators Between Contract Management and
Governance Generally

Contract Management	Governance
- Enforcement of Set of Terms	- Continuous Setting and Resetting of Terms
- Limited (Contract, Project) & Unilateral Management	- Varied & Joint Management
- Non Performance Viewed As Breach and Damages	- Non Performance Viewed as Matter of Management
- Arms Length Interaction	- Trust Based Interaction
- Self Limiting, Lower Transaction Costs	- No Self Limits, Higher Transaction Costs
- Cohesive Negotiations and Complete Value Trading	- Incomplete Value Trading Across Multiple Negotiations
- Rational Decision making	- Bounded Rationality in Decision making
- Change Viewed as Outside of Transaction	- Change Viewed as Integral Part of Transaction
- Performance of Requirements	- Achievement of Outcomes
- Risks Generally and Prospectively Allocated	- Risks Specifically and Contemporaneously Managed

Copyright James River Consulting LLC

Downside of Governance

Surveys conducted by outsourcing advisory firms have found that outsourcing customers spend on average about 7% of total contract value on governance, but the range of spend figures can go as high as 11%.[18] The eSCM states that governance costs should be between 2% and 12%.[19] The wide fluctuation in the cost of governance found in surveys should not be surprising, as governance is not self-limiting in the way contracts management is. Whereas contract management takes place within the explicit framework of a contract document and consists of monitoring performance and administering customer-provider interactions, governance has no self-limiting characteristics. The size and cost of governance can be as much or as little as the parties perceive is needed to achieve desired outcomes. If objectives are not being met, the logical response is to increase the amount of governance. At the end of the day, governance must govern itself, an inherent flaw that itself creates governance on top of governance and further increases costs.

Unfortunately, increasing the amount of governance does not mean greater success in outsourcing. A 2007 survey by prominent outsourcing consultancy EquaTerra concluded that there is no correlation between the amount spent on governance and satisfaction with governance.[20] The same 2007 EquaTerra survey generated another interesting result: While almost half of respondents said that a strong contract was the most important driver of outsourcing success, only one third replied that outsourcing governance was most important.[21]

Finally, the organizational and personnel competencies required to conduct governance can be very difficult and costly to develop or obtain, as governance is multidisciplinary. Whereas contracts management mostly comprised of legal, business administration and, project management skills, governance can also encompass professional skills in finance, systems engineering, human resources, industrial psychology, and risk management. Organizations must think long and hard about whether they are capable of governing large, complex service deals in ways that are not bound by contract.

Organizational Constraints on Governance

Strategic sourcing, which began in the 1990's, has become a widely adopted approach to procurement among corporations and government agencies. Strategic sourcing is the organized, systematic, and collaborative identification of suppliers for long-term agreements to purchase needed goods and services.[22] It involves some degree of centralized direction or coordination of buying across all business units, including adherence to prescribed processes and criteria for selecting suppliers and negotiating commercial terms, designation of suppliers for purchasing segmented commodities, evaluation of supplier performance using key metrics, and overall alignment of supplier relationships with strategic plans.

Administration of strategic sourcing is heavily dependent on the use of contracts as a way to define and maintain supplier relationships. Whereas strategic sourcing can be easily and effectively cascaded down through organizations by documenting sourcing policies and incorporating them into contract terms, governance dynamics are much less formal and more exposed to both organizational communication failures and rogue managers who have not bought into strategic sourcing. Without the ability to cascade strategic sourcing through contracts, organizations must find other methods of integrating sourcing strategy with governance; otherwise governance becomes the very thing that strategic sourcing is meant to curb.

Constraints on governance can also come from internal corporate stakeholders like the chief financial officer and the general counsel. Financial rules and operational risk management policies may require that supplier relationships be well defined and documented by contract, and that suppliers be legally bound to act according to requirements, i.e., insurance policies and government regulations. Modern law department best practices usually include the use of standard contracts to limit liability and ensure compliance, as well as to make the most efficient use of internal and external legal resources by creating a system for exceptions management. Governance decision-making that strays from contracts can preempt these policies. Further, legally satisfying these policies may still only be possible through the execution of written contract terms.

Figure 13-3 graphically depicts how governance is constrained relative to contracts within the context of a corporate (or governmental) enterprise.

Figure 13-3

Constraints on Governance in the Context of Corporate/Agency Policies and Rues

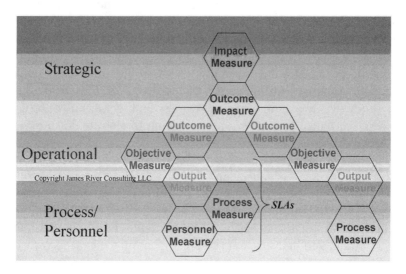

PERFORMANCE-BASED ACQUISITION

The U.S. government has evolved its own method for managing long, complex services contracts. Originally called "performance-based contracting," then later performance based services contracting (PBSC), –performance-based acquisition (PBA) is defined as "acquisition structured around the results to be achieved as opposed to the manner by which the work is to be performed," reflecting the government's history of specifying how providers should perform services.[23]

Management of services under PBA takes the form of six disciplines called Performance Based Management.™ The latter four of these disciplines are governance, communications, risk management, and performance monitoring. Like the eSCM, Performance Based Management includes identifying stakeholders, establishing governance bodies with charters, and defining decision-making and dispute resolution processes. However, unlike the eSCM, Performance Based Management does not universally promote joint decision-making. Some "decision frameworks" are recognized as resting wholly with one party or another and are not open to joint effort. Risk management in Performance Based Management includes identification of the risks of contracting for services, the readiness (competency) of an agency to employ performance based acquisition management, and project management against cost, schedule, and performance goals.[24]

PERFORMANCE MEASUREMENT: CONTRACT-BASED GOVERNANCE

Government governance of outsourcing and services contracts is constrained by the regulatory framework surrounding all government contracting, the Federal Acquisition Regulation (FAR). The FAR's "full and open competition" standard for sourcing obligates the government to define its requirements in a statement of work (SOW) or PBA performance work statement (PWS), or direct contractors in a PBA statement of objectives (SOO) to define requirements and provide a solution. The exchange of documentation (whether at the time of initial award or as a task order under a contract) becomes a written contract that defines the delivery of services and the relationship between the parties for the life of the contract. Authority to change the terms of the contract or to conduct further transactions is delegated exclusively to the agency contracting office. Any changes in performance terms must be within the "general scope" of the contract and become signed amendments to the contract using standardized forms. In summary, the rigidity of contract formation in the FAR disallows the free, collaborative relational governance that is championed by outsourcing advisory firms and academics in the private sector.

Because of the FAR, government must rely on governance methods that are based in contract terms and can be managed by contracting officers. In fact the government does exactly that. It governs services contracts by relying on the sophisticated and extensive use of "performance measures."

Performance Outcome-Process Hierarchy

As far back as the early 1990's the Office of Federal Procurement Policy (OFPP), Office of Management and Budget (OMB), provided guidance to government agencies on management of services through performance measures.[25] In 1993 the Government Performance and Results Act required agencies to implement measurement of outcomes, outputs, and service levels achieved in services contracts.[26] Since that time, government agencies and the OFPP have further developed definitions and methods for imple-

The Future of Contract Administration: Purpose Driven Governance™

menting performance measures in services contracts.[27] Currently, the sixth discipline of Performance Based Management,™ project monitoring, represents the role of performance measurement in the governance of government services contracting.

In the private sector, performance measures are popularly known as "service level agreements" or SLAs. By and large SLAs address single attributes of services at an operational level, such as timeliness of response or error rates in an activity. SLAs are mostly applied to information technology systems or labor-intensive services like transportation because those services are easily measurable using objective criteria. Government performance measurement is more sophisticated and involves a hierarchy of measures.

Figure 13-4 provides an overview of the PBA performance measurement hierarchy.

Figure 13-4
Overview of PBA Performance Measurement Hierarcy

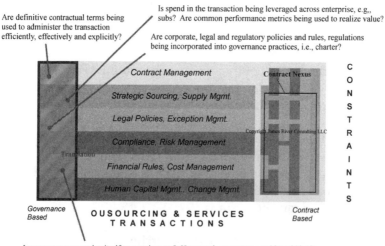

Under PBA, the "outcomes" required to achieve an agency's strategic planning goals are identified, and performance targets are set for them. Outcomes may be reduced to multiple lower level outcomes using a tree diagram. Next "objectives" are identified that must be fulfilled to produce the lowest level outcomes. Objectives are closest to the description of services in the provider statement of work. Measurements for the objectives are created with their own targets. At the bottom of the PBA measurement hierarchy, "outputs" produced from the provision of services are measured. Output measurements contain both targets and performance "indicators" (metrics) and resemble SLAs. Objectives may represent minimum standards of industry or they may contain targets negotiated by the agency and the supplier. Where appropriate, measures of the "processes" and "personnel" by which outputs are generated are also used.

By causally linking these several levels of performance measures, government contracting officers can determine both whether a provider is delivering good service and whether the service is supporting strategic goals. A provider may deliver services fulfilling output and objective measurements, yet outcome measurements fall short, indicating that performance targets are unsustainable, the outsourcing may need to be rescoped, or the outsourced operations may need to be transformed.

Balance Between Contracts and Governance

Performance measurements under PBA would seem to do a very good job of striking a balance between relational governance and contracts. Contracting officers are able to manage services delivery at a strategic level, a hallmark of governance. While performance measures are made a part of the formal contractual relationship between the buyer and seller, they also create the opportunity for the buyer and seller to address their business relationship in a dynamic fashion. Performance measures are highly effective in driving value in services contracting as well as providing a well-defined system for making changes to negotiated service terms, two other hallmarks of governance. Finally, because they exist within the framework of a contract document, performance measures do not present the same costs risks found in governance.

Further Developments in PBA Governance

In a January, 2007 report the Acquisition Advisory Panel authorized under the Services Acquisition Reform Act (SARA) of 2003 recommended that PBA be divided into "transactional" and "transformational" acquisitions. It recommended that for transformational acquisitions, the government should allow vendor-proposed, outcome-based solutions that vendors would be free to adjust post-contract award, bringing PBA much closer to commercial sector outsourcing governance models.[28] The Procurement Round Table proposed abandoning existing services acquisition rules in the FAR in favor of "relational contracting." The proposal contained several innovative changes to the FAR meant to improve the government's capabilities in managing long, complex services agreements: selection of contractors based on competency instead of responsiveness to requirements; joint development of the contract work statement with the provider; joint management of the operations budget; advance agreement on cost limits; cost-plus-fee pricing instead of fixed pricing; the setting and adjustment of expectations ex post contract; and incorporation of mandatory dispute resolution procedures.[29]

PURPOSE DRIVEN GOVERNANCE™: A BEST PRACTICES APPROACH TO GOVERNANCE

What, then, should corporations and government agencies consider as best practices in governing outsourcing and other long, complex services engagements? When should negotiating and enforcing contract terms be enough governance? When should governance practices far removed from contracts management be followed, and how much should be invested in them? Can relational governance and classic contract law complement each other and be used as part of a single governance strategy?

While there are several methodologies available to help organizations design more effective relational governance, there are none that answer threshold questions about using relational governance in a larger context of contract management alternatives, constraints on governance, and alternatives to governance. Purpose Driven Governance™ is a methodology that seeks to craft, negotiate, and implement optimal governance for outsourcing and long, complex services.[30] By first looking at the goals driving the outsourcing or services engagement, then working through a sequence of questions in a decision workflow, Purpose Driven Governance™ enables parties to determine the best governance practices for an outsourcing or services engagement. Results of the decision workflow can be presented by one party at the negotiating table, or both parties can jointly work through the methodology. The conclusions about governance reached through the workflow can also flow into many other critical decisions about the outsourcing or services engagement, including acquisition planning, negotiation strategy, vendor selection, and setting expectations among stakeholders and between the parties.

Governance = Decision-Making + Control

Governance is decision-making. Decision-making in outsourcing and services engagement can congregate around one of several distinct models, each containing its own set of practices. At the root, what distinguishes these models of governance is the type of decision-making they require.

Governance can be based on the established model of contracts and contracts management in which buyer and seller negotiate terms and hold each other to them. Final decisions must be reached prior to contract execution; otherwise there is no benefit in having a written contract. It requires rational or "classic" decision-making, meaning that the decision-maker has access to all of the information needed to make a decision, knows the choices and has had the opportunity to fully deliberate about the decision. The decisions made are intended to stand with little or no change, unless the parties intend to renegotiate at a later time.

Alternatively, governance can be guided through "programmatic" decision-making mechanisms incorporated into a contract as terms. Decision-making mechanisms are not the terms of service delivery per se but the rules by which terms of service are decided. Dispute resolution clauses are the best known example of these mechanisms in contracts. The purpose of decision-making mechanisms in contracts is to lead the parties in making rational decisions about terms.

Relational governance follows a "non-programmatic" decision-making model in which the parties make administrative-type decisions in an environment of complexity and change and with limited information and opportunity to deliberate. This type of decision-making is often perceived as inconsistent with written contracts because there really isn't any one set of terms, or bargain, defining the service.

Figure 13-5 places different governance tools and methods on a spectrum between classic transactional contract law and modern relational governance theory.

Figure 13-5
Governance Tools and Methods Spectrum

Governance is also control. To rise to the level of governance, decisions must have a controlling effect on the actions of the parties to a transaction. How decisions are made within organizations and how they are communicated and implemented is the subject of a great deal of available research and commentary in the field of management science, particularly on decision rights and organizational structures.

The ways that outsourcing governance models control parties to outsourcing are distinguishable from each other by how the models establish authority behind governance decisions.

Control by contract-based governance is based on laws, courts, arbitrators, and police forces to enforce judgments. Informal controls, namely the threat of litigation, carries a big price tag and can create bad publicity for executive management in the customer company championing an outsourcing project and for the provider among its other customers. Theoretically speaking, contract-based controls do not require any governance structures, charters, or rules for making decisions.

Programmatic decision mechanisms in contracts are a form of decision rights. Unlike relational governance, it is the terms of the decision-making provision in the contract that produce the decision, not the judgment of the persons following the terms. But unlike definitive contracts, decisions themselves are not terms. The semi-contractual practice of defining decision rights as contract terms rests in a kind of governance estuary where the limits of contract management and judicial enforcement meet and mix with simple forms of relational governance that may or may not involve organizational structures, charters, or management plans. Judicial enforcement of decision- making provisions is not straightforward. Seeking remedies before tribunals can involve outcomes in which arbitrators and courts fill in missing terms or deny other rights under the contract because terms for decision-making procedures have not been followed. Opportunities for morally hazardous behaviors and ex officio change management can occur during programmatic decision-making. At the same time though, the provisions build flexibility into contracts, allowing the parties to mutually adjust terms in response to changing assumptions and to unilaterally consider embedded commercial options.

Relational governance exemplifies transaction cost economics. The parties essentially sort out their rights between themselves instead of legally defining them up front in a contract and seeking to enforce contractual rights later. In a word, profit motive replaces the rule of law. Authority backing the decisions must in the end come from executive management (which takes authority from the board of directors) for both parties. Organizational structures, governance charters, and explicit management rules for decision-making take on paramount importance in relational governance. Otherwise enforcement of decisions will be inefficient and inconsistent.

Principles of Optimal Governance

Preferable and Optimal Governance

The overarching principle of Purpose Driven Governance™ is the preference always to make rational governance decisions about outsourcing and other services engagement and to incorporate decision-making into the contract as definitive terms at the earliest possible point in the outsourcing life cycle.[31] This preference holds true even when governance practices other than definitive terms are determined to be optimal. Under the methodology, governance through decision-making mechanisms and relational practices should be conducted with the secondary objective of, or at least recognition of the potential for, ultimately reaching rational governance decisions that can then be set forth in contractual language. The preference is not meant to dilute implementation of these other means of governance or to call their use into question. Preferring contract-based governance means recognizing opportunities for more rational decision-making that can be created by good non-contract–based governance practices.

If rational decision-making and complete terms for services delivery and the business relationship are not possible, contract terms defining programmatic decision-making are the next most preferable governance practice. But just as bounded rationality makes definitive contract terms impossible in a given outsourcing scenario, a given outsourcing scenario may not allow for good programmatic decision-making. Further, decision-making mechanisms in contracts are subject to issues of legal enforceability. Some mechanisms in contracts are more likely legally enforceable than others, depending on how they are written and the decisions they render. In these instances, under Purpose Driven Governance,™ relational governance, even highly relational governance such as value management in the eSCM, may be the optimal governance approach. As noted above, relational governance can be found optimal without determining that it will necessarily create a basis from which the parties ultimately can make rational decisions. The relational governance only needs to provide the best decision-making.

Further, while the preference for contract-based governance in Purpose Driven Governance™ is strong, it is not absolute and is subject to consideration of the other principles of Purpose Driven Governance.™ In some cases, contract-based governance may not constitute optimal governance for an outsourcing scenario even when contract based governance is possible.

Mutual Assent and Trust

Whether contract or non-contract–based, all governance requires some amount of negotiated or non-negotiated mutual assent. Not all mutual assent is the same. Purpose Driven Governance™ recognizes that different governance approaches are driven by different forms and degrees of mutual assent. Assent to contractual governance can be as cut and dry as exchanging solicitation and proposal documents during the bid process. Arm's-length negotiation can be more advantageous if one or both parties have concluded that a contract management model is the optimal form of governance or it is anticipated that the other party will object to relational governance. Where a mix of contractual and relational governance is being considered, a structured negotiation approach becomes more advantageous. Otherwise the end result of negotiations may be either a set of terms based on less than rational decision-making, an incomplete contract, or moral hazards.[32]

Highly relational (non-contractual) governance, such as value management in the eSCM, is heavily dependent on mutual assent. Unlike negotiated governance terms, highly relational governance exists purely as administrative decision-making and must be assented to fully and on a continuing basis. To drive this continuing assent, both the long-term business goals and short-term commercial interests of both the buyer and seller must align with a relational governance model. For this reason, relational governance is unlikely to be effective in incomplete contract scenarios where non-contractual governance is adopted because the parties have failed for whatever reasons to agree on terms.

In recent years, management thought leaders have focused on the concept of trust in business dealings between customers and suppliers. Recognizing a need for trust in business dealings is another way of recognizing the need for the deeply committed mutual assent that is needed in relational-type transactions. Purpose Driven Governance™ defines trust in outsourcing as the amount of mutual assent required to make the most rational decisions possible about services delivery and the business relationship, leaving open the opportunity for obtaining mutual assent either in the form of a negotiated contract or through interactive management.

Constraints and Opportunities

The potential for the effectiveness of any form of governance is not determined just by buyers and sellers but by frameworks surrounding the outsourcing: organization charts, corporate policy manuals; legal and regulatory frameworks; and the outsourcing life cycle.

Buyer and seller corporate organizations and corporate policies pose constraints on governance. It is harder to navigate and reconcile these constraints when governance is relational because decisions and decision-making are unspecified and undocumented.

Governance potential is also dependent on identifying the best opportunities for engaging in governance during an outsourcing engagement. Purpose Driven Governance™ identifies opportunities for governance using the stages of outsourcing across the entire outsourcing life cycle. Relational and incomplete contract theories do something similar when they define governance as ex ante or ex post contract. While it is obvious that opportunities for non-contractual governance are typically greatest in the ex post contract stages, it may be that relational governance will quickly become less effective upon completion of the transition stage, or that relational governance practices will be most effective if employed alongside of negotiated contract terms throughout the operations stage.

Applying governance within the framework of the outsourcing life cycle also accounts for shifts in bargaining power between buyer and seller. Buyers have greater bargaining power ex ante contract while sellers have greater bargaining power ex post contract, meaning that buyers and sellers may differ in what they see as governance opportunities.

Goals and Impacts

Outsourcing governance, like the outsourcing itself, should serve a customer's strategic business goals. Purpose Driven Governance™ recognizes that governance supports achievement of goals in two ways. One of relational governance's biggest assets is realignment of outsourcing services with strategic goals over time and in response to changing assumptions. Governance also aligns outsourcing with goals through the type of impact it has on services delivery and the business arrangement. While goals may call for the assessment of penalties for performance, assessing penalties through relational governance is very difficult.

Example of How Purpose Driven Governance™ Works

A national manufacturer and retailer of orthopedic implant devices (e.g., artificial knees) receives complaints from hospitals about deliveries of its products not arriving in time for surgeries. In several cases the surgery was begun and then halted because the implant was not on hand. The manufacturer manages its own network of warehouses and delivery vehicles. Lead times between initial order and delivery vary widely due to the unpredictable scheduling of surgeries and the uneven ordering procedures among the hospitals.

The manufacturer has decided to outsource the in-house storage and delivery operations to an outside service provider that has a niche in the delivery of time-critical medical supplies. The goal for outsourcing the operations is to build, within three months, the capability to deliver implants in a timely manner 100% of the time. What constitutes timely is difficult to define, other than getting the implants in the hands of surgical teams in operating rooms before an operation begins. Cost savings are not a concern in the short term, but the implant industry is becoming crowded and downward pressure on prices is growing. The manufacturer's existing processes and systems will need to be transformed to meet the lofty target of 100% timeliness. The envisioned storage and delivery capability will be industry leading, so no useful benchmarks for it are thought to exist. Integration of the provider with the manufacturer's retained business may meet resistance from employees. Federal regulations governing the interstate transport of implants may exist or come into being. The malpractice insurance providers for the hospitals have in the past asked to audit the supply of implants and may object to outsourcing to a third party.

Governance will only be beneficial if it promotes collaboration between buyer and seller in the transition and transformation stages of the outsourcing life cycle, and ultimately achievement of the stated business outcome, i.e., 100% timely delivery. Attempts at negotiation and enforcement of definitive service delivery terms prior to reaching the steady state of the outsourced services would be counterproductive. Imposing financial penalties on the provider for failure to meet the delivery target will not support the buyer's goals (industry leading, cost non-factor in the short term). Imposing penalties will also not facilitate compliance with regulatory constraints or additional requirements from hospital insurance companies.

Both the manufacturer and the provider are motivated by their respective commercial interests to collaborate, so the mutual assent required for relational governance is present. The parties can and should negotiate a subset of terms during the usual negotiation stage. The parties must at least partially negotiate an SLA for delivery, in particular how delivery will be measured based on the 100% timeliness target. SLA negotiation could prove difficult. The provider has little interest in agreeing to the 100% target other than to win the business, yet measurement of the service will require participation by both parties, which requires mutual assent. Other terms, such as volume and geographic scope, third-party liability for failed deliveries, and termination rights including backsourcing, should be well known and negotiable prior to contract execution and can be put into the written contract.

Rules for decision-making on certain terms, including price, can also be stated in the contract. A baseline price with an adjustment mechanism using accounting of proven and allowable provider cost increases can be drafted. In addition, a decision-making mechanism to resolve disputes about changes to the manufacturer's operations to optimize the provider's performance can be included in the written contract.

Upon reaching the steady-state stage, the manufacturer should have several governance options for itself in the contract. If the outsourcing services fail to meet the 100% target, the manufacturer might adjust the 100% target based on feedback from operations personnel for both buyer and seller. Or the manufacturer might terminate the outsourcing and backsource the transformed operations.

If the manufacturer and/or the provider are not confident that the outsourcing can be effectively governed, one possible alternative is to enter into a value-added reseller arrangement whereby the provider becomes the customer-facing company and assumes the responsibility to the customer (hospitals) for delivery.

Purpose Driven Governance™ vs. Current Governance Approaches

Conflict Between Contracts and Governance

Relational governance and contract management appear to conflict on their face. Part of the appearance of conflict comes from the false assumption that contracts are inherently adversarial and that the only purpose of a contract is to perfect legal rights for bringing claims in court. Viewing governance as existing across a spectrum, and defining optimal governance as the selective or combined implementation of governance practices based on contractual and non-contractual models, removes the appearance of conflict. Further, contractual governance is an effective model even if the parties waive all rights to sue each other.

Probably the harshest criticism of contracts as a means of outsourcing governance is that they destroy trust. The argument can be traced back to the false assumption about the purpose of contracts. First and foremost contracts serve to memorialize what the parties expect from each other. The process of articulating the services and the relationship causes the parties to think through what they expect and what they think is expected of them.

Third-Party Governance

Governance advisory services are primarily marketed as an independent and all- encompassing type of governance that begins in the planning stages and continues throughout the life of an outsourcing engagement. The amount of authority that third-party advisory firms sometimes possess has become a sore point with the service provider industry. Further, these firms overly focus on governance organizational structures and titles and ignore what governance practices are most effective. Looking at governance as a set of best practices, and considering governance within the framework of an outsourcing life cycle, governance should be utilized as a tool rather than as a bureaucratic entity.

Single-Model Governance

Without a strategy for implementing governance, predictably the same governance approach will be followed in all cases. Without strategy, any guidance for implementing governance must come from external benchmarks, such as the amount of spend on governance as a percentage of contract value. Approaching governance at a strategic level by examining the goals to be served, as a part of overall strategic planning for outsourcing, avoids these pitfalls and yields many planning, sourcing, and operational advantages.[33]

SUMMARY

A strategic, methodological approach to implementing governance, such as Purpose Driven Governance,™ can generate better value for both the customer and the provider by tying governance to business goals, identifying optimal governance practices, and reducing governance's transaction costs.

Tying governance into outsourcing strategy and strategic sourcing of services prevents parties from straying from business use. The success or failure of outsourcing projects can be fairly evaluated.

The cost, difficulty, and predicted effectiveness of governance become factors in strategic outsourcing planning and are no longer implemented as an afterthought. Viewing governance as a spectrum of choices and providing a structured way for determining particular practices removes the false dilemma of having to either govern by contract or govern by purely relational means. Not only is it inaccurate to say that contracts and relationship management are in conflict, it falls short of the truth to characterize contracts and relational management as complementing each other. Both approaches are related and serve the same goals and objectives. Probably most importantly, a strategic and methodological approach to governance streamlines governance and safeguards against its becoming a money pit. Having criteria and a workflow processes with which to fashion governance also takes full advantage of existing corporate competencies and draws in other internal and external resources as needed. In-house legal departments, internal customers, risk managers, procurement officials, and contract management staff can all become participants in governance in a coordinated manner. Through Purpose Driven Governance,™ both buyers and sellers become involved in the governance planning process and mutually assent to and put governance into practice.

ENDNOTES

1   To date there is no good single-industry definition of outsourcing governance. The International Association of Outsourcing Professionals (IAOP) defines governance as "the oversight and management of all aspects of the outsourcing relationship," a definition so broad as to provide little guidance. *Outsourcing Professional Body of Knowledge*, Version 8.0 (Revised February 2008, IAOP), p. 157.

2   Cullen, S., & Willcocks, L. *Intelligent IT Outsourcing: Eight Building Blocks to Success*, Section 7.3 Relationship Management. Elsevier Ltd., 2003.

3   Vantage Partners Study Managing Outsourcing Relationships: Essential Practices for Buyers and Providers. (2006). http://vantagepartners.com/researchandpublications/viewpublications.aspx?id=500

4   Edwards, V., and Nash, R. Relational Contracting: A Proposal for a New Approach to Performance Based Acquisition. *Contract Management* 32-40, August, 2006.

5   Poppo, L., and Zenger, T. Do Contracts and Relational Governance Function as Substitutes or Complements? Vol. 23 Issue 8, *Strategic Management Journal* 711-712, August, 2002. The Poppo and Zenger article is the seminal work on the relationship of contracts and governance in outsourcing. After summarizing the academic work arguing against the use of both governance and contracts, the authors, citing other sources, argue that contracts and governance not only complement each other but strengthen each other in a feedback loop (called "complimentarity"), which they substantiate with a survey of key informants. Contracts safeguard against attempts to realize short-term gains and carry the parties through until they have developed trust. Contracts can be written to create bilateral frameworks for cooperation instead of specifying requirements. In return, governance can respond to unforeseen disturbances when contracts cannot, and governance can fine tune complex contracts through amendment. Additionally, contracts serve as a sort of "pre-nuptial" agreement when the marriage between a customer and provider comes to an end. pp. 712-713.

6   Hefley, W., and Loesche, E. The eSCM-CL v1.1: Model Overview Part 1 (Carnegie Mellon University Information Technology Qualification Service Center (ITSQC) September 27, 2006). http://itsqc.cmu.edu/downloads/document.asp?id=18
7   eSCM-CL v1.1: Model Overview Part 1 p. 2.
8   eSCM-CL v1.1: Model Overview Part 1 p. 3.
9   eSCM-CL v1.1: Model Overview Part 1.
10 The eSCM-CL v1.1: Practice Details Part 2 - Sourced Services Management (Carnegie Mellon University Information Technology Qualification Service Center (ITSQC) September 27, 2006). http://itsqc.cmu.edu/downloads/document.asp?id=19
11 FAR Subpart 42.3—Contract Administration and Functions. http://www.acqnet.gov/far/current/html/Subpart%2042_3.html#wp1078235
12 eSCM-CL v1.1: Model Overview Part 1, p. 35
13 eSCM-CL v1.1 Part 2 Value Management. pp. 91-112
14 eSCM-CL v1.1 Part 2 mgt08 Review Service Performance, p. 284
15 eSCM-CL v1.1 Part 2 mgt08 Review Service Performance, p. 285 Activity b.5
16 eSCM-CL v1.1 Part 2 mgt05 Problem & Incident Monitoring. p. 274
17 eSCM-CL v1.1 Part 2 rel04 Issue Management, p. 82.
18 *Managing Sourcing Relationships: Essential Practices for Buyers and Providers* 43. In the Vantage survey, respondents spent an average of 7.2% of annual contract value on governance and between 3% and 7%. The report also cites survey figures from research firms that go as high as 11%.
19 eSCM-CL v1.1 Part 2 mgt01 Perform Sourcing Management p. 262
20 Outsourcing Management and Governance: Building a Foundation for Outsourcing Success., 5 (June, 2006, Updated May, 2007, EquaTerra). EquaTerra's survey looked at the relationship between spend on governance and overall outsourcing satisfaction. It found that almost half of respondents spent between 1-4% of total contract value on governance and one quarter spent 4-7%; governance spend did not drop off in succeeding years; and that a governance spend of 4-7% returned slightly more satisfaction. The survey did not find any correlation between governance spend and satisfaction with governance itself. http://www.equaterra.com/fw/main/Outsourcing-Management-and-Governance-Building-a-Foundation-for-Outsourcing-Success-15C361.html?LayoutID=
21 Outsourcing Management and Governance 16-17, Figure 9.
22 Slaight, T., & Goffre, J. Chapter 6: Strategic Sourcing: Where Did It Come From? What Has It Accomplished? Where Is It Going?, p. 99. *The Supply Management Handbook*, J. Cavinato, ed. (McGraw Hill Professional, 2006).
23 FAR 2.101 Performance-based acquisition (PBA), http://www.acqnet.gov/far/current/html/Subpart%202_1.html#wp1145507.
24 OMB Circular No. A-11, Part 7, June 2008. http://www.whitehouse.gov/omb/circulars_a11_current_year_a11_toc/
25 CIB 91-18, OFPP Policy Letter 91-2 — Service Contracting, March 14, 1991. Retrieved from http://www.whitehouse.gov/omb/rewrite/procurement/policy_letters/92-1_092392.html
26 Government Performance and Results Act of 1993, Public Law 103-62, Section 1115. http://govinfo.library.unt.edu/npr/library/misc/s20.html
27 Primer on Performance Measurement. OMB, Revised February 28, 1995. Retrieved from http://govinfo.library.unt.edu/npr/library/resource/gpraprmr.html; Performance Based Management: Eight Steps to Develop and Use Information Technology Performance Measures Effectively. GSA, January 23, 1997 Retrieved from http://www.estrategy.gov/documents/eight_steps_to_develop_use_IT.doc; How to Measure Performance: A Handbook of Techniques and Tools. DoE Performance Based Management Special Interest Group, October 1995. Retrieved from http://www.orau.gov/pbm/documents/handbook1a.html; Guidebook for Performance-Based Service Acquisitions (PBSA) in the Department of Defense December 2000 http://www.acq.osd.mil/dpap/Docs/pbsaguide010201.pdf
28 Report of the Acquisition Advisory Panel to the Office of Federal Procurement Policy and the United States Congress, Recommendation 2, p. 198, January 2007 retrieved from http://www.acquisition.gov/comp/aap/documents/Introduction%20and%20Executive%20Summary.pdf
29 Ibid., note 4 at 32-40.
30 Purpose Driven Governance is a trademark of James River Consulting LLC. For more information about the methodology, contact Eric Esperne, President, James River Consulting at eesperne@jamesriverllc.com.
31 Barthelemy, J. The seven deadly sins of outsourcing." Academy of Management Executive, Vol. 17, No. 2 (2003). Writing a poor contract is identified as the third of the seven deadly

sins. Barthelemy, who is widely published on the subject of outsourcing, recommends that contracts should be written precisely and as completely as possible prior to outsourcing. "The notion that outsourcing vendors are partners and that contracts play a minor role was popularized by a landmark IT outsourcing deal. In 1989, Eastman Kodak outsourced a large part of its IT operations to IBM, Digital Equipment, and Businessland. As the relationships between Eastman Kodak and its vendors were both cooperative and based on loose contracts, it has been wrongly inferred that tight contracts were not necessary to be successful with outsourcing." p. 90.

32   Chandar, S., and Zeleznikow, J. A Structured Approach to Negotiating Information Technology Outsourcing Agreements. Proceedings of the Fifth IASTED International Conference Law and Technology, September 24-26, 2007, Berkeley, CA.

33   For another method of integrating outsourcing contract terms and relationship management, see C. Gellings, Outsourcing Relationships: The Contract as IT Governance Tool. Proceedings of the 40th Hawaii International Conference on Systems Sciences, IEEE Computer Society, January 3-6, 2007, Waikoloa, Hawaii. Gellings creates an IT outsourcing model comprising five attributes (strategy alignment, delivery of value, performance management, risk management, and control & accountability), and then matches corresponding contract terms and relationship management activities to each.

GLOSSARY OF KEY TERMS

acceptance
(1) The taking and receiving of anything in good part, and as if it were a tacit agreement to a preceding act, which might have been defeated or avoided if such acceptance had not been made. (2) Agreement to the terms offered in a contract. An acceptance must be communicated, and (in common law) it must be the mirror image of the offer.

acquisition cost
The money invested up front to bring in new customers.

acquisition plan
A plan for an acquisition that serves as the basis for initiating the individual contracting actions necessary to acquire a system or support a program.

acquisition strategy
The conceptual framework for conducting systems acquisition. It encompasses the broad concepts and objectives that direct and control the overall development, production, and deployment of a system.

act of God
An inevitable, accidental, or extraordinary event that cannot be foreseen and guarded against, such as lightning, tornadoes, or earthquakes.

actual authority
The power that the principal intentionally confers on the agent or allows the agent to believe he or she possesses.

actual damages
See compensatory damages.

affidavit
A written and signed statement sworn to under oath.

agency
A relationship that exists when there is a delegation of authority to perform all acts connected within a particular trade, business, or company. It gives authority to the agent to act in all matters relating to the business of the principal.

agent
An employee (usually a contract manager) empowered to bind his or her organization legally in contract negotiations.

allowable cost
A cost that is reasonable, allocable, and within accepted standards, or otherwise conforms to generally accepted accounting principles, specific limitations or exclusions, or agreed-on terms between contractual parties.

alternative dispute resolution
Any procedure that is used, in lieu of litigation, to resolve issues in controversy, including, but not limited to, settlement negotiations, conciliation, facilitation, mediation, fact-finding, mini-trials and arbitration.

amortization
The process of spreading the cost of an intangible asset over the expected useful life of the asset.

apparent authority
The power that the principal permits the perceived agent to exercise, although not actually granted.

as is

A contract phrase referring to the condition of property to be sold or leased; generally pertains to a disclaimer of liability; property sold in as-is condition is generally not guaranteed.

assign

To convey or transfer to another, as to assign property, rights, or interests to another.

assignment

The transfer of property by an assignor to an assignee.

audits

The systematic examination of records and documents and/ or the securing of other evidence by confirmation, physical inspection, or otherwise, for one or more of the following purposes: determining the propriety or legality of proposed or completed transactions; ascertaining whether all transactions have been recorded and are reflected accurately in accounts; determining the existence of recorded assets and inclusiveness of recorded liabilities; determining the accuracy of financial or statistical statements or reports and the fairness of the facts they represent; determining the degree of compliance with established policies and procedures in terms of financial transactions and business management; and appraising an account system and making recommendations concerning it.

base profit

The money a company is paid by a customer, which exceeds the company's cost.

best value

The best trade-off between competing factors for a particular purchase requirement. The key to successful best-value contracting is consideration of life-cycle costs, including the use of quantitative as well as qualitative techniques to measure price and technical performance trade-offs between various proposals. The best-value concept applies to acquisitions in which price or price-related factors are not the primary determinant of who receives the contract award.

bid

An offer in response to an invitation for bids (IFB).

bid development

All of the work activities required to design and price a product and service solution and accurately articulate it in a proposal for a customer.

bid phase

The period of time that a seller of goods and/or services uses to develop a bid/proposal, conduct internal bid reviews, and obtain stakeholder approval to submit a bid/proposal.

bilateral contract

A contract formed when an offer states that acceptance requires only the accepting party's promise to perform. In contrast, a unilateral contract is formed when an offer requires actual performance for acceptance.

bond

A written instrument executed by a seller and a second party (the surety or sureties) to ensure fulfillment of the principal's obligations to a third party (the obligee or buyer) identified in the bond. If the principal's obligations are not met, the bond ensures payment, to the extent stipulated, of any loss sustained by the obligee.

breach of contract

(1) The failure, without legal excuse, to perform any promise that forms the whole or part of a contract. (2) The ending of a contract that occurs when one or both of the parties fail to keep their promises; this could lead to arbitration or litigation.

buyer

The party contracting for goods and/or services with one or more sellers.

cancellation

The withdrawal by the buyer of the requirement to purchase goods and/or services.

capture management

The art and science of winning more business.

capture management life cycle

The art and science of winning more business throughout the entire business cycle.

capture project plan

A document or game plan of who needs to do what, when, where, how often, and how much to win business.

change in scope

An amendment to approved program requirements or specifications after negotiation of a basic contract. It may result in an increase or decrease.

change order/purchase order amendment

A written order directing the seller to make changes according to the provisions of the contract documents.

claim

A demand by one party to contract for something from another party, usually but not necessarily for more money or more time. Claims are usually based on an argument that the party making the demand is entitled to an adjustment by virtue of the contract terms or some violation of those terms by the other party. The word does not imply any disagreement between the parties, although claims often lead to disagreements. This book uses the term dispute to refer to disagreements that have become intractable.

clause

A statement of one of the rights and/or obligations of the parties to a contract. A contract consists of a series of clauses.

collaboration software

Automated tools that allow for the real-time exchange of visual information using personal computers.

collateral benefit

The degree to which pursuit of an opportunity will improve the existing skill level or develop new skills that will positively affect other or future business opportunities.

compensable delay

A delay for which the buyer is contractually responsible that excuses the seller's failure to perform and is compensable.

compensatory damages

Damages that will compensate the injured party for the loss sustained and nothing more. They are awarded by the court as the measure of actual loss, and not as punishment for outrageous conduct or to deter future transgressions. Compensatory damages are often referred to as "actual damages." See also incidental and punitive damages.

competitive intelligence

Information on competitors or competitive teams that is specific to an opportunity.

competitive negotiation

A method of contracting involving a request for proposals that states the buyer's requirements and criteria for evaluation; submission of timely proposals by a maximum number of offerors; discussions with those offerors found to be within the competitive range; and award of a contract to the one offeror whose offer, price, and other consideration factors are most advantageous to the buyer.

condition precedent

A condition that activates a term in a contract.

condition subsequent

A condition that suspends a term in a contract.

conflict of interest

Term used in connection with public officials and fiduciaries and their relationships to matters of private interest or gain to them. Ethical problems connected therewith are covered by statutes in most jurisdictions and by federal statutes at the federal level. A conflict of interest arises when an employee's personal or financial interest conflicts or appears to conflict with his or her official responsibility.

consideration

(1) The thing of value (amount of money or acts to be done or not done) that must change hands between the parties to a contract. (2) The inducement to a contract– the cause, motive, price, or impelling influence that induces a contracting party to enter into a contract.

contract negotiation

The process of unifying different positions into a unanimous joint decision, regarding the buying and selling of products and/or services.

contract negotiation process

A three-phased approach comprising planning, negotiating, and documenting a contractual agreement between two or more parties to buy or sell products and/or services.

constructive change

An oral or written act or omission by an authorized or unauthorized agent that is of such a nature that it is construed to have the same effect as a written change order.

contingency

The quality of being contingent or casual; an event that may but does not have to occur; a possibility.

contingent contract

A contract that provides for the possibility of its termination when a specified occurrence does or does not take place.

contra proferentem

A legal phrase used in connection with the construction of written documents providing that an ambiguous provision is construed most strongly against the person who selected the language.

contract

(1) A relationship between two parties, such as a buyer and seller, that is defined by an agreement about their respective rights and responsibilities. (2) A document that describes such an agreement.

contract administration

The process of ensuring compliance with contractual terms and conditions during contract performance up to contract closeout or termination.

contract closeout

The process of verifying that all administrative matters are concluded on a contract that is otherwise physically complete—in other words, the seller has delivered the required supplies or performed the required services, and the buyer has inspected and accepted the supplies or services.

contract fulfillment

The joint buyer/seller actions taken to successfully perform and administer a contractual agreement and meet or exceed all contract obligations, including effective changes management and timely contract closeout.

contract interpretation

The entire process of determining what the parties agreed-to in their bargain. The basic objective of contract interpretation is to determine the intent of the parties. Rules calling for interpretation of the documents against the drafter, and imposing a duty to seek clarification from the drafter, allocate risks of contractual ambiguities by resolving disputes in favor of the party least responsible for the ambiguity.

contract management

The art and science of managing a contractual agreement(s) throughout the contracting process.

contract type

A specific pricing arrangement used for the performance of work under a contract.

contractor

The seller or provider of goods and/or services.

controversy

A litigated question. A civil action or suit may not be instigated unless it is based on a "justifiable" dispute. This term is important in that judicial power of the courts extends only to cases and "controversies."

copyright
A royalty-free, nonexclusive, and irrevocable license to reproduce, translate, publish, use, and dispose of written or recorded material, and to authorize others to do so.

cost
The amount of money expended in acquiring a product or obtaining a service, or the total of acquisition costs plus all expenses related to operating and maintaining an item once acquired.

cost of good sold (COGS)
Direct costs of producing finished goods for sale.

cost accounting standards
Federal standards designed to provide consistency and coherency in defense and other government contract accounting.

cost-plus-award-fee (CPAF) contract
A type of cost-reimbursement contract with special incentive fee provisions used to motivate excellent contract performance in areas such as quality, timeliness, ingenuity, and cost-effectiveness.

cost-plus-fixed-fee (CPFF) contract
A type of cost-reimbursement contract that provides for the payment of a fixed fee to the contractor. It does not vary with actual costs, but may be adjusted if there are any changes in the work or services to be performed under the contract.

cost-plus-incentive-fee (CPIF) contract
A type of cost-reimbursement contract that provides for a fee that is adjusted by a formula in accordance with the relationship between total allowable costs and target costs.

cost-plus-a-percentage-of-cost (CPPC) contract
A type of cost-reimbursement contract that provides for reimbursement of the allowable costs of services performed plus an agreed-on percentage of the estimated cost as profit.

cost-reimbursement (CR) contract

A type of contract that usually includes an estimate of project cost, a provision for reimbursing the seller's expenses, and a provision for paying a fee as profit. CR contracts are often used when there is great uncertainty about costs. They normally also include a limitation on the buyer's cost liability.

cost-sharing contract

A cost-reimbursement contract in which the seller receives no fee and is reimbursed only for an agreed-on portion of its allowable costs.

cost contract

The simplest type of cost-reimbursement contract. Governments commonly use this type of arrangement when contracting with universities and nonprofit organizations for research projects. The contract provides for reimbursing contractually allowable costs, with no allowance for profit.

cost proposal

The instrument required of an offeror for the submission or identification of cost or pricing data by which an offeror submits to the buyer a summary of estimated (or incurred) costs, suitable for detailed review and analysis.

counteroffer

An offer made in response to an original offer that changes the terms of the original.

customer revenue growth

The increased revenues achieved by keeping a customer for an extended period of time.

customer support costs

Costs expended by a company to provide information and advice concerning purchases.

default termination

The termination of a contract, under the standard default clause, because of a buyer's or seller's failure to perform any of the terms of the contract.

defect

The absence of something necessary for completeness or perfection. A deficiency in something essential to the proper use of a thing. Some structural weakness in a part or component that is responsible for damage.

defect, latent

A defect that existed at the time of acceptance but would not have been discovered by a reasonable inspection.

defect, patent

A defect that can be discovered without undue effort. If the defect was actually known to the buyer at the time of acceptance, it is patent, even though it otherwise might not have been discoverable by a reasonable inspection.

definite-quantity contract

A contractual instrument that provides for a definite quantity of supplies or services to be delivered at some later, unspecified date.

delay, excusable

A contractual provision designed to protect the seller from sanctions for late performance. To the extent that it has been excusably delayed, a seller is protected from default termination or liquidated damages. Examples of excusable delay are acts of God, acts of the government, fire, flood, quarantines, strikes, epidemics, unusually severe weather, and embargoes. See also forbearance and force majeure clause.

depreciation

The amount of expense charged against earnings by a company to write off the cost of a plant or machine over its useful live, giving consideration to wear and tear, obsolescence, and salvage value.

design specification

(1) A document (including drawings) setting forth the required characteristics of a particular component, part, subsystem, system, or construction item. (2) A purchase description that establishes precise measurements, tolerances, materials, in-process and finished product tests, quality control, inspection requirements, and other specific details of the deliverable.

direct cost

The costs specifically identifiable with a contract requirement, including but not restricted to costs of materials and/or labor directly incorporated into an end item.

direct labor

All work that is obviously related and specifically and conveniently traceable to specific products.

direct material

Items, including raw material, purchased parts, and subcontracted items, directly incorporated into an end item, which are identifiable to a contract requirement.

discount rate

Interest rate used in calculating present value.

discounted cash flow (DCF)

Combined present value of cash flow and tangible assets minus present value of liabilities.

discounts, allowances, and returns

Price discounts, returned merchandise.

dispute

A disagreement not settled by mutual consent that could be decided by litigation or arbitration. Also see claim.

e-business

Technology-enabled business that focuses on seamless integration between each business, the company, and its supply partners.

EBITDA

Acronym for earnings before interest, taxes, depreciation, and amortization, but after all product/service, sales, and overhead (SG&A) costs are accounted for. Sometimes referred to as operating profit.

EBITDARM

Acronym for earnings before interest, taxes, depreciation, amortization, rent, and management fees.

e-commerce
A subset of e-business, Internet-based electronic transactions.

electronic data interchange (EDI)
Private networks used for simple data transactions, which are typically batch- processed.

elements of a contract
The items that must be present in a contract if the contract is to be binding, including an offer, acceptance (agreement), consideration, execution by competent parties, and legality of purpose.

enterprise resource planning (ERP)
An electronic framework for integrating all organizational functions, evolved from manufacturing resource planning (MRP).

entire contract
A contract that is considered entire on both sides and cannot be made severable.

e-procurement
Technology-enabled buying and selling of goods and services.

estimate at completion (EAC)
The actual direct costs, plus indirect costs, allocable to a contract, plus the estimate of costs (direct or indirect) for authorized work remaining.

estoppel
A rule of law that bars, prevents, and precludes a party from alleging or denying certain facts because of a previous allegation or denial or because of its previous conduct or admission.

ethics
Of or relating to moral action, conduct, motive, or character (such as ethical emotion). Also, treating of moral feelings, duties, or conduct; containing precepts of morality; moral. Professionally right or befitting; conforming to professional standards of conduct.

e-tool

An electronic device, program, system, or software application used to facilitate business.

exculpatory clause

Contract language designed to shift responsibility to the other party. A "no damages for delay" clause would be an example of one used by buyers.

excusable delay

See delay, excusable.

executed contract

A contract that is formed and performed at the same time. If performed in part, it is partially executed and partially executory.

executed contract (document)

A written document, signed by both parties and mailed or otherwise furnished to each party, that expresses the requirements, terms, and conditions to be met by both parties in the performance of a contract.

executory contract

A contract that has not yet been fully performed.

express

Something put in writing, for example, "express authority."

fair and reasonable

A subjective evaluation of what each party deems as equitable consideration in areas such as terms and conditions, cost or price, assured quality, timeliness of contract performance, and/or any other areas subject to negotiation.

Federal Acquisition Regulation (FAR)

The government-wide procurement regulation mandated by Congress and issued by the Department of Defense, the General Services Administration, and the National Aeronautics and Space Administration. Effective April 1, 1984, the FAR supersedes both the Defense Acquisition Regulation (DAR) and the Federal Procurement Regulation (FPR). All federal agencies are authorized to issue regulations implementing the FAR.

fee

An agreed-to amount of reimbursement beyond the initial estimate of costs. The term "fee" is used when discussing cost-reimbursement contracts, whereas the term "profit" is used in relation to fixed-price contracts.

firm-fixed-price (FFP) contract

The simplest and most common business pricing arrangement. The seller agrees to supply a quantity of goods or to provide a service for a specified price.

fixed cost

Operating expenses that are incurred to provide facilities and organization that are kept in readiness to do business without regard to actual volumes of production and sales. Examples of fixed costs are rent, property tax, and interest expense.

fixed price

A form of pricing that includes a ceiling beyond which the buyer bears no responsibility for payment.

fixed-price-incentive (FPI) contract

A type of contract that provides for adjusting profit and establishing the final contract price using a formula based on the relationship of total final negotiated cost to total target cost. The final price is subject to a price ceiling, which is negotiated at the outset.

fixed-price-redeterminable (FPR) contract

A type of fixed-price contract that contains provisions for subsequently negotiated adjustment, in whole or in part, of the initially negotiated base price.

fixed-price with economic price adjustment

A fixed-price contract that permits an element of cost to fluctuate to reflect current market prices.

forbearance

An intentional failure of a party to enforce a contract requirement, usually for an act of immediate or future consideration from the other party. Sometimes forbearance is referred to as a nonwaiver or as a one-time waiver, but not as a relinquishment of rights.

force majeure clause

A contract clause intended to protect the parties in the event that part of their contract cannot be performed due to causes outside the control of the parties and could not be avoided by the exercise of due care. Excusable conditions for non-performance, such as strikes and acts of God (e.g., typhoons), are covered by this clause.

fraud

An intentional perversion of truth to induce another, in reliance on it, to part with something of value belonging to him or her or to surrender a legal right. A false representation of a matter of fact, whether by words or conduct, by false or misleading allegations, or by concealment of that which should have been disclosed, that deceives and is intended to deceive another so that he or she will act upon it to his or her legal injury. Anything calculated to deceive.

free on board (FOB)

A term used in conjunction with a physical point to determine (a) the responsibility and basis for payment of freight charges and (b) unless otherwise agreed, the point at which title for goods passes to the buyer or consignee. FOB origin–The seller places the goods on the conveyance by which they are to be transported, with the cost of shipping and risk of loss are borne by the buyer. FOB destination–The seller delivers the goods on the seller's conveyance at destination, with the cost of shipping and risk of loss borne by the seller.

functional specification

A purchase description that describes the deliverable in terms of performance characteristics and intended use, including those characteristics that at a minimum are necessary to satisfy the intended use.

general and administrative (G&A)

(1) The indirect expenses related to an overall business. Expenses for a company's general and executive offices, executive compensation, staff services, and other miscellaneous support purposes. (2) Any indirect management, financial, or other expense that (a) is not assignable to a program's direct overhead charges for engineering, manufacturing, material, and

so on, but (b) is routinely incurred by or allotted to a business unit, and (c) is for the general management and administration of the business as a whole.

generally accepted accounting principles (GAAP)

A term encompassing conventions, rules, and procedures of accounting that are "generally accepted" and have "substantial authoritative support." The GAAP have been developed by agreement on the basis of experience, reason, custom, usage, and, to a certain extent, practical necessity, rather than being derived from a formal set of theories.

General Agreement on Tariffs and Trade (GATT)

A multinational trade agreement, signed in 1947 by 23 nations, encouraging free trade among its members.

gross profit margin

Net sales less the cost of good sold.. Also called gross margin, gross profit or gross loss.

gross profit margin % or ratio

Gross profit margin divided by net sales.

gross sales

Total revenues at invoice value before any discounts or allowances.

horizontal exchange

A marketplace that deals in goods and services that are not specific to a single industry.

imply

To indirectly convey meaning or intent; to leave the determination of meaning up to the receiver of the communication based on circumstances, general language used, or conduct of those involved.

incidental damages

Any commercially reasonable charges, expenses, or commissions incurred in stopping delivery; in the transportation, care, and custody of goods after the buyer's breach; or in connection with the return or resale of the goods or otherwise resulting from the breach.

indefinite-delivery/indefinite-quantity (IDIQ) contract
A type of contract in which the exact date of delivery or the exact quantity, or a combination of both, is not specified at the time the contract is executed; the contract includes provisions to later stipulate these elements of the contract.

indemnification clause
A contract clause by which one party engages to secure another against an anticipated loss resulting from an act or forbearance on the part of one of the parties or of a third person.

indemnify
To make good; to compensate; to reimburse a person in case of an anticipated loss.

indirect cost
Any cost not directly identifiable with a specific cost objective but subject to two or more cost objectives.

indirect labor
All work that is not specifically associated with or cannot be practically traced to specific units of output.

intellectual property
The kind of property that results from the fruits of mental labor.

Internet
The World Wide Web; an electronic communications network.

interactive chat
A feature provided by automated tools that allow users to establish a voice connection between one or more parties and to exchange text or graphics via a virtual bulletin board.

intranet
An organization-specific internal secure network.

joint contract
A contract in which the parties bind themselves both individually and as a unit.

liquidated damages
A contract provision providing for the assessment of damages on the seller for its failure to comply with certain performance or delivery requirements of the contract; used when the time of delivery or performance is of such importance that the buyer may reasonably expect to sustain damages if the delivery or performance is delinquent.

mailbox rule
The idea that the acceptance of an offer is effective when deposited in the mail if the envelope is properly addressed.

marketing
Activities that direct the flow of goods and services from the producer to the consumers.

market intelligence
Information on competitors or competitive teams operating in the marketplace or industry.

market research
The process used to collect and analyze information about an entire market to help determine the most suitable approach to acquiring, distributing, and supporting supplies and services.

memorandum of agreement (MOA)/ memorandum of understanding (MOU)
The documentation of a mutually agreed-to statement of facts, intentions, procedures, and parameters for future actions and matters of coordination. A "memorandum of understanding" may express mutual understanding of an issue without implying commitments by the parties to the understanding.

method of procurement
The process used for soliciting offers, evaluating offers, and awarding a contract.

modifications

Any written alterations in the specification, delivery point, rate of delivery, contract period, price, quantity, or other provision of an existing contract that are accomplished in accordance with a contract clause; may be unilateral or bilateral.

monopoly

A market structure in which the entire market for a good or service is supplied by a single seller or firm.

monopsony

A market structure in which a single buyer purchases a good or service.

NCMA CMBOK

An acronym for the National Contract Management Association's Contract Management Body of Knowledge; definitive descriptions of the elements making up the body of professional knowledge that applies to contract management.

negotiation

A process between buyers and sellers seeking to reach mutual agreement on a matter of common concern through fact-finding, bargaining, and persuasion.

net marketplace

Two-sided exchange where buyers and sellers negotiate prices, usually with a bid-and-ask system, and where prices move both up and down.

net present value (NPV)

The lifetime customer revenue stream discounted by investment and operational costs.

net sales

Gross sales minus discounts, allowances, and returns.

North American Free Trade Agreement (NAFTA)

A trilateral trade and investment agreement between Canada, Mexico, and the United States ratified on January 1, 1994.

novation agreement

A legal instrument executed by (a) the contractor (transferor), (b) the contractor's successor in interest (transferee), and (c) the buyer by which, among other things, the transferor guarantees performance of the contract, the transferee assumes all obligations under the contract, and the buyer recognizes the transfer of the contract and related assets.

offer

(1) The manifestation of a willingness to enter into a bargain, so made as to justify another person in understanding that his or her assent to that bargain is invited and will conclude it. (2) An unequivocal and intentionally communicated statement of proposed terms made by one party to another. An offer is presumed revocable unless it specifically states that it is irrevocable. An offer once made will be open for a reasonable period of time and is binding on the offeror unless revoked before the other party's acceptance.

oligopoly

A market dominated by a few sellers.

operating expenses

Selling, general and administrative (SG&A) expenses plus depreciation and amortization.

opportunity

A potential or actual favorable event.

opportunity engagement

The degree to which a company or its competitors are involved in establishing a customer's requirements.

opportunity profile

A stage of the capture management life cycle during which a seller evaluates and describes an opportunity in terms of what it means to the customer, what it means to the seller company, and what is required to succeed.

option

A unilateral right in a contract by which, for a specified time, the buyer may elect to purchase additional quantities of the supplies or services called for in the contract or may elect to extend the period of performance of the contract.

order of precedence

A solicitation provision that establishes priorities so that contradictions within the solicitation can be resolved.

organizational breakdown structure (OBS)

An organized structure that represents how individual team members are grouped to complete assigned work tasks.

outsourcing

A contractual process of obtaining another party to provide goods and/or services that were previously provided internally by an organization.

overhead

An accounting cost category that typically includes general indirect expenses that are necessary to operate a business but are not directly assignable to a specific good or service produced. Examples include building rent, utilities, salaries of corporate officers, janitorial services, office supplies, and furniture.

overtime

The time worked by a seller's employee(s) in excess of the employee's normal workweek.

parol evidence

Oral or verbal evidence; in contract law, the evidence drawn from sources exterior to the written instrument.

parol evidence rule

A rule that seeks to preserve the integrity of written agreements by refusing to permit contracting parties to attempt to alter a written contract with evidence of any contradictory prior or contemporaneous oral agreement (parol to the contract).

payments

The amount payable under a contract supporting data required to be submitted with invoices, and other payment terms such as time for payment and retention.

payment bond

A bond that secures the appropriate payment of subcontractors for their completed and acceptable goods and/or services.

performance-based contract (PBC)

A documented business arrangement in which the buyer and seller agree to use a performance work statement, performance-based metrics, and a quality assurance plan to ensure contract requirements are met or exceeded.

performance bond

A bond that secures the performance and fulfillment of all the undertakings, covenants, terms, conditions, and agreements contained in a contract.

performance specification

A purchase description of the deliverable in terms of desired operational characteristics. Performance specifications tend to be more restrictive than functional specifications in that they limit alternatives that the buyer will consider and define separate performance standards for each such alternative.

performance work statement (PWS)

A statement of work expressed in terms of desired performance results, often including specific measurable objectives.

post-bid phase

The period of time after a seller submits a bid/proposal to a buyer through source selection, negotiations, contract formation, contract fulfillment, contract closeout, and follow-on opportunity management.

pre-bid phase

The period of time that a seller of goods and/or services uses to identify business opportunities prior to the release of a customer solicitation.

pricing arrangement

An agreed-to basis between contractual parties for the payment of amounts for specified performance; usually expressed in terms of a specific cost-reimbursement or fixed-price arrangement.

prime/prime contractor
The principal seller performing under a contract.

private exchange
A marketplace hosted by a single company inside a company's firewall and used for procurement from among a group of preauthorized sellers.

privity of contract
The legal relationship that exists between the parties to a contract that allows either party to (a) enforce contractual rights against the other party and (b) seek a remedy directly from the other party.

procurement
The complete action or process of acquiring or obtaining goods or services using any of several authorized means.

procurement planning
The process of identifying business needs that can best be met by procuring products or services outside the organization.

profit
The net proceeds from selling a product or service when costs are subtracted from revenues. May be positive (profit) or negative (loss).

program management
Planning and execution of multiple projects that are related to one another.

progress payments
An interim payment for delivered work in accordance with contract terms; generally tied to meeting specified performance milestones.

project management
Planning and ensuring the quality, on-time delivery, and cost of a specific set of related activities with a definite beginning and end.

promotion
Publicizing the attributes of a product/service through media,

personal contacts, and presentations, e.g., technical articles/ presentations, new releases, advertising, and sales calls.

proposal

Normally, a written offer by a seller describing its offering terms. Proposals may be issued in response to a specific request or made unilaterally when a seller feels there may be an interest in its offer (also known as an unsolicited proposal).

proposal evaluation

An assessment of both a proposal and the offeror's ability (as conveyed by the proposal) to successfully accomplish the prospective contract. An agency evaluates competitive proposals solely on the factors specified in the solicitation.

protest

A written objection by an interested party to (a) a solicitation or other request by an agency for offers for a contract for the procurement of property or services, (b) the cancellation of the solicitation or other request, (c) an award or proposed award of the contract, or (d) a termination or cancellation of an award of the contract if the written objection contains an allegation that the termination or cancellation is based in whole or in part on improprieties concerning the award of the contract.

punitive damages

Damages awarded to a plaintiff over and above what will compensate for his or her loss. Unlike compensatory damages, punitive damages are based on an actively different public policy consideration, that of punishing the defendant or setting an example for similar wrongdoers.

purchasing

The outright acquisition of items, mostly off-the-shelf or catalog items, that are manufactured outside the buyer's premises.

quality assurance

The planned and systematic actions necessary to provide adequate confidence that the performed service or supplied goods will serve satisfactorily for the intended and specified purpose.

quotation

A statement of price, either written or oral, that may include, among other things, a description of a product or service; the terms of sale, delivery, or period of performance; and payment. Such statements are usually issued by sellers at the request of potential buyers.

reasonable cost

A cost is reasonable if, in its nature and amount, it does not exceed that which would be incurred by a prudent person in the conduct of competitive business.

request for information (RFI)

A formal invitation to submit general and/or specific information concerning a potential future purchase of goods and/or services.

request for proposals (RFP)

A formal invitation that contains a scope of work and seeks a formal response (proposal), which describes both methodology and compensation, to form the basis of a contract.

request for quotations (RFQ)

A formal invitation to submit a price for goods and/or services as specified.

request for technical proposals (RFTP)

A solicitation document used in two-step sealed bidding. Normally in letter form, it asks only for technical information; price and cost breakdowns are forbidden.

revenue value

The monetary value of an opportunity.

risk

Exposure or potential of an injury or loss.

sealed-bid procedure

A method of procurement involving the unrestricted solicitation of bids, an opening, and award of a contract to the lowest responsible bidder.

selling, general & administrative (SG&A) expenses
The administrative costs of running a business.

severable contract
A contract divisible into separate parts. A default of one section does not invalidate the whole contract.

several
A circumstance when more than two parties are involved with a contract.

single source
One source among others in a competitive marketplace that, for justifiable reason, is found to be most worthy to receive a contract award.

small business concerns
A small business is one that is independently owned and operated, and is not dominant in its field; a business concern that meets government size standards for its particular industry type.

socioeconomic programs
Programs designed to benefit particular groups. They represent a multitude of program interests and objectives unrelated to procurement objectives. Some examples of these are preferences for small business and for American products, required sources for specific items, and minimum labor pay levels mandated for contractors.

solicitation
A process through which a buyer requests bids, quotes, tenders, or proposals orally, in writing, or electronically. Solicitations can take the following forms: a request for proposals (RFP), a request for quotations (RFQ), a request for tenders, an invitation to bid (ITB), an invitation for bids, and an invitation for negotiation.

solicitation planning
The preparation of the documents needed to support a solicitation.

source selection

The process by which a buyer evaluates offers, selects a seller, negotiates terms and conditions, and awards a contract.

Source Selection Advisory Council

A group of people who are appointed by the Source Selection Authority (SSA). The Council is responsible for reviewing and approving the source selection plan (SSP) and the solicitation of competitive awards for major and certain less-than-major procurements. The Council also determines the proposals that are in the competitive range and provides recommendations to the SSA for final selection.

source selection plan (SSP)

A document that describes the selection criteria, the process, and the organization to be used in evaluating proposals for competitively-awarded contracts.

specification

A description of the technical requirements for a material, product, or service that includes the criteria for determining that the requirements have been met. There are generally three types of specifications used in contracting: (1) performance, (2) functional, and (3) design.

stakeholders

Individuals in a company who control the resources that are needed to pursue opportunities or deliver solutions to customers.

standard

A document that establishes engineering and technical limitations and applications of items, materials, processes, methods, designs, and engineering practices. It includes any related criteria deemed essential to achieve the highest practical degree of uniformity in materials or products, or interchangeability of parts used in those products.

standards of conduct

The ethical conduct of personnel involved in the acquisition of goods and services. Within the federal government, business must be conducted in a manner above reproach and, except as authorized by law or regulation, with complete impartiality and without preferential treatment.

statement of work (SOW)
That portion of a contract describing the actual work to be done by means of specifications or other minimum requirements, quantities, performance date, and a statement of the requisite quality.

statute of limitations
The legislative enactment prescribing the periods within which legal actions may be brought on certain claims or within which certain rights may be enforced.

stop work order
A request for interim stoppage of work due to nonconformance, funding, or technical considerations.

subcontract
A contract between a buyer and a seller in which a significant part of the supplies or services being obtained is for eventual use in a prime contract.

subcontractor
A seller who enters into a contract with a prime contractor or a subcontractor of the prime contractor.

supplementary agreement
A contract modification that is accomplished by the mutual action of the parties.

technical factor
A factor other than price used in evaluating offers for award. Examples include technical excellence, management capability, personnel qualifications, prior experience, past performance, and schedule compliance.

technical leveling
The process of helping a seller bring its proposal up to the level of other proposals through successive rounds of discussion, such as by pointing out weaknesses resulting from the seller's lack of diligence, competence, or inventiveness in preparing the proposal.

technical/management proposal
That part of an offer that describes the seller's approach to meeting the buyer's requirement.

technical transfusion
The disclosure of technical information pertaining to a proposal that results in the improvement of a competing proposal. This practice is not allowed in federal government contracting.

term
A part of a contract that addresses a specific subject.

termination
An action taken pursuant to a contract clause in which the buyer unilaterally ends all or part of the work.

terms and conditions (Ts and Cs)
All clauses in a contract, including time of delivery, packing and shipping, applicable standard clauses, and special provisions.

unallowable cost
Any cost that, under the provisions of any pertinent law, regulation, or contract, cannot be included in prices, cost-reimbursements, or settlements under a government contract to which it is allocable.

uncompensated overtime
The work that exempt employees perform above and beyond 40 hours per week. Also known as competitive time, deflated hourly rates, direct allocation of salary costs, discounted hourly rates, extended workweek, full-time accounting, and green time.

Uniform Commercial Code (UCC)
A U.S. model law developed to standardize commercial contracting law among the states. It has been adopted by 49 states (and in significant portions by Louisiana). The UCC comprises provisions that deal with specific commercial subject matters, including sales and letters of credit.

unilateral
See bilateral contract.

unsolicited proposal

A research or development proposal that is made by a prospective contractor without prior formal or informal solicitation from a purchasing agency.

variable costs

Costs associated with production that change directly with the amount of production (e.g., the direct material or labor required to complete building or manufacturing a product).

variance

The difference between projected and actual performance, especially relating to costs.

vertical exchange

A marketplace that is specific to a single industry.

waiver

The voluntary and unilateral relinquishment by a person of a right that he or she has. See also forbearance.

warranty

A promise or affirmation given by a seller to a buyer regarding the nature, usefulness, or condition of goods or services furnished under a contract. Generally, a warranty's purpose is to delineate the rights and obligations for defective goods and services and to foster quality performance.

warranty, express

A written statement arising out of a sale to the consumer of a consumer good, pursuant to which the manufacturer, distributor, or retailer undertakes to preserve or maintain the utility or performance of the consumer good or provide compensation if there is a failure in utility or performance. The creation of an express warranty does not require that formal words such as "warrant" or "guarantee" be used or that a specific intention to make a warranty be present.

warranty, implied

A promise arising by operation of law that something sold is fit for the purpose for which the seller has reason to know that it is required. Types of implied warranties include implied warranty of merchantability, title, and wholesomeness.

warranty of fitness

A warranty by the seller that goods sold are suitable for the special purpose of the buyer.

warranty of merchantability

A warranty that goods are fit for the ordinary purposes for which the goods are used and conform to the promises or affirmations of fact made on the container or label.

warranty of title

An express or implied (arising by operation of law) promise that the seller owns the item offered for sale and, therefore, is able to transfer a good's title and that the goods, as delivered, are free from any security interest of which the buyer at the time of contracting has knowledge.

Web portals

A public exchange in which a company or a group of companies lists products or services for sale or provides other transmission of business information.

win strategy

A collection of messages or points designed to guide a customer's perception of an organization, its solution, and its competitors.

work breakdown structure (WBS)

A logical, organized, decomposition of the work tasks within a given project, which typically uses a hierarchical numeric coding scheme.

World Trade Organization (WTO)

A multinational legal entity that serves as the champion of global fair trade, which was established April 15, 1995.

REFERENCES

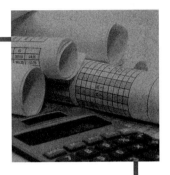

Albert, Neil F, *Developing a Work Breakdown Structure*, McLean, VA: MCR LLC, June 16, 2005.

Anderson, Mark and Nelson, David, *Developing an Averaged Estimate at Completion (EAC) Utilizing Program Performance Factors and Maturity*, Arlington, VA: Tecolote Research, Inc., June 14-17, 2005.

Atkinson, William, *Beyond the Basics*, PM Network Magazine, May 2003 (Project Management Institute).

Badgerow, Dana B., Garrett, Gregory A., DiClementi, Dominic F. and Weaver, Barbara M., *Managing Contracts for Peak Performance*, Vienna, VA: National Contract Management Association, 1990.

Barkley, Bruce T. and Saylor, James H, *Customer Driven Project Management: A New Paradigm in Total Quality Implementation*, New York: McGraw-Hill, 1993.

Black, Hollis M, *Impact of Cost Risk Analysis on Business Decisions*, Huntsville, Ala.: Boeing, June 14-17, 2005.

Bonaldo, Guy, *Interview with Business 2.0 Magazine*, Business Intelligence, February 2003.

Bossidy, Larry and Charan, Ram, *Confronting Reality: Doing What Matters to Get Things Right*, New York: Crown Business, 2004.

Bruce, David L., Norby, Marlys and Ramos, Victor, *Guide to the Contract Management Body of Knowledge, 1ˢᵗ ed.*, Vienna, VA: National Contract Management Association, 2002.

Christensen, David S. and Templin, Carl, *An Analysis of Management Reserve Budget on Defense Acquisition Contracts*, Cedar City: Southern Utah University, 2000.

Cleland, David I., *Project Management: Strategic Design and Implementation*, New York: McGraw-Hill, 1994.

Cleland, David I. and King, William R, *Project Management Handbook, 2ⁿᵈ ed.*, New York: Van Nostrand Reinhold, 1988.

Coleman, Richard L., Gupta, Shishu S. and Summerville, Jessica R., *Two Timely Short Topics: Independence and Cost Realism*, Chantilly, VA: Northrop Grumman, The Analytical Sciences Corporation and Intelligence Community Cost Analysis Improvement Group, June 16, 2005.

Coleman, Richard L. and Summerville, Jessica R., *Advanced Cost Risk*, Chantilly, Va.: Northrop Grumman, The Analytical Sciences Corporation, June 16, 2005.

Coleman, Richard L. and Summerville, Jessica R., *Basic Cost Risk.* Chantilly, VA: Northrop Grumman, The Analytical Sciences Corporation, June 15, 2005.

Collins, Jim, *Good to Great: Why Some Companies Make the Leap... and Others Don't*, New York: Harper Collins, 2001.

Coulson-Thomas, Colin, *Creating the Global Company*, New York: McGraw-Hill, 1992.

Covey, Stephen R., *The Seven Habits of Highly Effective People*, New York: Simon and Schuster, 1989.

Defense Acquisition University, *Cost Estimating Methodologies*, Fort Belvoir, VA: April, 2005.

Fisher, Roger, Kopelman, Elizabeth and Schneider Andrea K., *Beyond Machiavelli: Tools for Coping with Conflict*, Cambridge: Harvard University Press, 1994.

Fleming, Quentin W., *Earned Value Management (EVM) Light...But Adequate for All Projects*, Tustin, Calif.: Primavera Systems, Inc., November 2006.

Fleming, Quentin W. and Koppelman, Joel M., *The Earned Value Body of Knowledge*, Presented at the 30th Annual Project Management Institute Symposium, Philadelphia, PA, October 10-16, 1999.

Flett, Frank, *Organizing and Planning the Estimate*, McLean, VA.: MCR LLC, June 12-14,2005.

Galorath, Daniel D., *Software Estimation Handbook*, El Segundo, Calif.: Galorath Inc. (n.d.).

Government Accountability Office, *Cost Assessment Guide, GAO-07-11345P*, Washington, D.C.: July 2007.

Garrett, Gregory A., *Achieving Customer Loyalty*, Contract Management Magazine, August 2002 (National Contract Management Association).

Garrett, Gregory A., *Cost Estimating and Contract Pricing*, Chicago: CCH, 2008.

Garrett, Gregory A., *Performance-Based Acquisition: Pathways to Excellence*, McLean, VA: NCMA, 2005.

Garrett, Gregory A., *World-Class Contracting, 4th ed.*, Chicago: CCH, 2007.

Garrett, Gregory A., *Managing Complex Outsourced Projects.*, Chicago: CCH, 2004.

Garrett, Gregory A., *Contract Negotiations: Skills, Tools, & Best Practices*, Chicago: CCH, 2005.

Garrett, Gregory A., *Managing Subcontracts: Optimizing the U.S. Government Supply Chain*, New York: Thomson-West, 2009.

Garrett, Gregory A., *Risk Management for Complex U.S. Government Contracts and Projects*, Ashburn, VA: NCMA, 2009.

Garrett, Gregory A. and Bunnik, Ed., *Creating a World-Class PM Organization*, PM Network Magazine, Project Management Institute, September 2000.

Garrett, Gregory A. and Kipke, Reginald J., *The Capture Management Life-Cycle: Winning More Business*, Chicago: CCH, 2003).

Garrett, Gregory A. and Rendon, Rene G., *Contract Management Organizational Assessment Tools*, McLean, VA: NCMA, 2005.

Garrett, Gregory A. and Rendon, Rene G., *U.S. Military Program Management: Lessons Learned and Best Practices*, McLean, VA: Management Concepts, 2007.

Harris, Phillip R. and Moran, Robert T., *Managing Cultural Differences*, Houston: Gulf Publishing Company, 1996.

Hassan, H. and Blackwell, R., *Global Marketing*, New York: Harcourt Brace, 1994.

Hirsch, W. J., *The Contracts Management Deskbook*, New York: American Management Association, 1986.

Horton, Sharon, *Creating and Using Supplier Scorecards*, Contract Management Magazine, McLean, VA: NCMA, September 2004, pp. 22-25.

Johnson, Jim, et al., *Collaboration: Development and Management – Collaborating on Project Success*, Software Magazine, Sponsored Supplement, February-March 2001.

Kantin, Bob, *Sales Proposals Kit for Dummies*, New York: Hungry Minds, 2001.

Kerzner, Harold, *In Search of Excellence in Project Management*, New York: Van Nostrand Reinhold, 1998.

Kirk, Dorothy, *Managing Expectations*, PM Network Magazine, August 2000, Project Management Institute.

Kratzert, Keith, *Earned Value Management (EVM): The Federal Aviation Administration (FAA) Program Manager's Flight Plan*, Washington, D.C.: Federal Aviation Administration, January 2006.

Kumley, Alissa, et al., *Integrating Risk Management and Earned Value Management: A Statistical Analysis of Survey Results*, N.p.: June 14-17, 2005.

Lewis, James P, *Mastering Project Management: Applying Advanced Concepts of Systems Thinking, Control and Evaluation, Resource Allocation*, New York: McGraw-Hill, 1998.

Liker, Jeffrey K. and Choi, Thomas Y., *Building Deep Supplier Relationships*, Harvard Business Review, Boston, MA: December 2004, pp. 104-113.

McFarlane, Eileen Luhta, *Developing International Proposals in a Virtual Environment*, Journal of the Association of Proposal Management, Spring 2000.

Monroe, Kent B., *Pricing: Making Profitable Decisions, 2nd ed.*, New York: McGraw-Hill Publishing Co., 1990.

Moran, J. and Riesenberger, M., *The Global Challenge*, New York: McGraw-Hill, 1994.

The Desktop Guide to Basic Contracting Terms, 4th ed., Vienna, VA: The National Contract Management Association, 1994.

O'Connell, Brian, *B2B.com: Cashing-in on the Business-to-Business E-commerce Bonanza*, Holbrook, Mass.: Adams Media Corp., 2000.

Ohmae, Kenichi, *The Borderless World: Power and Strategy in the Interlinked Economy*, New York: Harper Collins, 1991.

Patterson, Shirley, *Supply Base Optimization and Integrated Supply Chain Management*, Contract Management Magazine, McLean, VA: NCMA, January 2005, pp. 24-35.

Project Management Institute Standards Committee, *A Guide to the Project Management Body of Knowledge*, Upper Darby, Pa.: Project Management Institute, 2001.

Impossible Certainty: Cost Risk Analysis for Air Force Systems, Arlington, VA: RAND Corp., 2006.

Cost Programmed Review of Fundamentals (CostPROF): Basic Data Analysis Principles – What to Do Once You Get the Data, Vienna, VA: SCEA (Society of Cost Estimating and Analysis), 2003.

Tichy, Noel, *The Leadership Engine*, New York: Harper Business Press, 1997.

Webster's Dictionary, The New Lexicon of the English Language, New York: Lexicon Publications, Inc., 1989.

Zubrow, Dave, *Earned Value Management (EVM): Basic Concepts*, Pittsburgh, PA: Carnegie Mellon Software Engineering Institute, 2002.

Zubrow, Dave, *Implementing Earned Value Management (EVM) to Manage Program Risk*, Pittsburg, PA.: Carnegie Mellon Software Engineering Institute, 2002.

References

INDEX

Best practices
government property, 163
NCR, 27
   customer-focused
     teams, 28
   GlobalPM®, 28
   professional
     development, 29
   project manager
     involvement, 28
   shared lessons
     learned, 29
supply chain, 152

Case study
Hewlett-Packard, 29
NCR, 27

Contract administration
challenge, 70
contract type, 6
personnel, 2
workload, 2

**Contract administration
process**
input, 10
   change requests, 11

contract, 10
invoices, 11
project plan, 10
schedule, 10
work results, 10
output, 16
   completion of
     work, 18
   documentation, 16
   payment, 18
tools and techniques, 11
   contract analysis, 11
   contract closeout
     process, 15
   contract planning, 11
   dispute resolution
     process, 14
   government property
     management, 15
   kickoff meeting, 12
   payment process, 14
   performance
     measurement and
     reporting, 13
   pre-performance
     conference, 12
   project management
     discipline, 11

supply chain
management, 15
Contract changes
advance change adjustment
agreement, 84
best practices, 85
change control board, 79
contract changes
authority, 77
contract changes process, 74
contract
administration, 76
contract closeout, 76
procurement planning, 74
solicitation, 75
solicitation planning, 75
source selection, 75
contract manager's letter, 82
controlling contract
changes, 77
types of contract changes, 71

Contract claims
discovery, 130
documentary
evidence, 132
expert witnesses, 130
entitlement, 121
contractor claims, 121
government claims, 121
other claims, 122
final decisions, 122
appeals, 123
quantum, 127
methods of proving
damages, 127
types of claims, 133
changes clause, 134
cost overrun, 141
delay and disruption, 140

loss of efficiency, 142
lost profit, 143
termination, 137
unabsorbed
overhead, 135

Contract financing
techniques, 90
advance payments, 91
grants and loans, 90
progress payments, 92
provisional payments, 91
types of payment, 93
fast payment, 95
prompt payment, 94

Contract interpretation
guidelines, 272
contract as a whole, 273
definition of key
terms, 273
duty to seek
clarification, 276
extrinsic evidence, 275
interpretation against
drafter, 276
order of precedence, 274
parol evidence rule, 275

**Contracting policies,
reviews, and audits**
audits and other
reviews, 283
subcontract audits, 286
contractor purchasing system
review, 279
generally, 276
preparing for policy
changes, 279

Contract termination and closeout

closeout, 236
  administrative, 237
discharge, 222
termination, 224
  default, 226
  timeliness, 234

Earned value management

application thresholds, 194
contract
  implementation, 195
DOD reviews and
  reports, 214
    contract funds status
      report, 216
    contract performance
      report, 215
    cost data report, 217
    integrated baseline
      review, 214
    integrated master
      schedule, 216
    software resources data
      report, 218
understanding EVM
  systems, 195
    authorizing work, 196
    budgeting work, 200
    changes, 209
    cost accumulation, 203
    internal audit/
      verification, 210
    organizing work, 195
    performance
      measurement, 204
    scheduling work, 197
    variance analysis, 208

Future of contract administration

balance between contracts
  and governance, 301
contract-based
  governance, 299
contract management, 290
developments in PBA
  governance, 301
downside of
  governance, 295
governance models, 292
organizational constraints on
  governance, 296
performance-based
  acquisition, 298
performance outcome-
  process hierarchy, 299
philosophy of
  governance, 293
principles of optimal
  governance, 305
    constraints and
      opportunities,   307
    example, 308
    goals and impacts, 308
    mutual assent and
      trust, 306
    preferable and optimal
      governance, 305
purpose-driven
  governance, 302
    vs. current
      approaches, 310

Government property management

best practices, 163
challenges, 163

consumption, 185
contractor plans or
systems, 166
disposal, 188
identification, 171
movement, 185
process or outcome
essentials, 165
storage, 186

**Integrated project
management**
awakening phase, 23
enterprising phase, 26
implementing phase, 24
integrating phase, 27
professionalizing phase, 25

**Integrated project
management life-cycle**
customer needs and
goals, 31
four major inputs, 33
integrated project
management
discipline, 34
translating customer
needs, 32
understanding customer
needs, 32
integrated project
management discipline, 41
essentials, 41
graduate degree
programs, 43
masters certificate
programs, 43
lessons learned, 30
project communications, 36
four major inputs, 37

making project
communications
work, 36
project teamwork, 38
developing project
teamwork, 39
four major inputs, 40
integrated project
management
discipline, 41
supplier value chain, 34
four major inputs, 35
integrated project
management
discipline, 36
making projects
succeed, 34

Managing Litigation Risk
during contract
formation, 252
financial risk, 254
risk in contract
terms, 252
during contract
performance, 256
direction from
unauthorized
persons, 256
risk in contract
changes, 257
risk of potential
litigation, 258
importance, 250
settlement
considerations, 266
when litigation appears
possible, 262

Opportunity and risk management
inputs, 58
  elements of
    opportunity, 58
  elements of risk, 59
  people, 58
opportunity, defined, 48
output, 67
risk, defined, 48
risk in federal acquisitions
  management, 48
tools and techniques, 61
  opportunity and risk
    management
    model, 61
  project doability
    analysis, 65
  risk management plan
    outline, 62
  risk mitigation form, 64

Profit analysis
measures of profitability, 99
  days of sales
    outstanding, 108
  EBITDA, 112
  gross profit, 101
  internal rate of
    return, 105
  measured operating
    income, 106
  return on assets, 102
  return on investment, 100
  weighted guidelines
    method, 109
profitability, 97

Supply chain
best practices, 152
challenges, 146